Parchment Barriers

Parchment Barriers

Political Polarization and the Limits of Constitutional Order

Edited by Zachary Courser,
Eric Helland, and Kenneth P. Miller

University Press of Kansas

© 2018 by the University Press of Kansas
All rights reserved

Published by the University Press of Kansas (Lawrence, Kansas 66045),
which was organized by the Kansas Board of Regents and is operated
and funded by Emporia State University, Fort Hays State University,
Kansas State University, Pittsburg State University, the University of Kansas,
and Wichita State University.

Library of Congress Cataloging-in-Publication Data is available.
ISBN 978-0-7006-2713-4 (cloth : alk. paper)
ISBN 978-0-7006-2714-1 (pbk. : alk. paper)
ISBN 978-0-7006-2715-8 (ebook)

British Library Cataloguing-in-Publication Data is available.

Printed in the United States of America

10 9 8 7 6 5 4 3 2 1

The paper used in this publication is recycled and contains 30 percent
postconsumer waste. It is acid free and meets the minimum requirements
of the American National Standard for Permanence of Paper
for Printed Library Materials Z39.48-1992.

Contents

Acknowledgments

The editors gratefully acknowledge the help and assistance of the people and institutions that made this book possible. We extend our sincere appreciation to David Dreier, longtime member of the US House of Representatives and former chair of the Rules Committee, who established the Dreier Roundtable at Claremont McKenna College. This work is the first major research project undertaken by the Roundtable, and it has benefited greatly from Mr. Dreier's unwavering and generous support of our efforts.

This project would not have been possible if not for the financial support of the Annenberg Foundation and the William and Flora Hewlett Foundation. Our thanks to Larry Kramer, president of the Hewlett Foundation, for his advice and guidance during the early stages of the project.

We are indebted to the outstanding group of scholars who joined this project and are grateful for the excellent collaborations we enjoyed in building this book together. This volume represents the coordinated work of academics in a diversity of disciplines—political science, economics, and law—and its insights are thanks to their scholarship, dedication, and collegiality.

The concept and chapters were developed during two different conferences, one in California and the other at James Madison's Montpelier. Our thanks to Kat Imhoff, president of the Montpelier Foundation, for helping make our final conference such a success, and for sharing the unique legacy of James Madison's home and estate with our group. Our thanks to Hiram Chodosh, Gary Schmitt, Steven Teles, and Craig Volden for their insights and suggestions during the conferences. Also, our thanks to Claremont McKenna College students Mohamad Batal, Jessica Davis, and Jessica Jin for their research assistance as Dreier Fellows.

Lastly, we are grateful to David Congdon and his team at the University Press of Kansas for their enthusiasm and support for this project.

Parchment Barriers

CHAPTER 1

Introduction

Zachary Courser, Eric Helland, and Kenneth P. Miller

We live in an age of polarization. The United States of America has become the "Divided States of America"—divided into entrenched, powerful, rival, partisan camps. Surveys confirm that Americans, especially the most politically active, have become more sharply separated along ideological lines. Most conservatives now identify as Republicans and most liberals as Democrats, and the number of persons holding consistently conservative or consistently liberal views is rising.[1] In Congress, the two parties have pulled apart. As measured by key roll call votes, the 114th Congress (2015–2017) had the highest level of partisan polarization of any Congress in a century,[2] the number of moderate members is declining, and bipartisan cooperation on major legislation is increasingly rare. Recent presidents have contributed to the nation's polarization. Republican George W. Bush ran for office claiming to be "a uniter, not a divider," and Democrat Barack Obama famously said, "[W]e are not a collection of red states and blue states. We are the United States of America."[3] But their actions often contradicted these aspirations, and the nation's partisan divisions hardened during their presidencies. The 2016 election of Republican Donald J. Trump introduced a new intensity to the nation's polarization. Democrats immediately formed a "resistance" to the president, and some called for his impeachment within weeks of his inauguration. Similarly, although the judiciary was designed to be insulated from politics, it too has been affected by polarization to the point where it is now seen as an important element of partisan control of government. Most federal judges are viewed as either liberal or conservative; nominations to the federal courts, especially the US Supreme Court, are seen in partisan terms; and Senate confirmation votes divide along partisan lines. The states, too, are polarizing. Most states have become more consistently conservative or liberal—more solidly "red" or "blue"—and are forming partisan alliances to support or resist federal policies on ideological grounds. Partisan polarization clearly defines contemporary American politics and causes concern on all sides about the direction of the nation's political life.

How should we view this condition? What is the nature of our contemporary polarization? What is causing it? How do our divisions affect our governing institutions? Is polarization truly a problem or not? And, if so, in what ways? In this book, scholars from the disciplines of political science, economics, and law approach these questions by exploring the relationship between our current political polarization and the nation's constitutional design.

The architects of the Constitution were fundamentally concerned about political division. They believed that democratic governments were prone to factional conflict—indeed, the "violence of faction." James Madison warned in *Federalist* 10 that:

> A zeal for different opinions concerning religion, concerning government, and many other points, as well of speculation as of practice; an attachment to different leaders ambitiously contending for pre-eminence and power; or to persons of other descriptions whose fortunes have been interesting to the human passions, have, in turn, divided mankind into parties, inflamed them with mutual animosity, and rendered them much more disposed to vex and oppress each other than to co-operate for their common good.[4]

Madison believed that such factions were inevitable in a free society. In his view, the challenge was to develop a system of government that would make it difficult for majority factions to form, gain control of government, and overpower their opponents. The Constitution thus contained numerous means for controlling factional division, restraining pure majority rule, and preventing concentrations of power. These features included federalism, indirect elections, separately elected institutions, separation of powers, bicameralism, the presidential veto, and numerous other checks and balances.

This constitutional structure was masterfully designed, but Madison knew that it was vulnerable to an encroaching and impetuous "spirit of power." In *Federalist* 48, for example, he noted the difficulty of limiting the power of Congress due to its popular nature. Madison cautioned against trusting in "parchment barriers"—mere words on paper—to protect a constitutional system against encroachments by the legislative power.[5] He argued that a "more adequate defense is indispensably necessary for the more feeble, against the more powerful, members of the government."[6] Indeed, Madison believed that the popular power of the legislative branch was such a danger to the Constitution that "the people ought to indulge all their jealousy and exhaust all their precautions" in restraining it.[7] In other words, the people themselves shared the responsibility to defend the constitutional structure and preserve constitutional limits. In our own day, the rise of mass politics and the intensification of partisan polarization have empowered other members of the government, including, especially, the executive. These developments have made it even more difficult to resist the pull of democratic power and to preserve the constitutional order. The Framers of the Constitution armed us with the tools to resist the usurpations of popular power, but these limitations rest upon our acceptance that liberty requires power to be restrained, and that democratic power should not extend beyond constitutional norms.

To be sure, the same James Madison who warned against the dangers of faction in the 1780s, soon thereafter, with Thomas Jefferson, participated in founding the nation's first party system. In the early 1790s, Madison became convinced that a new political party was needed to challenge the policies of Alexander Hamilton and the Federalists. He and Jefferson formed what is known as the Democratic-Republican Party, the forerunner to the modern Democratic Party. When the Republican Party later formed in the 1850s, the nation settled in to the present two-party system. Over time, many have concluded that, in addition to checking the government, parties are needed to inform, organize, and mobilize voters. Indeed, parties have become an indispensable feature of American government. The question is thus not whether parties have any value, but whether under present conditions, "partyism" or "factious spirit" or, in current terms, "polarization," endangers the nation's constitutional design.

DEFINING POLITICAL POLARIZATION

The *Oxford English Dictionary* defines political polarization simply as "division into two sharply contrasting groups or sets of beliefs."[8] By this definition, political polarization is not new. Throughout its history, the nation has "divi[ded] into two sharply contrasting groups or sets of beliefs" on a series of major issues. One such divide, regarding the status of slavery, was so deep and intractable that it caused the nation to descend into civil war. The United States has also been divided over the ratification of the Constitution itself, the introduction of the New Deal in the 1930s, the effort to end racial segregation, the prosecution of wars in Vietnam and Iraq, and many other consequential questions.

In the past, however, the nation's polarization has been limited by several factors. First, policy cleavages have often cut across party lines. The two major parties have often experienced internal divides on policy questions—to the point where sometimes they have been almost as deeply divided internally as from each other. Second, the parties have generally polarized over a single issue or a related cluster of issues at a time—that is, while sharply divided on a few controversial questions, they could cooperate on others. Third, despite their differences, most Americans generally have shared a broad set of cultural, political, and legal assumptions, including many shared understandings of the Constitution. Today, these three limits on partisan polarization have weakened as the nation's political life is increasingly defined by partisan sorting, conflict across a larger range of issues, and erosion of consensus on fundamentals.

Sorting

Levels of partisan polarization have varied greatly over the course of the nation's history. At times, the parties have been sharply divided; at other times, they have overlapped so extensively that it was difficult to find differences between them. The middle of the twentieth century was a period of relatively low partisan polarization. American politics featured broad bipartisan consensus on many economic, social, and foreign policy issues. During this era, the Democratic Party included a large conservative faction, located mainly but not exclusively in the South, and many Republicans identified as liberals. As a consequence, policy conflicts did not divide neatly along party lines, and many voters "split their tickets" between Democrats and Republicans on Election Day.

This pattern of low partisan polarization began to break down during the 1960s, which was marked by revolutions in civil rights, the status of women, sexual mores, and environmentalism, as well as intense antiwar activism. As the Democratic Party began to embrace more liberal positions on these issues, conservative Democrats, especially in the South, began to gravitate to the Republican Party. The Republican Party, in turn, became more consistently conservative, alienating liberal Republicans and inducing them to join the rival team. Scholars debate the causes of this division but agree that the public has sorted ideologically between the two parties, which are now more clearly separated and defined on major policy questions.

Broadening of Conflict

Through a process scholars have called "conflict extension," partisan polarization has expanded to include a broader swath of political issues.[9] In the past, party polarization tended to focus on a single contested issue or set of issues, with party coalitions organizing around the party's stance on that fundamental controversy. On other issues, party members could disagree. In this former system, a new issue or cluster of issues could emerge and "displace" the formerly dominant issue. When that occurred, the party would coalesce around the new dominant issue, but party members could continue to disagree on other matters. Today, however, the two parties no longer organize and polarize around a single issue or a small set of issues; instead, they are polarized across a much broader issue domain.

Eroding Consensus on Fundamentals

The spread of polarization to a broader set of issues has corresponded with an erosion of consensus on fundamental cultural, political, and legal questions, many of which implicate the terms of the Constitution itself. Although debates over the Constitution have persisted throughout the nation's history, we now are experiencing new depths of partisan division over the proper role of government and the definition of constitutional rights. Many of these issues are not amenable to compromise, and committed partisans on both left and right are motivated to prevail on them by any means necessary. Intense fights over issues that partisans consider fundamental place enormous stress on the constitutional structure.

Is Polarization Necessarily a Problem?

Polarization has its defenders. During the mid-twentieth century, many argued that the country needed more polarization—they lamented the two parties' internal divisions, ideological incoherence, and overlap. In the 1960s, Alabama governor George Wallace famously complained that there wasn't "a dime's worth of difference" between the two parties.[10] Many scholars agreed, arguing that the parties needed to differentiate themselves in order to give voters clearer policy choices, and, after elections, to provide the majority party the mandate and means to govern more effectively. In 1950, for example, a committee of the American Political Science Association issued a report calling for the nation to move "toward a more responsible two-party system"—that is, a system in which parties are more differentiated and disciplined.[11] Indeed, it is true that polarization can help mobilize voters and guide their voting choices. Similarly, polarization can sometimes facilitate government policymaking, at least under circumstances when one party controls the presidency and both houses of Congress. Moreover, as Joseph M. Bessette argues in chapter 9, polarization can be a necessary step toward resolution of certain fundamental policy questions.

Experience has shown, however, that our polarization also can have negative consequences. In recent years, political polarization has been marked by persistent disagreement between the parties, incivility, tribalism, decreasing cooperation across party lines, the near-extinction of moderate elected officials, and, especially in times of divided party control, gridlock. More fundamentally, as several of the following chapters illustrate, our present polarization places chronic stress on our constitutional system, which is premised on institutional loyalty, deliberation, consensus building, and compromise.

Thus, while polarization may be benign, or beneficial, or even necessary under some circumstances, it also can be destructive. This book asks whether our present conditions of polarization are affecting our constitutional system in ways that should cause us alarm. The chapters that follow provide a diverse scholarly range of perspectives on the relationship between polarization and the nation's constitutional system. The first seven chapters examine in turn the Madisonian constitutional design, Congress, the presidency, the judiciary, the federal bureaucracy (or "administrative state"), federalism, and political parties. A recurring theme in these chapters is that the constitutional design is under sustained pressure to yield to the desires of partisan majorities, and American institutions are straining against their constitutional limits to govern in a highly polarized political environment. The book's final chapter presents a different perspective, making a case for the value of polarization in American politics, at least under some circumstances.

CHAPTER SUMMARIES
Madisonian Constitutional Design

American government in a period of polarization necessarily emphasizes the veto points of the Constitution: those checks that each institution possesses to stop or delay political action. In chapter 2, George Thomas reexamines James Madison's constitutional design and reminds us that checks and balances were not meant to be the centerpiece, nor were they intended to produce political paralysis. Rather, Madison was more concerned about the American political system being effective and most likely to achieve a government capable of promoting the general welfare, as stated in the preamble to the Constitution. Checks and balances were to present political actors with the resources of time and space within which to refine the public's immediate concerns into a fuller idea of the public good, not simply to stymie political action.

Thomas notes that the successful operation of the Constitution relies on intermediary institutions like the press, parties, and leaders to educate and shape the public's political sensibilities. As political stalemates force leaders to focus on achieving policy goals at the expense of constitutional norms, we are beginning to see pathologies emerge that diminish the public's commitment to democratic norms. The 2016 presidential election evinced no positive constitutional vision from either candidate. Donald Trump's victory was built on a populist message at times deeply at odds with constitutional norms and a conventional understanding of the American political system. With the threat of illiberal democracy upon us, and polarization leading us away from the possibility of compromise, Thomas encourages us to think of the Constitution in more instrumental terms. We ought to consider constitutional reform with an open mind and recognize that the goal of constitutional government is effective government that promotes the general welfare. And, in thoughtfully contemplating reform, we should also pay heed to how our civil society is failing to produce the leadership and educative resources necessary for a Madisonian constitutional order to succeed.

Congress

Madison assumed that Congress would be the centerpiece of the constitutional system he designed, that it would jealously guard its prerogatives and attempt to consolidate all political power within its grasp. In chapter 3, Kathryn Pearson demonstrates that polarization has weakened Congress within the separation of powers and has undermined its effectiveness in responding to critical problems that affect the national interest. As parties have become more ideologically homogenous since the 1990s, power has shifted from committees and minority interests to majority party leaders. Members are less concerned with institutional prerogatives and the constitutional legitimacy of their actions than they are about achieving policy goals in an uncompromising ideological fashion. The result has been a significant reduction in the productivity of Congress in passing legislation and an emphasis on a new kind of leadership-driven irregular legislative order that undermines deliberation and compromise. With moderates no longer having an effective role in legislating, there is little need for negotiation, and policy is increasingly formulated by a handful of the majority leadership without bipartisan support.

The Presidency

In chapter 4, according to Benjamin Kleinerman, while intense partisan conflict has existed throughout American history, this animosity did not prevent the government from working. During the twentieth century, the role of the president has evolved to include control over policy as party leader, and executives increasingly attempt to enact their party's policy goals through administrative control. Ideological polarization has motivated both parties to prefer obstructionism to compromise, focusing contemporary congressional leaders on framing the next election, with their presidential candidate as a quasi-parliamentary leader, rather than following the regular constitutional order of deliberation, debate, and compromise. In the Constitution's system of separated powers, the president is ill-equipped to serve as a parliamentary leader, and of necessity must rely on his powers as head of the administration—or on informal powers derived from public opinion—to accomplish his policy goals. The result is a disfiguration of the constitutional order that transfers the mantle of representation from Congress to the executive and grants legitimacy to a mere partisan majority rather than to a deliberative process that considers the public as a whole. Drawing on the historical development of the executive branch, Kleinerman observes that an executive acting as a parliamentary leader, and shifting the responsibility of representative from Congress to the executive, pushes our politics toward ideological polarization, partisan obstruction, and uncompromising assertions of power over compromise.

The Judiciary

Within the separation of powers, the judiciary is intended to stand apart from partisan consideration and popular pressures to uphold the paramount law that is the Constitution. Amanda Hollis-Brusky demonstrates in chapter 5 that in a prolonged era of polarization the courts cannot but reflect and respond to the stark and uncompromising partisan differences that exist in American politics. Moreover, as the political process stagnates, the judiciary is increasingly called on to resolve political disputes and policy questions that cannot be settled by ordinary political means. Under these unorthodox circumstances, the Supreme Court becomes an attractive venue for partisan actors to achieve their policy goals, while judicial selection and the Court's docket turn into objects of partisan political intrigue. The result is a judiciary that is increasingly receptive to resolving the concerns of party activists, interest groups, and legislators, rather than exercising independent judgment and remaining detached from partisan considerations.

This adaptation compromises the Madisonian constitutional order by placing responsibility for representation and policymaking in the hands of an unelected minority, and undermining the representative powers of Congress and the executive. Hollis-Brusky reminds us that as policy becomes "juridified"—when it becomes a legal rather than a political process—it necessarily degrades the democratic quality of our politics and threatens domination by a handful of elites. Supreme Court decisions are more difficult to alter or overturn than legislation as they are insulated from political control, and thus narrow the choices and alternatives for political actors working within a regular constitutional order. Despite these unintended consequences, Hollis-Brusky sees that both sides of the political divide have adapted to this new judicial order, with conservatives calling for "judicial engagement" and liberals for "activism" from the courts. These adaptations are a reflection of the growing divide in our country and the deep political rift that exists within the public. Therefore, the path back to the Madisonian constitutional order lies not in a reform of the courts but in a change of our politics.

The Administrative State

The Framers of the Constitution could not have anticipated how vast and powerful federal administrative agencies would become in the modern era. In chapter 6, Eric Helland and Kenneth P. Miller describe the establishment of an "administrative state" as a central feature of the federal government and analyze how polarization has affected its operation. Although the architects of the administrative state hoped that it would be insulated from partisan politics, they grafted it into the Madisonian constitutional system so that all three branches exert some degree of control over its actions. Partisans now seek to use these institutional controls over agencies to shape policy.

When examining how partisan polarization has affected institutional control of agencies, it is important to take into account whether one party controls both Congress and the presidency. The effects of polarization are quite different when government is unified than when control of the branches is divided between the two parties. The Obama and early Trump eras illustrate these dynamics. In the first two years of the Obama administration, Democrats exercised unified control over the presidency and Congress. Through party discipline across the two branches, they expanded federal administrative responsibilities by enacting the Affordable Care Act, Dodd-Frank, and other measures—all over Republican opposition. When Republicans took control of the House of Representatives in 2011, however, the dynamics shifted into an extended partisan stalemate over control of the administrative state. Under conditions of partisan gridlock, Congress's ability to exercise oversight over the administrative state diminished, and the president increasingly used his control over agencies—his "pen" and his "phone"—to adopt major policies in areas ranging from immigration to environmental regulation unilaterally, without securing bipartisan consensus in Congress.

Presidential policymaking through administrative action is vulnerable to override, however, as events following the 2016 election demonstrated. With the election of Donald Trump, Republicans gained unified control of government and were able to reverse many Obama-era administrative policies through a combination of congressional and executive action. In contrast to the expansion of agency powers under President Obama, President Trump and his advisors sought to "deconstruct" the administrative state. Meanwhile, the judiciary has entered the fray. For many years, courts have extended deference to agency decision-making, loath to substitute their own judgment for the complex and often arcane disputes that arise from administrative rulemaking. But in recent years, the judiciary has begun to assert a stronger check on unilateral assertion of executive power through administrative fiat.

The frustrations of polarized politics have led activists to seek policy change through administrative action, an approach that has lacked bipartisan consensus and generated resistance in the courts. The interbranch struggle for control of policymaking through the administrative state has been less stable than lawmaking by conventional constitutional means and, in turn, has contributed to polarization.

States and the Federal System

The Madisonian constitutional order envisions the national government bounded not only by the branches of government countering each other but also by the several state governments' exercise of their own sovereign powers. In *Federalist* 51, Madison anticipated a "double security" arising to protect the rights of the people, deriving from "two distinct governments" countering each other's ambitions and maintaining each within their proper sphere of power.[12] In chapter 7, Michael S. Greve shows us that polarized politics has pushed relations between the states and the executive to eschew formal institutional arrangements. Instead of working within the limitations the Constitution places on the national government, states negotiate with the president on a series of political settlements that achieve short-term policy goals at the expense of legal legitimacy. The inability to achieve policy change through the regular constitutional order has accelerated the transformation of a formal federal system into what Greve calls presidential government. Polarization at the state level has disabled individual states from resisting the pull of presidential government.

Following this trajectory, relations between the state and federal government become informal, highly personalized negotiations centered on executive power. Policy becomes transacted in an extralegal process of high-level state and presidential officials working to resolve policy questions. Greve sees states acting as blocs to advance their interests, appealing to the president and the courts, or sometimes resisting them if they see their interests threatened by executive power. Although this informal system of state and federal relations has proved tolerably effective in "getting things done," it comes at a high price: it is less representative in a broad sense. Instead of distinct governments representing the people in a constitutionally defined formal legal and legislative process, national policies are increasingly enacted in an improvised and informal process by the president. Greve warns that this tendency—if left unchecked—will make American politics more vulnerable to executive control and the corruptions of an unpopular politics that favors discrete interests and oppresses minorities through political, economic, and social controls.

Political Parties

The Framers of the Constitution did not anticipate the formation of political parties, and indeed looked upon party spirit as a threat to the deliberative capacities of the constitutional order. Despite these misgivings, political parties proved to be indispensable tools for organizing public opinion and mobilizing voters during elections. Congressional government is scarcely imaginable without the device of party caucuses to organize a buzzing confusion of interests into policy considerations that are digestible by an often distracted public. However, as Zachary Courser demonstrates in chapter 8, instead of parties working to facilitate the constitutional order as envisioned by Madison, they now chafe against its limits on majority power. Whereas nineteenth-century parties accepted and respected these republican limitations as protections for liberty and minority rights, today's parties seek to overcome them as undemocratic and illegitimate. The conflict between today's democratic parties and the republican Constitution has resulted in much of the gridlock in American politics today.

American parties increasingly operate under parliamentary assumptions of unlimited majority control of government, disdaining compromise and deliberation with minority interests, and asserting only the interests of a partisan majority. In our highly polarized era, partisans disdain compromise in favor of the chance to fully affect their will under conditions of unified party government; they seek the unlikely governing coalition of the executive, congressional supermajorities, and a politically sympathetic judiciary. Courser warns that the growing appetite for uncompromising partisan power over the federal government—fed by the frustrations of prolonged political gridlock—may tempt partisans to operate outside established constitutional norms to achieve their policy ends. We may run the risk of impetuous majorities working to oppress or ignore minority interests, impair rights, and undermine constitutional legitimacy in pursuit of their partisan ends, all under a banner of democratic rule.

A Case for Polarization

Madison himself was not immune to the allure of partisanship, and in fact he contributed to the polarization of politics in his own generation as a political actor. In the concluding chapter, Joseph M. Bessette offers a defense of polarizing politics as a means of enacting reforms that cannot be achieved through normal constitutional order. Polarization need not always be considered negative when it is a reflection of real and meaningful differences in the public over fundamental constitutional considerations that cannot be resolved through compromise. Drawing on the examples set by Madison and Abraham Lincoln, Bessette suggests that fundamental questions of the regime sometimes require leaders to polarize opinion in order to facilitate political change. Seeing a threat to the republican order of the Constitution from the Federalists, Madison worked to sharpen political divisions and delegitimize the opposition. In concert with like-minded politicians such as Thomas Jefferson, Madison helped to build a partisan apparatus to wrest political control away from the Federalists to secure the Constitution and preserve the ideals of the revolution.

    Lincoln polarized public opinion in order to arrest the decline of respect for natural rights that the scourge of slavery had encouraged in American politics. He recognized that the founding generation had seen the evils of slavery but had tolerated them to achieve political union. Further political compromises to maintain this union had obscured the evil of slavery and had pushed toleration to its limits. Northern leaders such as Senator Stephen Douglas sought further compromise on the question of slavery as being fully a matter of majority opinion and not principle, justifying the preservation of the union as the paramount political interest. While accepting the legality of slavery, Lincoln pushed against Douglas's banal approach to moral compromise to polarize public opinion around the question of slavery's morality. Lincoln saw the accommodation of slavery as a moral question necessarily undermining the principles of the Declaration of Independence and believed that Douglas's policy of compromise would degrade American politics to mere calculations of self-interest. Unable to find a political compromise that acknowledged the evil of slavery, Lincoln led the union to reestablish itself and transform the Constitution.

In both of these critical junctures in American politics, extraordinary leaders were able to mold public opinion in defense of republican government, relying on their superior talent of practical political wisdom to guide them. In our own political moment, as this book demonstrates, there are many alarms that suggest another such critical juncture may be upon us.

CONCLUSION

This book provides various perspectives on how polarization is affecting our constitutional order. Although the contributors have a range of views about the character of our contemporary partisan polarization and the balance of its benefits and harms, they agree that polarization is now a defining feature of the nation's politics and is placing strains on our institutions and political life. Following the tumultuous 2016 presidential election, we see polarization persisting with continued legislative gridlock driven by uncompromising partisans and continued strains on the constitutional order. We may take heart that periods of polarization have, despite their tumult and excess, often led to positive political reform. There is hope that our current moment may lead to such reform under the established principles of republican government enshrined in the Constitution.

NOTES

1. Pew Research Center, "Political Polarization in the American Public: How Increasing Ideological Uniformity and Partisan Antipathy Affect Politics, Compromise, and Everyday Life," June 12, 2014, last accessed May 10, 2018, http://www.people -press.org/2014/06/12/political-polarization-in-the-american-public.

2. Voteview, "The End of the 114th Congress," December 18, 2016, last accessed May 12, 2018, https://voteviewblog.com/category/114th-congress.

3. "Gov. Bush: 'I'm a Uniter, not a Divider,'" CNN.com transcripts, aired February 29, 2000, last accessed May 10, 2018, http://transcripts.cnn.com/TRAN SCRIPTS/0002/29/se.01.html; and "Barack Obama's Caucus Speech," the *New York Times* online, January 3, 2008, last accessed May 10, 2018, https://www.nytimes.com /2008/01/03/us/politics/03obama-transcript.html.

4. James Madison, *Federalist* 10, in Alexander Hamilton, James Madison, and John Jay, *The Federalist Papers*, ed. Clinton Rossiter (New York: Mentor, 1999), 47.

5. Madison, *Federalist* 48, 276.

6. Madison, *Federalist* 48, 277.

7. Madison, *Federalist* 48.

8. *Oxford English Dictionary, s.v.* "polarization," last accessed May 8, 2018, http://www.oed.com/view/Entry/146757.

9. Geoffrey C. Layman and Thomas M. Carsey, "Party Polarization and 'Conflict Extension' in the American Electorate," *American Journal of Political Science* 46, no. 4 (October 2002): 786–802.

10. Howard Raines, "George Wallace, Segregation Symbol, Dies at 79," *New York Times* online, September 14, 1998, last accessed May 10, 2018, https://www.nytimes.com/1998/09/14/us/george-wallace-segregation-symbol-dies-at-79.html.

11. American Political Science Association (APSA), *Toward a More Responsible Two-Party System, a Report* (Menasha, WI: American Political Science Association, 1950).

12. Madison, *Federalist* 51, 291.

CHAPTER 2

The Madisonian Constitution, Political Dysfunction, and Polarized Politics

George Thomas

Americans are increasingly called on to recognize that the Constitution they purportedly revere is dysfunctional and that the chief problem with the Constitution is the Madisonian framework, with its separation of powers and checks and balances, which, to draw from Woodrow Wilson's century-old criticism of the Constitution, holds us in a state of "inactive equilibrium."[1] Indeed, critics have posited that the Madisonian framework enables a "vetocracy," in Francis Fukuyama's words, generating an ineffective and dysfunctional government that may be a sign of American political decay.[2] Political polarization compounds these pathologies. As Jane Mansbridge writes, "Our polarization is exacerbated by our Constitution's extreme separation of powers, with its many veto points."[3] Against this growing criticism, others have praised the Madisonian system for these very features: in a deeply polarized country, it prevents bare majorities from acting too hastily. Thomas Petri, a former member of Congress, insists that given our sharp polarization, the separation of powers is "functioning as the architects of our Constitution intended."[4] Yet whether our separation of powers is functioning as intended is far from clear. This insistence too readily assumes that "vetocracy" was a healthy element in Madison's constitutional design. Such an understanding, increasingly common, misconstrues Madison's institutional thinking. It places checks and balances at the centerpiece of his constitutional system when, in fact, it was only one part of it. Before he thought of checks and balances, Madison thought of making governmental institutions effective by way of the separation of powers. Madison's constitutional framework was not meant to produce stalemate, but rather to foster effective government able to provide for the public welfare.

As Madison put it in the too-often overlooked *Federalist* 57: "The aim of every political constitution is, or ought to be, first to obtain for rulers men who possess most wisdom to discern, and most virtue to pursue, the common good of society."[5] Madison, to be sure, continued, "And in the next place, to take the most effectual precautions for keeping them virtuous whilst they continue to hold their public trust." This second statement can certainly be interpreted as a nod to checks and balances. But what Madison places first is notable: leadership for the common good. One tends to think of our Madisonian separation of powers as preoccupied with containing power, but separate institutions were designed to effectively meet the governing tasks assigned to them. Even what we take to be checks and balances were, as understood by Madison, meant to nurture better government in the long run and not create stalemate.

This chapter will first explore how Madison's vision of "ambition countering ambition" sought to cultivate the public interest. Madison's framework may no longer serve the ends he envisioned for it, but it is helpful to consider how his institutional design was meant to effectively serve numerous ends. Critics often focus on specific elements—they want a more democratic, more efficient, or more responsible government. A Madisonian vision helps us think about the balance and tension between the different attributes we want from our political institutions. Having elucidated the Madisonian foundation, this chapter turns to Madisonian failings—features of the Madisonian framework that have not worked as Madison hoped. This failure is particularly true of Congress, which is at the center of concerns about political dysfunction: what Sandy Levinson has called "the crisis of governance."[6] Political polarization may exacerbate the dysfunctional elements of the Madisonian system; yet it is helpful to conceptually separate "dysfunction" from "polarization." By "dysfunction" I mean the institutional inability of the government to respond effectively to persistent and pressing issues of public policy. This can be due to "gridlock," which refers to the multiple veto players within American political institutions where action can be brought to a halt by one of the veto players. By "polarization" I refer to the extreme ideological division of the parties. The symptoms of institutional dysfunction—problems of effective and responsible governance, including "veto points" that allow for "gridlock"—are enduring features of American constitutionalism that predate our polarized present. Perhaps the troubles that beset American politics are due to the peculiar collision of polarization and the Madisonian Constitution, as Thomas

Mann and Norman Ornstein argue. [7] But these concepts do not necessarily line up together. Thus, conceptually separating these issues can help us get the diagnosis right. Suggested reforms run from altering constitutional institutions to changing the character of the Republican Party. Efforts to mitigate polarization may not address deeper questions of dysfunction, and, in fact, if we think historically, it may be that political polarization is necessary to bring about fundamental political and constitutional reforms.

Finally, even if we think Madisonian institutions are dysfunctional, a Madisonian mind-set is still helpful to contemplating political reform. Madison was an imaginative political scientist and political actor whose thinking was shaped by political experience. Most importantly, Madison's synoptic vision is a model for thinking about how different elements of the constitutional order fit together, particularly as we aspire to secure a number of ends that do not easily coexist. In this regard, Madison did not think his constitutional framework was "a machine that would go of itself."[8] Indeed, it would require public leaders and citizens to carry it forward. In a polarized age where the basic institutions of liberal democracy are under pressure, educating the public mind may be more important than ever, yet it is part of the Madisonian system that receives only occasional attention.

POLITICAL INSTITUTIONS AND
THE MADISONIAN FRAMEWORK

It may seem odd to assess our current political problems by starting with Madison's thoughts leading up to the Constitution of 1787; yet it is helpful. Madison's "Vices of the Political System of the United States," written in April 1787 as part of the call for political reform, highlighted the inadequacies and ineffectiveness of the Articles of Confederation in not providing the requisite power and effectiveness in "matters where common interest requires it."[9] In defending the new Constitution, Madison labored to persuade his fellow citizens that "the defects of the existing Confederation" would not be overcome "by a government of less energy than that before the public."[10] As Madison continued, this required "a firm national government" that would be "adequate to the exigencies of government and the preservation of the union."[11] Madison's constitutional design was, first and foremost, meant to provide the basis of an energetic and powerful government capable of meeting the demands placed on it. I do not want to rehash Madison's constitutional theory, as much of it is familiar. Yet there is enough misunderstanding to justify revisiting the thinking that undergirds Madison's constitutional design when it comes to power checking power. The Madisonian undertaking of power checking power is most evident in the large republic and the separation of powers (and checks and balances).

The Extended Republic

Madison recognized that different opinions and interests were an inevitable feature of a liberal democratic political order. The "latent causes of faction" were "sown in the nature of man."[12] Madison did not operate under the illusion that giving us "perfect equality" in our political rights would do away with different interests and opinions, the root of political polarization. Recognizing the inevitability of different interests and opinions, Madison argued for the institutional and sociological advantages of a large republic. Madison doubted that we could trust a "statesman" to always adjust such clashing interests and ideas as to render them "subservient to the public good," though this would be ideal.[13] Instead, he thought we could control their effects, channeling clashing opinions and interests toward the public good. Madison thought two features were particularly important to such a political sociology: scale and representation. A large republic would increase the variety of interests and opinions. With numerous competing interests and opinions, ambition would counteract ambition, making it unlikely that any one group could dominate. This countenanced a disharmony of opinions and interests, but might also foster deliberation and reflection precisely because it allowed disharmony. The inevitability of numerous opinions and interests might then have the benefit of softening and moderating opinions.

Representation itself in the extended republic would also moderate the clash of interests and opinions. Representatives would "refine and enlarge the public views," not necessarily out of the goodness of their hearts, or because factions would forgo self-interest.[14] On the contrary, self-interested motives, in accord with Madison's theory, were turned into a virtue. As Jonathan Rauch argues, "Effective action, in this system, depends on nothing but a series of forced compromises."[15] As such, representatives would be a better indicator of the "public voice" than the "people themselves."[16] Madison even argued that one of the great virtues of the Constitution was "*the total exclusion of the people, in their collective capacity*" from any share of the government.[17] Madison insisted on this point even while repeatedly insisting that the people were the font of all legitimate power—the root of political authority—and their "great happiness" the object of government. But constitutional design is meant to refine and educate the public rather than simply act on the public's immediate wants and interests, an important factor in our polarized age. Placing space between the immediate wants of the public and the government's ability to act on these wants might suggest, at first glance, the virtue of gridlock. For Madison it suggested that institutional design would require compromise and coalition building in the pursuit of "the real welfare of the people."[18] This was the aim of the separation of powers.

Separation of Powers

That dividing power into different branches was a means of preventing concentrated and abusive power—and preserving liberty—should not obscure that the separation was meant to secure governmental competence.[19] From the perspective of constitutional design, the separate institutions have unique responsibilities: they serve different functions, interests, and principles. Consider the executive. The execution of the laws required energy, which in turn required unity. Madison insisted, "Energy in Government requires not only a certain duration of power, but the execution of it by a single hand."[20] The president would need to make quick decisions that could be quickly enforced, as well as to steadily administer the laws. Thus, the institution was structured in a way that would ensure executive "virtues," which necessitated a single executive with duration in office and adequate support. A multiple executive would make it more difficult to render decisive judgments when necessary; it would also make it more challenging for the people to hold the executive branch responsible for its judgments. Who are we to hold accountable when multiple people occupy the office?

Institutional form was meant to cultivate the most effective use of executive power, a provision that holds true for the other institutions of government as well. As Hamilton argues in *Federalist* 70, we ought to favor "a single Executive and a numerous legislature," given what we desire from each institution based on its function in the constitutional scheme. He continues: "In the legislature, promptitude of decision is oftener an evil than a benefit. The differences of opinion, and the jarrings of parties in that department of the government . . . often promote deliberation and circumspection, and serve to check excesses in the majority."[21] These are virtues in the legislature, which is representing different views and crafting law. Similarly focusing on institutional function, Madison explains why stability and a six-year term are beneficial in the Senate by contrasting it with the more immediately democratic House, in which representatives serve a two-year term. Madison argues that the Senate provides a check on the House—combining stability with liberty: "The cool and deliberate sense of the community" is more likely to be secured if legislation has to pass through the Senate, ameliorating the more immediately democratic, and possibly passionate, House.[22] The House "is so constituted as to support in the members an habitual recollection of their dependence on the people."[23] Both institutions have their virtues. The Senate's six-year term grants it stability and a longer view—even over the president's four-year term. The House, in contrast, is representative of more immediate democratic wishes and turns over quickly—every two years—and, for this reason, differs from the Senate, where only one-third of its membership is up for reelection every two years. The different branches of government also depend on different constituencies—or, we might say, different versions of the people—which shape their institutional perspective. The president has a national vision, whereas the House is much more parochial, but gives us diverse perspectives when combining the views of all its members.

Yet these different branches "are by no means totally separate and distinct from each other."[24] Power is also contrived to limit the reach of each branch, "keeping each other in their proper places."[25] Here, in perhaps the most famous of *The Federalist Papers*, Madison argues, "Ambition must be made to counteract ambition."[26] To this end, the offices and institutions of government are arranged "in such a manner as that each may be a check on the other—that the private interest of every man may be sentinel over the public rights."[27] Yes, this is to keep the different branches of government within the limits of their constitutional power. By design the Madisonian system fosters conflict and tension but does so to better preserve the constitutional scheme and promote better government. The system of checks and balances requires the building of political coalitions, which includes refining and shaping public opinion, moderating positions, and compromising with other interests in crafting public policy. In this vein, Madison speaks of the "mild voice of reason, pleading the cause of an enlarged and permanent interest."[28]

Forgive an elementary tutorial in Madisonian constitutionalism. And yet I think it's a helpful reminder that the Madisonian system was meant to produce a functional and effective government. Whether it does so more than two hundred years later in a radically altered society is the question I consider next. But even if reform is necessary, Madison's capacious vision is a helpful reminder that the Constitution was a means of achieving multiple and disparate ends.

THE CONTEMPORARY SEPARATION OF POWERS: POLITICAL OBSTRUCTION AND POLITICAL OPPORTUNITY

Congress sits at the center of complaints about America's dysfunctional separation of powers.[29] Since 2011, Congress has not been able to pass a budget by normal means, relying instead on short-term emergency resolutions, which are the subject of ugly partisan dispute, often allowing a small number of representatives to effectively hold Congress hostage. Fortunately, in the fall of 2015, up against yet another deadline, Congress was able to pass a budget that would keep the US government afloat until mid-March 2017, when a new president would occupy the White House, placing budget concerns safely out of the presidential election. Even then, a supermajority of Republicans in the House voted against the budget, underscoring our deep divisions. With unified party government after the election of Donald Trump, the Republicans struggled in the first year of his administration to repeal the Affordable Care Act (ACA), to agree on a budget, or to pass tax reform, all things the president promised to do in his first 30 days in office with a Republican Congress. In the first year of the Trump administration, the major achievements of the Republican Party were limited to the confirmation of Neil Gorsuch to the Supreme Court and the passage of an unpopular tax reform bill.

Against these criticisms, defenders of the Madisonian Constitution argue that a longer view yields a more positive picture than the current chorus of dysfunction suggests. Shep Melnick points out that the Madisonian system was able to respond quite effectively to the fiscal crisis of 2008 and the Great Recession more generally. He also points to a number of major governmental expansions in the last two decades: the No Child Left Behind Act, Medicare drug benefits, and the McCain-Feingold Act, to name just a few. And all of this congressional activity does not include foreign and defense policy at a time when the United States was engaged in wars in Iraq and Afghanistan, both approved by Congress. We can add to this list the creation of the Department of Homeland Security, the creation of the Consumer Financial Protection Bureau, and the ACA.[30] Focusing on the Great Recession and fiscal policy more generally, Pietro Nivola and Jonathan Rauch, both from the Brookings Institution, suggest that the American system has worked reasonably well, particularly in comparative perspective.[31] Rauch, in particular, notes how the Madisonian system still forces compromise, though he does worry that hardening polarization and an "anti-compromise" mentality in the name of "pure" political principles—particularly in the Republican Party—are threats to the Madisonian system.

In fact, in the face of increased "gridlock" in the past few Congresses due to the polarized conflict between former president Barack Obama and the Republican Congress, Melnick points to policy and governmental innovation outside of Congress, arguing that "gridlock" focuses too narrowly on major legislative enactments, neglecting innovative "policy entrepreneurs" in the executive and judicial branches. The American administrative state has been built by a piecemeal fashion, and innovations from the executive and judiciary are a crucial part of the story, as Michael S. Greve illustrates in chapter 7. Melnick points to the existence of extra-legislative policy innovation on a number of fronts as well. An example of this process is a recent Title IX reform, launched by the now famous "Dear Colleague" letter from the Office of Civil Rights (OCR) in the Department of Education.[32] At the initiative of the OCR, the letter was an innovative interpretation of Title IX that required large-scale reforms of grievance procedures across colleges and universities dealing with sexual discrimination and sexual violence.[33] President Trump's education secretary Betsy DeVos withdrew the letter in 2017, citing concerns that the guidance created "regulatory burdens" without "affording notice and the opportunity for public comment."[34]

Melnick is right that even in the face of polarized parties and legislative intransigence, the government continues to be active on a number of fronts, and the executive branch and the courts are innovative policy makers. Yet, interestingly, for a defender of the Madisonian Constitution, Melnick does not pause to ask if this sort of innovation is a sign of constitutional dysfunction.[35] Although "veto points" may also be "opportunity points," there are also costs to such policy innovation. While political stalemate provides innovative actors an opportunity, it is also what makes haphazard policy innovation necessary. Indeed, I cannot help but point out that Melnick himself has been quite critical of the "Dear Colleague" letter with regard to Title IX precisely because he worries about its potential erosion of due process rights, given its somewhat suspect origins and its preoccupation with a narrow set of partisan interests "insulated from ordinary politics."[36] These policy innovations, moreover, are insecure under Trump; yet this is true of much policymaking within the administrative state, which is often driven by executive action.

We might think of some forms of "policy entrepreneurship" as akin to what Steven Teles has dubbed "kludgeocracy."[37] A *kludge* is an inelegant word that points to an inelegant and complicated solution in computer programming. As Teles argues, the complexity of the American system of government is the source of much of our dysfunction and—like Melnick—contends that "veto points" only capture part of the problem because they are not simply points that allow numerous political actors to "stymie action." Rather, we can see "veto points" as tollbooths: the keeper gets to "extract a price for his willingness to allow legislation to keep moving," thereby allowing individual members to protect pet projects or add on "special interest" programs as the price for joining legislation.[38] Congressional lawmaking, then, as William Howell and Terry Moe put it, often resembles "cobbled-together packages that were literally not designed to achieve their loftily stated purposes."[39] Add to haphazard policymaking the proliferation of networks around particular policy issues in which interest groups, administrative agencies, and courts collaborate with legislators to create, negotiate, and protect policy. Moreover, policy negotiated around these different networks does not necessarily cohere. The result is that our decentralized separation of powers "gives representation to the views of interest groups and activist organizations that collectively do not add up to a sovereign American people."[40] The proliferation of money in politics—and the connections with interest groups—only compounds this problem. All of this has led Fukuyama to argue that we are witnessing the "repatrimonialization" of the American state.[41]

From a Madisonian perspective, the crucial point is that Madison's analysis of Congress within the constitutional scheme has turned out to be inaccurate. Madison argued, "In a republican government, the legislative authority necessarily predominates." He went so far as to insist, "The legislative department is everywhere extending the sphere of its activity, and drawing all power into its impetuous vortex."[42] In fact, these quotations reflect Madison's insistence that we counterbalance and limit the legislature precisely because it will naturally be the dominant branch of government. Contrary to his institutional expectations, not only have executive and judicial power grown over the years, but Congress has often willingly yielded its power—so much so that it raises questions about legislative deference to the executive and to the courts. Although Madison's "ambition counteracting ambition" was designed to connect the self-interest of the office holder to the power of the institution, the incentives for Congress to defend its institutional prerogatives have not worked as Madison anticipated. Individual members of Congress, driven by electoral concerns, do not necessarily have clear self-interest in defending the institutional and constitutional prerogatives of the institution. Individual members of Congress have an incentive to act parochially rather than taking into consideration broad public interest. Howell and Moe capture this problem: "Congress is made up of hundreds of members, each a political entrepreneur in her own right, each dedicated to her own reelection and thus to serving her own district or state. Although all have a common stake in the institutional power of Congress, this is a collective good that, for well-known reasons, can only weakly motivate their behavior."[43]

Madison's misjudgment about the primacy of Congress parallels his misjudgment about the executive.[44] Madison envisioned a limited role for the president, and he argued for a circumscribed view of executive power that has been deeply at odds with the development of American institutions.[45] While this dynamic gainsays Madison's particular expectation of the balance within the system, this development is not necessarily at odds with the Madisonian system. Presidents have embodied Madison's insistence that "the interest of the man must be connected with the constitutional rights of the place."[46] The concerns of the president and the expectations placed on presidents have led to expansive claims of power by the executive. Even presidents who have come to office with a more Madisonian vision of executive power—Obama, for example—have found themselves defending and building executive prerogatives. We could call this institutionally induced hypocrisy; that is, the tendency to see things from an institutional perspective. It is not surprising that Obama had a more sympathetic take on executive power as president than he did as a senator. This is not a criticism; it is a feature of constitutional design. Obama turned to executive action most notably on immigration, which he described as "fixing our broken immigration system through executive action."[47] But he turned to executive power on a number of other fronts—gun control, education, and the environment—often with the justification that Congress was not acting or that it was beholden to special interests. Yet even with Republican control of both houses of Congress, Trump has continued to act by way of executive orders—most notably with his travel ban—but also on health care, trade, the environment, and religious liberty.

Like their predecessors, both Obama and Trump have been criticized for executive overreach—by both the left and the right. Interestingly, defenders and critics of executive power share something in common: they both see something dysfunctional in Congress. Critics of executive overreach, particularly in foreign affairs, have long sought to push Congress to more vividly defend its constitutional power against executive encroachment. They often lament that Congress has the tools but that it does not have the will to act. As a collective body, the self-interest of Congress may be in deferring fraught issues to the other branches of government—particularly enabling presidential initiative. Defenders of executive power argue that this deferral still leads to piecemeal policy solutions that are less effective than they could be.[48] Wherever one comes down on the proper balance of power between the executive and the legislature, a problem with the Madisonian framework remains.

The Republican Senate's refusal to hold hearings on Obama's Supreme Court nominee Merrick Garland, in hopes the 2016 presidential election would yield a Republican president and nominee, could be understood at first glance as an instance of congressional assertion against a recent history of congressional acquiescence on Supreme Court nominees and consistency with the Madisonian framework. To be sure, the Madisonian separation of powers can be frustrating because it refuses to place trust in "any one center." Rather, it divides power based on the logic that the system will be best preserved if all parties are given responsibility for its maintenance. The president has the power—indeed, the constitutional obligation—to appoint justices to the Supreme Court. But the Senate must consent. The Senate can of course vote a nominee down; it can also delay hearings. It has postponed consideration of nominees on several occasions—including election years in 1828, 1844, 1852, and 1968—so the incoming president would be able to make the appointment.[49] In the 1844 case, the Senate refused to confirm a number of nominees from former president John Tyler and then postponed consideration until after the election of 1844. The court had a vacancy for nearly two years.[50] Congress has also lowered the number of justices sitting on the Supreme Court from ten to nine to deny former president Andrew Johnson a Supreme Court appointment.[51] In the event of a clash between a recalcitrant Senate and a determined president, no "higher" or "ultimate" arbiter exists within the Madisonian framework, or, as Madison put it in somewhat different circumstances, the people themselves must be the judge.

The Republican Senate's refusal to consider Garland reflects our deep polarization, already evident in the court's 5–4 opinions on same-sex marriage, religious liberty, the ACA, and campaign finance, to name just a few. That Justice Antonin Scalia was a solid vote on the conservative side and Obama's appointment of Judge Garland would almost certainly have tipped the court in a more liberal direction only heightened the stakes. Indeed, the court might be even more important these days precisely because it is an avenue for pushing a political and constitutional agenda, as Amanda Hollis-Brusky illustrates in chapter 5.[52] The Senate successfully halted the process, wielding an effective "veto" against Obama's appointee, in order to preserve a political balance that favors Republicans, which was solidified with the confirmation of Judge Neil Gorsuch. While Obama, former secretary of state Hillary Clinton, and Democrats complained about constitutional obstruction from a Republican Senate, Senator Mitch McConnell gave new life to the old aphorism that the Court follows the election returns. He and his fellow Republicans explicitly treated the Court as part of a governing coalition: the winner of the presidential election should be given the opportunity to tip the balance on the Court in his or her favor. During the 2016 presidential election, both Clinton and Trump frequently spoke of the Court in political and partisan terms. Both, that is, spoke in terms of the policy commitments they hoped to secure by way of their judicial appointments. For example, Clinton spoke about a woman's right to choose, and Trump spoke of securing gun rights. There was less discussion of appropriate methods of constitutional interpretation or the role of the Court in the constitutional scheme than of policy objectives to be entrenched or repealed by way of judicial appointments. Much like the Senate, Clinton and Trump embraced the Court as an explicit part of their governing coalition rather than treating it as standing apart from ordinary politics. Unfortunately, neither candidate offered American citizens much of a positive constitutional vision but spoke to constitutional issues in terms of the judiciary, reinforcing the long trend of narrowing the Constitution to legal terrain as understood by courts.

At the same time, the presidential election of 2016 was a vivid reminder that maintaining our constitutional order depends on more than courts. Trump challenged basic constitutional norms: he repeatedly threatened to "lock up" a political opponent, questioned judicial independence and freedom of speech and the press, and hesitated on whether he would accept the election results should he lose. There is debate about how seriously we should take Trump's rhetoric, but his rhetoric is deeply disturbing. Even after being elected, Trump tweeted that those who burned American flags should be stripped of citizenship or punished in some fashion. Tweeting, as the essential means of presidential communication, may point to a kind of demagogic populism that is profoundly at odds with our Madisonian system, and the democratic debate and discourse it depends on. More than tweeting, Trump has acted in ways that raise profound questions about the separation of powers and the future of liberal democracy in America. Trump has continued to raise questions about the nature and value of an independent judiciary but has thus far not acted against judicial independence. He did, however, fire former FBI director James Comey in 2017— very likely because of the bureau's independence in investigating the Trump campaign's possible connections to Russian interference in the presidential election. And while Trump was well within his legal power to fire Comey, we should resist a legalistic understanding of abusing constitutional power and norms. As Hamilton put it in *Federalist* 65, an "abuse of the public trust" may be an injury to "society itself" and not simply a legal wrongdoing.[53]

So, while the 2016 presidential election results indicate the continued polarization of parties, the election raises deeper questions about the rise of "illiberal democracy."[54] Yascha Mounk and Roberto Foa also point to evidence of the softening of democratic norms and commitments among the American populace.[55] Whether or not Trump is a genuine populist, he seems to have very little commitment to liberal democracy or American constitutionalism. We are witnessing the powerful appeal of what Christopher Achen and Larry Bartels call the "folk theory" of democracy—the idea that the people's wants should rule simply, ungoverned or educated by mediating representative institutions.[56] But, as Achen and Bartels demonstrate, the people are ill-equipped to rule in this regard. Realistic democracy depends on the very sort of political dealings that we have been doing away with in recent years. Ironically, Jonathan Rauch notes this has very likely increased the polarization of the parties.[57]

Yet looking back, America has had freighted political debates about our foundational constitutional principles and commitments when the country was deeply polarized. This was true of Abraham Lincoln's election in 1860;

his first inaugural offered an interpretation of the Constitution on numerous fronts that rejected the Court's constitutional judgment in *Dred Scott*. In 1916, Supreme Court Justice Charles Evans Hughes stepped down from the Court to accept the Republican nomination and run against Woodrow Wilson in an extraordinarily close contest that featured constitutional issues. While Franklin Delano Roosevelt's election in 1936 was overwhelming, he pushed a partisan and constitutional agenda, which sought to bring the Court and country into line with his constitutional vision. Interestingly, these conflicts have been described as efforts to transform America's constitutional understandings, which grew out of political polarization. Many of our most important presidents—Thomas Jefferson, Abraham Lincoln, Theodore Roosevelt, Woodrow Wilson, Franklin Roosevelt, and Ronald Reagan—were polarizing figures. They sought to constitutionalize political principles that were deeply controversial in their day.[58] Polarization can become an engine of political and constitutional change or provide for party realignment.

While polarization can generate stalemate, a polarizing politics about fundamental constitutional and political issues may also be the way out—but it won't necessarily be quick. And, as much as partisanship is blamed for polarization and dysfunctional government, there is no doing away with partisanship. Yet we can distinguish between what Russell Muirhead dubs "high partisanship," partisanship on principled issues and broad goals that define a conception of the good, and low partisanship, which is rooted in electoral victory and denying opponents, but not much else.[59] Despite deep political divisions, indeed because of them, partisanship is a healthy feature of American democracy. Yet given the threat to our liberal democracy, we might recall a common commitment to constitutional norms. Even so, we cannot assume that we will all agree or that we can dissolve political conflict simply by turning to reason or the common good. In fact, we ought to be far more concerned with the temptation to turn to "leadership" that dispenses with the difficult business of politics and disagreement in the Madisonian scheme—promising, as Trump does, "to go in and get things done."[60] Leadership of this sort is a temptation that needs be resisted and a reminder of why Madison wanted "ambition to counteract ambition."

Constitutional Reform and a Madisonian Mind-Set

If the Constitution needs to be reformed, a Madisonian mind-set would be helpful. As Madison said to his fellow citizens, the revolutionary generation "reared the fabrics of governments which have no model on the face of the globe. They formed the design of a great Confederacy, which it is incumbent on their successors to improve and perpetuate. If their works betray imperfections, we wonder at the fewness of them. If they erred most in the structure of the Union, this was the work most difficult to be executed."[61] As you may have guessed, this was Madison urging his fellow citizens that the Articles were inadequate to the governance of the Union. In the spirit of the revolution, he argued that we should not to be beholden to a "blind veneration for antiquity" but rather should deliberate on the Constitution before us as an innovation to better secure the ends of the Union.[62] We could think of contemporary calls for constitutional reform in this Madisonian spirit and recall that Madison learned from experience. On many of the most important questions in framing the Constitution, Madison lost; yet he came to reconsider his position. Given our experience of the institutions he helped create, we have a much better sense of how they have actually worked, empirically speaking. In Madison's terms, the Constitution was a means to achieve political ends of the sort laid out in the Constitution's preamble, and therefore needs to be measured against its effectiveness in achieving these ends. No constitution will be perfect in this regard.

Thinking of the Constitution in instrumental terms will allow us to more readily consider constitutional reforms. Indeed, given the stalemate and conflict over a single Supreme Court nominee, we might consider the idea of term limits for justices. One proposed scheme, with bipartisan support, would provide for eighteen-year terms with two presidential appointments for every four-year term. Deliberations of this nature are central to our constitutional democracy, and a debate about them could be healthy—even in polarized times, which is not to deny politics, partisanship, and self-interest. If we cannot have such a dialogue around Supreme Court appointees, then it seems highly unlikely that we could debate more fundamental changes to the constitutional order, such as Howell and Moe's suggestion of a constitutional amendment giving the president "fast-track" authority on all policy matters, or Levinson's call for a new constitutional convention.[63] But there are also political reforms that do not require constitutional change, such as abolishing the Senate filibuster, which does not have grounding in the Madisonian Constitution, or even bringing back a reformed legislative veto to empower Congress against executive administration.[64] More difficult, but perhaps most pressing, is campaign finance reform.[65] Neither of these is a fundamental constitutional reform. These issues also cut across our polarized and partisan divide with strong support from the populace.

With regard to our partisan divide, I want to conclude on an aspect of the Madisonian Constitution that is too often neglected but may be at the root of our polarization: the necessity of educating the public. Many of our most pressing problems may be mental rather than institutional; they are problems of civil society as much as of institutional form.[66] Every constitution is incomplete: it will always depend on future citizens to carry the project forward. To this end, Madison thought education was necessary for cultivating the habits and mind-set in citizens and public officers—Madison referred to "national feelings," "liberal sentiments," and "congenial manners"—necessary to America's constitutional experiment.[67] Madison thought that "liberty" and "learning" would have to go together. Education would supplement America's political institutions by fostering a healthy civil society. As Thomas Jefferson put it, education will "form the statesmen, legislators and judges, on whom public prosperity and individual happiness are so much to depend."[68] Madison joined Jefferson in forging the University of Virginia to this end—and also called for the establishment of a national university—that would educate and shape the public mind, carrying the American experiment forward.[69]

"Learned institutions," however, were not the only place Madison thought the public mind could be shaped. Madison turned to representation itself, as I noted above, but more importantly to political parties and newspapers in this effort. The educative function of parties was also an area where Madison learned from experience, confronting his first constitutional failure in the 1790s. Madison began as a skeptic of parties, but ultimately accepted and defended the role of political parties as an essential feature of the constitutional system. Madison argued that insofar as differences in interests and ideas would persist, parties were unavoidable. But this reality could be turned to political advantage by "making one party a check on the other."[70] The parties themselves would articulate, temper, and refine popular understandings. The parties would become a source of popular education and empowerment—as would partisan newspapers and representatives. Our current political parties tend to misapprehend their importance, as is evident in chapter 8 by Zachary Courser. Parties, at their best, do not simply discover and articulate static interests and divisions. Rather, they are actively engaged in forming and organizing beliefs that seek to articulate important political differences. But they also play a moderating role in recognizing that politics requires compromise. At their best, parties are educative. But what happens when political leaders and the parties are not led by the most informed, but seem to be represented by what Edmund Burke called the "less inquiring" in public affairs?[71] What happens when our leadership class lacks the sort of political education envisioned by a Madison?

In our current historical moment, political parties are often vehicles for expressing unrefined popular opinion rather than operating as intermediary institutions educating and channeling it. This is perhaps most evident in the case of Trump. During the 2016 presidential campaign, Trump reflected a stunning ignorance of America's Constitution and the political process, at times voicing contempt for liberal democracy itself. Given this, many in the Republican Party found his ascendency deeply disturbing. Yet, given that he garnered the most votes in the Republican primary, it was also argued that it would be "undemocratic" to deny him the nomination. Understanding democracy as reflecting the immediate will of the people abdicates the educational role that intermediary institutions—like political parties—play in a healthy democracy. We stand to benefit from Madison's complex understanding of democracy and the necessity of informing public opinion as I have argued elsewhere.[72] America's constitutional democracy depends on a generally educated citizenry, but it does not depend on them to be constitutional and political experts. Rather, they are likely to take their cues from ideas generated by political and intellectual leaders, whom Madison referred to as "the cultivators of the human mind—the manufacturers of useful knowledge—the agents of the commerce of ideas—the censors of republican manners—the teachers of the arts of life and the means of happiness."[73] Madison anticipated that public opinion could be enlightened by the refinement of public views. This was an essential feature of republican leadership insofar as Madison insisted: "Public opinion sets bounds to every government, and is the real sovereign in every free one."[74] Yet the current state of the media, political parties, and representation often fosters the worst features of democracy rather than moderating them. Trump is only the most notable example of this.

Calls to reform the Madisonian system are not necessarily calls to more immediately act on popular understandings. Effective governance should not be confused with simple democracy. Indeed, scholars like Fukuyama argue that effective governance and the public good depend on governmental autonomy from popular opinion. Curiously, the United States might suffer from too much democracy in the rhetoric of campaigns and elections, and too little when it comes to policymaking. Reforms aimed at both limiting and enabling democracy would be Madisonian in the best sense, yielding a complex understanding of popular government that we ought to maintain. In particular, we should heed his prudent reminder that we aspire to secure multiple constitutional values, which necessarily requires compromise. Perhaps most of all, we should insist that civic education is not the preserve of the elite but essential to a healthy and balanced democracy.

These dysfunctions are not in the formal institutions of the Madisonian Constitution but in the civil society that supplements it. Advocates of constitutional reform persistently point to America's fiscal woes as evidence of structural constitutional dysfunction thanks to the separation of powers.[75] Yet our fiscal woes are also a failure of democratic education and citizenship. We let Americans demand low taxes and governmental programs rather than insisting that we must pay for the services we want. And representatives often do not function as educators in this regard, as Madison hoped they would. Achieving reforms here may be easier than altering our formal institutions, and such reforms may be more essential. With Trump's presidency, the United States may be in a battle for its constitutional soul. Such political moments are fraught with peril, but they have also been our greatest periods of constitutional reform and revitalization.

NOTES

1. Woodrow Wilson, *Constitutional Government in the United States* (New Brunswick: Transaction Press, 2002 [1908]), 199.

2. Francis Fukuyama, *Political Order and Political Decay: From the Industrial Revolution to the Globalization of Democracy* (New York: Farrar, Straus and Giroux, 2014), 502.

3. Jane Mansbridge, "Political Polarization Is Here to Stay," *Washington Post*, March 11, 2016.

4. Thomas Petri, "Our Government Is Messy, but That Doesn't Mean It Isn't Working," *Washington Post*, March 9, 2016.

5. James Madison, *Federalist* 57, in Alexander Hamilton, James Madison, and John Jay, *The Federalist Papers*, ed. Ian Shapiro (New Haven, CT: Yale University Press, 2009), 290.

6. Sanford Levinson, *Framed: America's 51 Constitutions and the Crisis of Governance* (New York: Oxford University Press, 2012).

7. Thomas E. Mann and Norman J. Ornstein, *It's Even Worse Than It Was: How the American Constitutional System Collided with the New Politics of Extremism* (New York: Basic Books, 2012).

8. James Russell Lowell, "The Place of the Independent in Politics," *The Complete Writings of James Russell Lowell*, vol. 7 (New York: Houghton, Mifflin, 1904), 252.

9. Marvin Meyers, ed., *The Mind of the Founder: The Sources of the Political Thought of James Madison*, 2nd ed. (Lebanon, NH: Brandeis University Press, 1981), 57.

10. Madison, *Federalist* 37, 179.

11. Madison, *Federalist* 40, 199.

12. Madison, *Federalist* 10, 48.

13. Madison, *Federalist* 10, 50.

14. Madison, *Federalist* 10, 45.

15. Jonathan Rauch, "Rescuing Compromise," in *What Would Madison Do? The Father of the Constitution Meets Modern American Politics*, ed. Benjamin Wittes and Pietro Nivola (Washington, DC: Brookings Institution, 2015), 98.

16. Madison, *Federalist* 10, 51.

17. Madison, *Federalist* 63, 322.

18. Madison, *Federalist* 45, 235. This analysis draws on my book: George Thomas, *The Madisonian Constitution* (Baltimore: Johns Hopkins University Press, 2008).

19. Madison, *Federalist* 47, 246.

20. Hamilton, *Federalist* 37, 181.

21. Hamilton, *Federalist* 70, 355, 357.

22. Madison, *Federalist* 63, 320. See *Federalist* 58 on the House.

23. Madison, *Federalist* 57, 291.

24. Madison, *Federalist* 47, 246.

25. Madison, *Federalist* 51, 263.

26. Madison, *Federalist* 51, 264.

27. Madison, *Federalist* 51, 258.

28. Madison, *Federalist* 42, 216.

29. William G. Howell and Terry M. Moe, *Relic: How Our Constitution Undermines Effective Government* (New York: Basic Books, 2016), 47.

30. R. Shep Melnick, "Gridlock and the Madisonian Constitution," in *What Would Madison Do?*, ed. Benjamin Wittes and Pietro Nivola (Washington, DC: Brookings Institution, 2015), 75–78.

31. Wittes and Nivola, "Overcoming the Great Recession: How Madison's 'Horse and Buggy' Managed," 51–67; and Wittes and Nivola, "Rescuing Compromise," in *What Would Madison Do?*, 95–110.

32. Melnick, "Gridlock and the Madisonian Constitution," 82.

33. Russlynn Ali, "Dear Colleague," US Department of Education, Office for Civil Rights, April 4, 2011, last accessed May 12, 2018, https://www2.ed.gov/about/offices/list/ocr/letters/colleague-201104.pdf.

34. Candice Jackson, "Dear Colleague," US Department of Education, Office for Civil Rights, September 22, 2017, last accessed May 12, 2018, https://www2.ed.gov/about/offices/list/ocr/letters/colleague-title-ix-201709.pdf.

35. Melnick, "Gridlock and the Madisonian Constitution," 79.

36. R. Shep Melnick, "The Odd Evolution of the Civil Rights State," *Harvard Journal of Law and Public Policy* 37, no. 1 (Winter 2014): 113.

37. Steve Teles, "Kludgeocracy in America," *National Affairs* (Fall 2013): 104–114.

38. Teles, "Kludgeocracy in America," 104.

39. William G. Howell and Terry M. Moe, *Relic: How Our Constitution Undermines Effective Government* (New York: Basic Books, 2016), 50.

40. Fukuyama, *Political Order and Political Decay*, 503.

41. Fukuyama, *Political Order and Political Decay*, 479.

42. Madison, *Federalist* 51, 264; and Madison, *Federalist* 48, 252.

43. Terry M. Moe and William G. Howell, "Unilateral Action and Presidential Power," *Presidential Studies Quarterly* 29, no. 4 (1999): 861–873.

44. William Galston, "Constitutional Surprises: What James Madison Got Wrong," in *What Would Madison Do?*, ed. Benjamin Wittes and Pietro Nivola (Washington, DC: Brookings Institution, 2015), 38–50.

45. I am referring to Madison's Helvidius essays, which offered a narrow view of executive power against Alexander Hamilton's Pacificus essays. See Thomas, *The Madisonian Constitution*, 166–167.

46. Madison, *Federalist* 51, 264.

47. Department of Homeland Security News Archive, "Executive Action," November 20, 2015, last accessed May 12, 2018, https://www.dhs.gov/immigration-action.

48. Even among critics of the Constitution some, like Levinson, favor Congress, while others, such as Howell and Moe, favor the president.

49. Henry J. Abraham, *Justices, Presidents, and Senators: A History of the U.S. Supreme Court Appointments from Washington to Clinton* (Lanham, MD: Rowman and Littlefield, 1999), 72, 79, 83, and 218, respectively. The obvious cases are 1828, when the Senate declined John Quincy Adams's appointment so that Andrew Jackson could have it; the Whig Senate denying John Tyler numerous appointments, which left a court seat vacant in 1844–1845; and 1852–1853 when the Senate denied consideration of former president Fillmore's nominee, leaving it to the Democrat, Franklin Pierce; and in 1968 Abe Fortas was nominated by former president Johnson, but the Senate delayed.

50. Abraham, *Justices, Presidents, and Senators*, 79.

51. Abraham, *Justices, Presidents, and Senators*, 93.

52. Thomas M. Keck, *Judicial Politics in Polarized Times* (Chicago: University of Chicago Press, 2015).

53. Hamilton, *Federalist* 65, 330–331.

54. Fareed Zakaria, "The Rise of Illiberal Democracy," 76 *Foreign Affairs* (1997): 22–43.

55. Yascha Mounk and Roberto Foa, "The Democratic Disconnect," *Journal of Democracy* 27, no. 3 (July 2016): 5–17; and "The Signs of Deconsolidation," *Journal of Democracy* 28, no. 1 (January 2017): 5–15.

56. Christopher A. Achen and Larry M. Bartels, *Democracy for Realists: Why Elections Do Not Promote Responsive Government* (Princeton, NJ: Princeton University Press, 2016).

57. Jonathan Rauch, "How American Politics Went Insane," *The Atlantic* (July/August 2016).

58. Russell Muirhead, *The Promise of Party in a Polarized Age* (Cambridge, MA: Harvard University Press, 2014), 205.

59. Muirhead, "Promise of Party," 202.

60. Sandy Fitzgerald, "Trump: My Policy Plans Are to Go In and Get Things Done," *Newsmax*, August 11, 2015.

61. Madison, *Federalist* 14, 71.

62. Madison, *Federalist* 14, 65.

63. Howell and Moe, *Relic*; and Sanford Levinson, *Our Undemocratic Constitution* (New York: Oxford University Press, 2006).

64. See Ilan Wurman, "Constitutional Administration," *Stanford Law Review* 69, no. 2 (February 2017): 359–434.

65. Lawrence Lessig, *Republic, Lost: How Money Corrupts Congress—and a Plan to Stop It* (New York: Twelve, 2011).

66. Rauch notes that an increasing number of Americans are "politiphobes" who believe that there are simple, obvious, and commonsense solutions to all of our problems that are beyond politics. Rauch, "How American Politics Went Insane."

67. James Madison, *Seventh Annual Message,* December 5, 1815, last accessed May 12, 2018, http://www.presidency.ucsb.edu/ws/index.php?pid=29457.

68. Thomas Jefferson, "Report of the Board of Commissioners for the University of Virginia to the Virginia General Assembly," August 4, 1818, last accessed May 10, 2018, https://founders.archives.gov/documents/Madison/04-01-02-0289.

69. George Thomas, *The Founders and the Idea of a National University: Constituting the American Mind* (New York: Cambridge University Press, 2015).

70. James Madison, "Parties," *National Gazette,* January 25, 1792, last accessed May 10, 2018, http://press-pubs.uchicago.edu/founders/print_documents/v1ch15s 50.html.

71. Edmund Burke, *Reflections on the Revolution in France and Other Writings* (New York: Everyman's Library, 2015), 728.

72. George Thomas, "Madison and the Perils of Populism," *National Affairs* 29 (Fall 2016): 142–156.

73. Quoted in Colleen A. Sheehan, *James Madison and the Spirit of Republican Self-Government* (New York: Cambridge University Press, 2009), 104.

74. Thomas, *The Founders and the Idea of a National University*, 9, 225.

75. See Benjamin Wittes, Pietro Nivola, and John J. DiIulio Jr., "Mr. Madison's Communion Suit: Implementation-Group Liberalism and the Case for Constitutional Reform," in *What Would Madison Do?*, 15–37.

CHAPTER 3

Rising Partisan Polarization in the US Congress

Kathryn Pearson

Political scientists and practitioners alike express deep concerns about partisan polarization in contemporary US Congress, pointing to partisan polarization as a dominant source of congressional dysfunction, gridlock, and record-low levels of approval.[1] Although the Constitution does not mention parties by name, James Madison's warnings about the "mischiefs of factions" did in fact target political parties.[2] In his farewell address, former president George Washington warned the new nation about the "baneful effects of the spirit of party," which he considered the "worst enemy" of popular government.[3]

From the outset, the Framers of the Constitution created an obstacle course for passing and enacting legislation, and over time legislators have added more hurdles, including the Senate filibuster.[4] As challenges to governing arose, congressional parties were often solutions to overcoming the collective action problem inherent in a legislative process involving both houses of the legislature and the president. Indeed, in his influential 1942 study of party government, political scientist E. E. Schattschneider concluded, "The political parties created democracy and modern democracy is unthinkable save in terms of the parties."[5]

In 1950 Schattschneider chaired the Committee for a More Responsible Two-Party System for the American Political Science Association (APSA).[6] The APSA report called for "responsible parties" at a time when Democrats in Congress lacked party unity, hindering their ability to translate large congressional majorities into policy change—even when Democrats also controlled the White House. Political scientist Austin Ranney outlined key criteria of responsible parties: they would make policy commitments to the electorate, be willing and able to carry them out when in office, develop alternatives to government policies when out of office, and differ sufficiently between themselves to provide the electorate with a choice.[7] While polarized parties and responsible parties are not synonymous, there is no doubt that the positions taken by today's polarized parties differ significantly, providing the electorate with stark choices and hindering Congress's ability to govern.

Since the 1950s, a sea change in Congress and in the electorate has taken place. By the 1990s, political scientists were no longer bemoaning weak congressional parties but were documenting and debating the rise of partisanship. In 1994, Republicans gained majority party control of the House and Senate for the first time in forty years. Parties seemed to be behaving more like responsible parties. Yet, political scientists and observers alike expressed concerns over growing partisan polarization as the two parties became increasingly homogeneous and far apart from one another on policy issues; partisan disagreement seemed increasingly bitter and dysfunctional.

A 2013 report of the APSA task force on negotiating agreement in politics focused on some of the deleterious effects of partisan polarization in Congress.[8] Indeed, the effects of partisan polarization extend well beyond strong intraparty agreement and interparty disagreement on policy issues. As polarization has increased, party leaders have gained strength and power, and committees have become less active in the policymaking process. Polarization has also caused procedural disputes, gridlock, delays in appropriations—resulting in budget shutdowns—as well as delays and vacancies in judicial confirmations.

Evidence for partisan polarization separating the two parties in the House and Senate is clear. Figure 1 shows the increase in members' party line voting—voting with their party on votes that divide the party—in the House of Representatives between 1987 and 2017. Scholars have found that polarization is asymmetric, with Republicans moving a greater distance to the right than Democrats have moved to the left.[9] Scholars also note that the partisan polarization has occurred in both economic and social dimensions, at least as indicated by the roll call record, meaning that socially conservative Republicans in Congress are also economically conservative, and vice versa. Moreover, Frances Lee demonstrates that the parties in the Senate are polarized not only on issues that tap a left-right ideological divide but also on issues that are nonideological and procedural in context.[10]

In the pages that follow, I trace the rise of partisan polarization. I begin with a brief overview of the evolving congressional literature on parties, and

Figure 1: Increasing Party Unity in the
US House of Representatives, 1987–2017

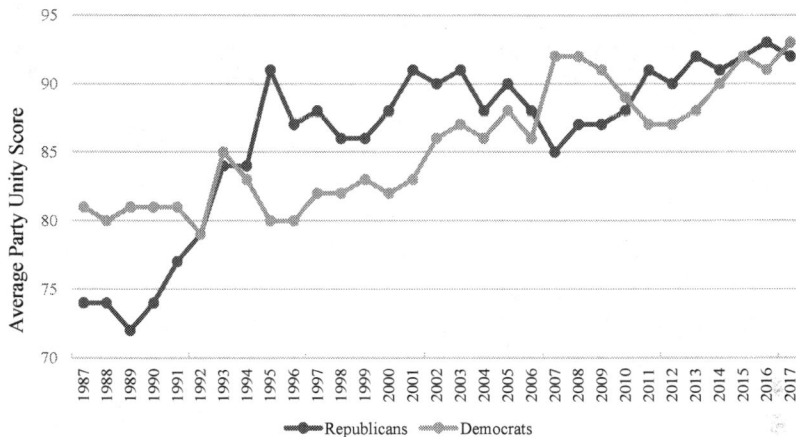

Source: Compiled from *CQ Weekly* data by author.

subsequently detail changes inside Congress and the concomitant increase in party leaders' strength. I then analyze the effects of partisan polarization on the legislative process in both chambers. While there are some benefits to partisan polarization in certain contexts, the effects are largely negative, diminishing members' abilities to represent many of their constituents, budget effectively, respond to the nation's most pressing problems, and compete with the president for influence.

SCHOLARSHIP ON PARTIES IN CONGRESS

In the wake of the institutional and political changes that transformed congressional parties beginning in the 1970s, a sea change in the literature on Congress occurred. By the 1990s, scholars were engaged in a heated and prolific debate over the role of congressional parties, marking a sharp contrast from congressional scholarship that focused on individual members and their committee roles, particularly from the late 1930s to the mid-1970s.[11] In his seminal work, *Congress: The Electoral Connection,* David Mayhew famously articulated the prevailing scholarly view of congressional parties in 1974: "The fact is that no theoretical treatment of the United States Congress that posits parties as analytic units will go very far."[12] Congressional parties, Mayhew argues, could help members with their electoral goals, but they did not pursue policy programs or pressure their members to vote with them. As Mayhew himself notes,[13] he was writing during the low point of intraparty cohesion in voting, and party cohesion began to rise significantly in the years that followed.

During the 1990s, scholars developed and analyzed two leading theories of congressional parties: conditional party government theory[14] and the party cartel theory.[15] David Rohde's *Parties and Leaders in the Postreform House*[16] reversed a long decline in scholarly interest in parties in the House of Representatives, detailing the revival of party activity and articulating the theory of conditional party government (CPG). According to CPG, members' willingness to cede power to their leaders depends on the homogeneity of members' preferences within their party caucus and the distance between the preferences of the two parties. CPG thus explains variation in party power, as parties became more divided, and leaders gained strength during the 1970s and 1980s. As more liberals were elected to the House, Democrats became an increasingly like-minded majority beginning in the late 1960s and the 1970s, and their ideological distance from Republicans grew, prompting them to enact a series of reforms to centralize power in the hands of majority party leaders and thereby achieving results favored by most majority party members.

When Republicans gained majority control of the House in 1995, party leaders centralized power with support from rank-and-file members. CPG helps explain this centralization of power: "Gingrich and his allies wanted to strengthen the GOP party leadership in order to gain greater control over the agenda and greater influence over the choices of Republican members. The party Conference was willing to grant these greater powers because the party had a high degree of preference homogeneity, which had been reinforced by the large and very conservative freshman class of 1994."[17] By contrast, Cox and McCubbins[18] model parties in the House as a legislative cartel, whereby the majority party is able to "usurp the rule-making power of the House"[19] and wield power over every stage of the legislative process to achieve majority party interests. They argue that parties are—and have consistently been—stronger than most scholars recognize.

Contemporary scholarship on congressional parties accelerated when Keith Krehbiel entered the debate by challenging scholars to prove that "apparent party effects"[20] are more than just the expression of members' ideological preferences and, by extension, that the two congressional parties are more ideologically sorted than in the past. In his 1993 article "Where's the Party?" Krehbiel questions whether parties matter at all once scholars take into account members' policy preferences, arguing that what scholars identify as party effects are instead "artifacts of preferences rather than evidence of party discipline, party cohesion, party strength, or party government." In the political science firestorm that followed Krehbiel's 1993 article, most of the scholarly work contrasted one or both of the partisan theories to Krehbiel's nonpartisan models of legislative institutions,[21] which emphasize the importance of the median voter on legislative procedures and outcomes.

Krehbiel's challenge instigated a "hunt for party discipline,"[22] and scholars began to systematically explain how parties exert influence in post-reform congressional politics.[23] Scholars were able to detect partisan effects in analyses of roll call votes and interest group scores that show higher levels of party support than their ideology would predict.[24] For example, Snyder and Groseclose found evidence of party discipline through an analysis of closely contested roll call votes.[25] They derived a scale of underlying preferences from lopsided votes—where party pressure should not matter—which they then used to derive party pressure when analyzing close votes, where pressure is likely to be applied. Pearson found that majority party leaders in the House indeed discipline their members, particularly in pursuit of a partisan policy agenda, rewarding members for their loyalty in voting with key committee assignments and by bringing their bills and resolutions to the House floor for consideration, but rarely rewarding loyalty with campaign contributions, instead focusing on protecting the most vulnerable in pursuit of majority party control.[26]

Frances Lee has demonstrated clear party effects and intense party conflict in the contemporary US Senate.[27] Lee analyzed legislative behavior in the Senate from 1981 to 2004, determining that ideological disagreement between Democrats and Republicans alone does not account for the high levels of party conflict. Instead, she argued that party competition and partisans' shared goals of undermining the other party help explain the divides she has found in the roll call record. Lee coded the substance of votes from 1981 to 2004 and analyzed voting behavior by senators on ideological, non-ideological, and explicitly procedural issues. She then demonstrated that there is a significant partisan divide in all types of votes, even though we would expect no such divide in non-ideological and procedural votes if the parties are divided primarily by ideology. Lee has argued that partisans' shared risk and goals underlie this partisan conflict, leading members of one party to discredit the opposition party—and opposition party president—on all issues, including integrity and competence. How did we get to this point?

INCREASING PARTY LEADERSHIP POWER:
DRIVING, AND DRIVEN BY, PARTISAN POLARIZATION

Polarization is driven by, and drives, a number of forces, including changes in the electorate among donors and activists, in the media, and within the insti-

tution. In these pages, I focus on the forces within the institution, particularly
the increased power of party leaders in Congress, and its implications.

From 1937 to the late 1960s, Democrats held the majority for all but four
years, yet Democratic leaders wielded relatively little power. During the "textbook Congress" era (1940s–1960s) when the institution ran according to set
norms of political behavior, strong committee chairs exerted considerable
control over the legislative agenda, and legislative outcomes were often dominated by a conservative coalition of southern Democrats and Republicans
who voted against the majority of northern Democrats on the floor and in key
committees, often thwarting majority party leaders' initiatives and presidential
proposals.[28] Conservative southern Democrats held a disproportionate number of chairmanships, as they typically represented districts that generated
no real Republican competition, and thus they tended to hold safe seats that
allowed them to serve for long periods of time.[29] With this committee gate-
keeping power, the conservative coalition often succeeded in blocking legislation favored by party leaders and liberal Democrats. Democratic leaders held
together procedural rather than policy majorities,[30] and majority party Democratic leaders lacked the institutional tools and the support of their members
to exert control over their party.[31]

In the late 1960s and early 1970s, political changes paved the way for institutional reforms that shifted power in the House from committee chairmen
to party leaders. As the Republican Party became viable in more areas in
the south, competitive two-party elections meant that southern conservatives
were increasingly likely to run as Republicans, and the remaining southern
Democrats' constituencies became more liberal over time.[32] Eventually, these
changes led to a decreased proportion of southern conservatives in the Democratic Caucus. An influx of new Democrats in the 1964 and 1974 elections
further augmented support for liberal policies and provided critical support
for institutional reforms. The 1974 elections added seventy-five new, mainly
liberal Democrats for a net gain of forty-eight Democratic seats. These so-
called Watergate babies hastened reforms already under way, as many of them
joined forces with liberal Democratic Study Group (DSG) members agitating
for reform. Junior members anxious to obtain power—combined with liberal
Democrats intent on passing a legislative program—formed a majority that
enabled Democrats to adopt several party and institutional reforms. These
reforms greatly enhanced the power of party leaders at the expense of committee chairs' power, while democratizing the House in ways that allowed junior members to exert power, particularly as subcommittees reinforced their
control and autonomy.[33] In 1973, the rules were reformed again, this time to

require an automatic secret ballot on committee chairs at the start of each Congress, making it easier for members to remove a recalcitrant committee chair. The effects were significant; three committee chairmen were deposed after the 1974 elections (Crook and Hibbing 1985).

The 1970s reforms endowed party leaders with power not possessed by a leader since former Speaker Joe Cannon (R-IL) was stripped of his by a group of progressive Republicans and minority party Democrats in 1910.[34] The reforms gave the Speaker much more control over the legislative agenda. In 1975, the Speaker was authorized to select the chairman and Democratic members of the House Rules Committee, rendering the Rules Committee an "arm of the leadership in fact as well as in theory," according to the Democratic Study Group report (1975, 4). With a 9–4 supermajority of handpicked, loyal Democrats, the Rules Committee would no longer thwart the leadership's legislative agenda by simply refusing to report a rule governing the consideration of legislation or granting favorable rules to legislation opposed by majority party leaders. In addition, the Speaker was given the power to refer legislation to more than one committee, to set time limits on committee consideration, and to expedite the consideration of legislation in committee and on the House floor.

In January 1987, James (Jim) Wright (D-TX) succeeded Tip O'Neill (D-MA) as Speaker of the House after O'Neill's retirement. The political landscape was ripe for a powerful Speaker to challenge then president Reagan, and rank-and-file Democrats were hungry for legislative victories and strong leadership. Wright articulated a partisan legislative agenda and immersed himself in the details, fortifying his own powers in the process of pursuing Democrats' legislative agenda.[35] Wright used procedural maneuvers to block Republican-supported alternatives and ensure the passage of Democratic legislation,[36] paving the way for future Speakers to increase their power. In October 1987, for example, Wright stretched the rules of the House to their limits to advantage Democrats during the consideration of a budget reconciliation bill. After the special rule governing consideration of the budget bill failed, Wright called for a "new legislative day" that would enable him to call up a new special rule on the same actual day that it had been crafted in the Rules Committee.[37]

With their large margins in the late 1980s and early 1990s, Democratic leaders assumed that they would direct the majority for the foreseeable future. The ideological homogeneity of the Democratic Caucus continued to increase during this period, and Democratic leaders and committee chairmen had less need for Republican votes to pass their legislation. Although the reforms of the 1970s were aimed at majority party Democrats, the reforms and their adoption and adaptation had significant implications for congressional Republicans.

The rise of Democratic leadership power led to a decline in minority party Republican influence. With an increasingly homogeneous Democratic Caucus and weakened committee chairs, the influence of the cross-party conservative coalition waned. Democrats were less likely to seek Republican support in committee and on the House floor. Shut out of the process, Republicans responded with increased partisanship and centralization. Newt Gingrich (R-GA) emerged as a leader of the "bomb thrower" wing of the party when he and other junior Republicans formed the Conservative Opportunity Society (COS) in 1983, a group devoted to "sharpening partisan distinctions of the House floor."[38] The COS gained attention for its frequent special order speeches attacking Democrats and, under the guidance of Bob Walker (R-PA), confrontational parliamentary tactics designed to make Democrats look bad. As the number of Republican moderates decreased and Republicans' frustration increased, Newt Gingrich moved from a fringe figure among House Republicans to a member of the party leadership in 1989.[39] As former Speaker James Wright shut Republicans out of the legislative process and the "bomb throwing" faction within the Republican Party increased, partisan conflict dominated much of the legislative process by the late 1980s. The bomb throwers focused on scoring political points that would translate into electoral victories rather than achieve small legislative achievements.[40]

Republicans gained fifty-two House seats and eight Senate seats in 1994, giving Republicans a majority in the House of Representatives for the first time in forty years and for the first time in the Senate since 1986. Republicans' surprising victory catapulted Newt Gingrich into the Speakership. The goals of the Republican leadership in the House shifted overnight as they abruptly—and surprisingly—assumed responsibility for governing, and faced pressure to maintain a majority in the next election. House Republican leaders' first task was to fulfill the partisan policy agenda they had articulated during the campaign in their "Contract with America," a platform of ten conservative legislative proposals.

Former Speaker Newt Gingrich wielded considerable power in the 104th Congress. New GOP committee chairs were term-limited to six years, making clear that party leaders, not committees, were in charge. Rather than relying on a Speaker-dominated Steering Committee, as Democrats had done, Gingrich handpicked committee chairs, violating seniority in key cases. Gingrich appointed Robert Livingston (R-LA) chair of the Appropriations Committee—even though he ranked fifth in committee seniority. Further, new rules gave committee chairs the power to appoint subcommittee chairs instead of relying on seniority, but chairs had to consult with the Speaker. For example, when William Clinger (R-PA), chairman of the Government Reform and Oversight Committee, appointed subcommittee chairs, at the behest of Gingrich he skipped over two more senior committee members to give posts to freshmen.

Party leaders, not committee chairs, determined the legislative agenda. Republicans, including committee chairs, were grateful to Gingrich for his role in the 1994 elections. Not one GOP committee chair had ever filled the role of committee chair during an era in which committee government was the norm, and, as a result, Gingrich encountered less resistance from committee chairs than his Democratic predecessors had. At times when committee chairs did resist, Gingrich simply established task forces that reported directly to him. This climate of GOP majority rule intensified partisan conflict. Scholars and journalists alike highlighted the acrimony in books such as *Party Wars, Fight Club Politics,* and *The Broken Branch.*[41]

After Republicans lost seats in the 1998 elections, former Deputy Whip Dennis Hastert emerged as the party's choice for Speaker in the 106th Congress. Despite the expectation that he would restore civility in the House and be more willing to work with Democrats, Hastert actually further centralized party leaders' power in the House and continued to shut Democrats out of the legislative process.[42]

The extent to which GOP term limits on committee chairs bolstered leaders' power became clear six years after they started, as large numbers of chairmanships were vacated. An interview process for prospective committee chairs by the leadership-dominated Steering Committee—on which the Speaker and the majority leader controlled seven of the twenty-eight votes—afforded Hastert considerable control over the process and gave those interested in chairing committees additional incentives to demonstrate their loyalty to the party. In November 2002, the Republican Conference passed a rule subjecting Appropriations subcommittee chairs to the same interview process, further enhancing leaders' power. When Hastert succeeded Gingrich, many observers expected leadership centralization to loosen a bit. Even with a style less intense than Gingrich's, Hastert actually expanded the power of the leadership. When George W. Bush was elected president in 2000, Hastert focused on passing their shared conservative policy agenda.

Despite their narrow majorities from 1995 to 2006, Republican leaders relied on their own members' votes to pass their legislative program instead of trying to attract support from centrist Democrats, even rebuffing the Blue Dog Democrats who initially expressed great interest in working with Republicans.

In a speech in October 2003, former Speaker Hastert made it clear that he was not interested in passing legislation that required significant Democratic support.[43] Hastert explained that he would not bring a bill to the House floor for a vote unless a majority of Republicans approved—a stipulation now referred to as the "Hastert rule." Although the "Hastert rule" receives media attention from time to time, particularly when leaders violate it, which does occur occasionally, it is actually neither a rule nor a new practice in the post-reform era. Yet, Democrats seeking to cooperate with Republicans in crafting policy were nonetheless quite frustrated during the Gingrich and Hastert speakerships.

In the 2006 elections, with a net gain of thirty seats, Democrats won majority party control for the first time in twelve years. And, Democrats' victory catapulted Nancy Pelosi (D-CA) from minority leader to Speaker of the House. Pelosi benefited from the leadership centralization that had occurred during the preceding twelve years of GOP control. By 2007, Pelosi had more tools and prerogatives than her Democratic predecessors had had—giving her significant influence over the legislative agenda and over the careers of rank-and-file members. Pelosi maximized her sway, pursuing partisan policy initiatives, fundraising for her colleagues, excluding the minority party from decision-making, and relentlessly attacking Republicans. Indeed, she was sometimes criticized for picking favorites.

Pelosi and the Democratic leadership controlled the agenda from the start. Bypassing committees, Democrats passed their "hundred hours agenda" consisting of legislation to tax the oil industry, to implement the 9/11 Commission's recommendations, to increase the federal minimum wage, to provide discounts for Medicare prescription drugs, to cut student loan costs, and to expand embryonic stem cell research well before the deadline. Externally and internally, Democrats had high expectations for the 111th Congress. In the eyes of her colleagues, at least, Pelosi and her leadership team demonstrated an impressive ability to unify Democrats in support of the president's agenda. When it came to former president Barack Obama's most important legislative priority, health care reform, Pelosi's role can hardly be overstated. She was critical in starting the process in the House before Obama became intricately involved. When key House Democrats threatened to withdraw their support over disagreements related to abortion funding, Pelosi worked out a deal to appease both sides. And, when it seemed that the House and Senate would not be able to reconcile their versions of reform after Senate Democrats lost their filibuster-proof majority, Pelosi's leadership became essential to crafting and executing a complicated legislative strategy that resulted in the bills that Obama ultimately signed into law.

Republicans gained sixty-four seats to win a 242–193 majority in the 2010 elections, their best showing since 1946, leading to the election of a Republican Speaker, John Boehner (R-OH), who would preside for nearly five tumultuous years until he announced his resignation on September 22, 2015. Although the enthusiasm generated by the "Tea Party" movement and its antigovernment rhetoric likely increased enthusiasm in the electorate for Republicans in the 2010 elections, the newly elected Tea Party members of the House, and eventually the Freedom Caucus members, hindered former Speaker Boehner's ability to lead the GOP conference. Republicans generally do not seek votes from Democrats, and Democrats are loath to provide them. But with unusually high levels of intraparty disagreement over strategy, Boehner faced challenges from both his own members and minority party Democrats.

In 2011, insurgent Tea Party Republicans made it very difficult for Boehner to forge budget compromises with then president Obama and then Senate majority leader Harry Reid (D-NV). In April of that year, Tea Party Republicans dug in their heels against a bill Boehner proposed to avert a government shutdown because they viewed the spending cuts as insufficient. A few months later, Tea Party members defected when Boehner brought a bill to the floor to raise the debt ceiling and establish a "supercommittee" to identify $1.5 trillion in budget cuts. In the final budget showdown of 2011 on New Year's Eve, Boehner was forced to violate the "Hastert rule" by passing a budget bill that the majority of his party opposed, as 63 percent of Republicans voted against the deal extending the Bush-era tax cuts for most earners and postponing scheduled budget cuts that he negotiated with the president and Senate Democrats. Three other bills Boehner brought to the floor in the 112th Congress also violated the "Hastert rule."[44]

After the bruising 112th Congress, Boehner showed a growing willingness to exert his power in the 113th Congress. He increased his own votes on the party's Steering Committee to five, decreasing the number of votes for the class of 2010, and in turn, reducing the influence of the Tea Party members. Boehner tried to persuade Tom Price (R-GA) to drop out of the race for party conference chair and, although he failed, Boehner helped Cathy McMorris Rogers (R-WA) win by a narrow margin. In a rare move, Boehner also removed four members from their powerful committees—three Tea Party members who often caused problems for him, and one moderate who also defected too frequently, from their plum committees.[45] Nonetheless, the 113th Congress started off with more headaches for the Speaker. He was reelected only after an attempted leadership "coup" was called off at the last minute and twelve Republicans voted against him.[46] Budget battles continued, and the federal government shut down for sixteen days in 2013. Congressional observers judged the 113th Congress harshly for its low productivity, and approval of Congress dipped to a record low of 9 percent approval during that period.[47] Nonetheless, Republicans maintained the majority in the House, winning their largest majority since the 71st Congress.

Although Boehner was reelected Speaker in the 114th Congress—with twenty-five Republicans supporting another candidate—he resigned less than a year later amid an intraparty battle over House Republicans' strategy to avert—or not—another government shutdown over defunding Planned Parenthood. Boehner could not effectively lead a Republican conference divided over political strategy and institutional loyalty, and he seemed to have had enough. Boehner's challenges and ultimate resignation demonstrate that even with considerable power, balancing the dual imperatives of the Speakership—responsibility for the institution and for one's party—is increasingly difficult in the context of divided government, polarized and competitive parties, and, perhaps most important, with a significant number of members who are less concerned about Congress's institutional legitimacy and place in the system of separated and shared powers than they are about particular policy goals.

When Speaker Paul Ryan (R-WI) reluctantly assumed the gavel, he stated that Congress needed to "return to regular order," and vowed to provide more opportunities for his fellow Republicans to legislate in committee and on the floor. Initially, he granted committee chairs a bit more latitude, and opened up the amendment process on some but not all bills. For the most part, however, Ryan has done little to advance regular order. He has encountered familiar hurdles reconciling the competing institutional demands of the speakership and the demands of Freedom Caucus Republicans who, at times, place ideological and strategic goals ahead of their commitment to Congress's role in the constitutional system. Speaker Ryan has faced challenges when trying to pass health care and budget legislation, although he led Republican efforts to pass significant tax policy changes in Congress, a key legislative priority of the White House and Republicans in Congress.

CONGRESSIONAL DYSFUNCTION IN A POLARIZED ERA
Polarized Procedure

As majority party leaders in each chamber have gained power and influence, and the parties act as competing teams, they increasingly use procedural rules to their advantage. In the House, this power comes at the expense of an open, representative, and transparent legislative process—and the minority party's ability to participate meaningfully in the process. Barbara Sinclair has identified a number of procedural mechanisms that majority party leaders use in the legislative process to stack the deck for their party's advantage, procedures that she dubs "unorthodox lawmaking" because they are complex and varied, and they deviate from our "textbook" understanding of the linear, legislative process.[48]

Polarization has significantly affected the House Rules Committee, and much of the action in the legislative process that advantages the majority party and excludes the minority party starts in the Rules Committee. The Rules Committee drafts "special rules," referred to simply as rules, which govern the consideration of nearly all legislation on the House floor. Rules may allow for an open amendment process, a restrictive amendment process—where only specific amendments are permitted—or no amendments at all. Rules may also waive points of order against violations of House rules in the process.

The transformation of the Rules Committee and its activities since the 1970s highlights how in a polarized environment the power of the majority party sacrifices congressional committees and minority party members. The 1975 reform giving the Speaker of the House the authority to appoint the majority party members of the Rules Committee, with caucus approval, significantly bolstered the responsiveness of committee members to party leaders and the agenda-setting power of the majority party leadership.[49] The reforms immediately consolidated majority party power at the expense of conservative southern Democrats. In the years that followed, the Rules Committee evolved to "manage the uncertainty" generated by an increasingly disgruntled minority and to provide critical advantages for the majority party by limiting the number of open rules, thereby preventing the minority party from amending legislation and steering it away from the policy preferences of the median majority party member.[50]

Although the Rules Committee has not undergone major reform since 1975, the committee nonetheless continued to evolve in important ways as polarization increased. Most significantly, the number of members' amendments permitted to be offered by special rules that are either open rules or make selected amendments in order has declined. In the past decade, the Rules Committee has dramatically increased the number of closed rules. Donald Wolfensberger has compiled data on closed rules, illustrating that their number has risen dramatically since the 94th Congress, when over 85 percent of rules were open rules. By the 111th Congress, over 95 percent of rules were closed.[51]

Party leaders view votes on rules and other procedural votes as a test of their loyalty.[52] Minority party members have no real ability to shape legislation during the legislative process and are often denied opportunities to amend

legislation or offer a minority party alternative. Minority party members may
offer a motion to recommit with or without instructions, but those are rarely
successful, and when they are successful, they kill the bill. The rise of closed
rules has also meant that majority party members have fewer opportunities
to offer amendments. Indeed, the lack of opportunities to offer amendments
was a key complaint of majority party Republican Freedom Caucus members
when Speaker Boehner resigned in 2015.

In addition to closed rules, the Rules Committee is increasingly likely to
issue "self-executing" rules at the behest of majority party leaders, particularly for important legislation.[53] This means that the content of legislation
automatically changes when the special rule, not the underlying legislation, is
approved by the chamber, typically without debate on what is changing. This
way, the leadership can alter bills marked up by committees without debate in
committee or on the House floor. Rules routinely waive points of order against
provisions in legislation that violate House rules, meaning that minority party
members cannot effectively protest violations in House rules.

In a highly polarized House, the powerful "arm of the leadership" seems to
have become a rubber stamp for the leadership instead, mainly issuing closed
rules on legislation approved by majority party leaders. By 2007, Speaker Pelosi faced such formidable challenges in persuading members to join the Rules
Committee that she appointed an unprecedented number of freshmen (four)
to the committee, and the committee dropped its "exclusive" designation so
that all members could add a committee assignment.

Party leaders have less power in the Senate, even as they develop new ways
to shut out the minority, such as "filling the amendment tree," whereby majority leaders use their privilege to be recognized first to offer amendments to
effectively block other members from doing the same. The mix of individual-
ism and partisanship in the Senate has made it very difficult for majority parties to pass their priority items without bipartisan support. The filibuster has
not always been a tool for minority parties. Before 1917 there was no cloture
rule to stop a filibuster in the Senate at all, yet by most accounts, fewer than
a dozen bills were killed by obstruction in first 120 years of US history. The
explosion of the Senate filibuster began in the 1960s, with senators engaging
in obstruction for individualistic purposes, but the widespread use of the filibuster for partisan purposes—blocking votes on the majority party's major
agenda items—began in the 1990s when norms of restraint had broken down
in the context of increasing polarization.[54] In the contemporary era—save six
months in 2009 when Democrats had sixty senators—the minority party has
found it easy to persuade at least forty-one senators to support a party-based
filibuster. The 110th Congress saw 112 cloture votes, as filibusters occurred

not just on major legislation, but on procedure, such as motions to proceed (to consider a bill). When the minority indicates it will filibuster, the majority leader will generally pull the bill from the floor until he sees whether he can get the sixty votes for cloture. The result has been gridlock in the absence of unified party control of government that includes sixty votes in the Senate.

THE WITHERING OF COMMITTEES
IN A POLARIZED CONGRESS

In the textbook Congress era, committees in Congress operated on a bipartisan basis, and, as detailed above, committee chairs enjoyed considerable power. Today, party leaders have substantially more power than committee chairs—particularly since the implementation of term limits in 1995—and committees typically make decisions on a partisan basis.[55]

Data collected by Barbara Sinclair clearly illustrate the diminished role of committees in the legislative process in a polarized House and Senate. When crafting major legislation, party leaders are much more likely to bypass the committee of jurisdiction altogether or make "postcommittee adjustments," thereby changing the content of the bill, in the contemporary era than in the past.[56] Sinclair found that in 1975–1976, no House committees of jurisdiction were bypassed, and only 4 percent of major Senate bills bypassed Senate committees of jurisdiction. The same year, 15 percent of major House bills and 4 percent of major Senate bills were subject to postcommittee adjustment. A steady growth in bypassing committees and postcommittee adjustments occurred between the mid-1970s and the contemporary era. Further, Sinclair noted that 34 percent of the House's major legislation and 45 percent of the Senate's major legislation bypassed the committee of jurisdiction, and 39 percent of major House legislation and 42 percent of major Senate bills were subject to postcommittee adjustment by 2009–2010.

Conference committees—the traditional method of resolving House-Senate differences to pass identical forms of legislation to send to the president—have all but disappeared in a polarized era. Indeed, congressional leaders avoided them for major legislation such as the Affordable Care Act, the Troubled Asset Relief Program, the Foreign Intelligence Surveillance Act, and omnibus appropriations bills, among others. The 100th Congress (1987–1988) had sixty-six conference committees. Twenty years later, in the 110th Congress (2007–2008), there were only seventeen conference committees.[57] This means that the House and Senate majority leaders meet in secret, without the requirements of a conference committee to hold public meetings—and thus provide some transparency—and without minority party input, to resolve differences and send amendments back and forth between chambers. Members are thus less likely to know what is actually in the final version of legislation.[58]

<h2 style="text-align:center">LEGISLATIVE PRODUCTIVITY IN AN ERA
OF DIVIDED GOVERNMENT</h2>

In a deeply polarized era, competitive parties view the president as the leader of his congressional party's team—what political scholars Thomas Mann and Norman Ornstein refer to as "parliamentary style parties"—which makes governing within the constraints of the US constitutional system difficult.[59] Even as a divided government has been more common than not, it hasn't always been this way. David Mayhew's 1991 study of major legislation over the previous decades suggests that divided government does not significantly affect legislative productivity or the number of major laws passed by Congress and signed into law by the president.[60] Since then, scholars have contested these findings, arguing that divided government does in fact depress legislative responsiveness to public mood[61] and productivity.[62] Although some may argue that productivity in and of itself is not necessarily a good thing (if the laws aren't "good" laws), Sarah Binder shows that the larger the ideological distance between the parties, the more likely Congress is to fail to pass and enact legislation on the national agenda, suggesting that the stalled legislation is important, whatever its content.

Examining the enactment of major laws during the Obama presidency suggests that, in a polarized era, divided government significantly reduces legislative productivity. Democrats enjoyed unified party control in the 111th Congress (2009–2010), and former president Obama signed several landmark bills into law, typically with little or no support from Republicans. After Democrats lost majority party control in the House in 2010 and in the Senate in 2012, legislative productivity slowed dramatically. According to *CQ Weekly*, the 112th Congress (2011–2012) set a record low for productivity, passing only 283 laws, and the 113th Congress (2013–2014) enacted only 286 laws.[63] Both sessions were far less productive than the preceding twenty Congresses, which averaged 564 bills signed into law.

A key reason for gridlock is disagreement between the president and the other party. House Republicans voted with Obama on only 11 percent of the votes on which the president expressed an opinion in 2015, and on 12 percent in 2013 and 2014—fewer than any record low since 1954. In 2015, House Democrats supported Obama on 86 percent of the votes where Obama had a preference.[64] In the Senate, Republicans voted with Obama on 53 percent of the votes he supported. Thirty of those seventy-five votes were Obama's own judicial and executive branch nominees, which were generally not controversial because the Republican majority leader, Mitch McConnell, did not allow nominations his party opposed to get to the floor.[65]

A LACK OF REPRESENTATION FOR MODERATES IN THE ELECTORATE

Moderates in Congress have all but disappeared. Only about 6 percent of Representatives and 13 percent of Senators in the 112th Congress can be described as moderates, defined as having a first dimension DW-NOMINATE score between 0.25 and 0.25. In 2015, the Blue Dog Coalition of conservative Democrats consisted of just fifteen members, down from fifty-four in 2009.[66] The disappearance of moderates in Congress is a problem for representation, because it means that many—if not most—voters are not well represented by their member of Congress, even when, as most do, they share the same party identification. A large number of, though not all, political scientists have found that most voters are moderates when it comes to their policy positions. Indeed, Bafumi and Herron as well as Clinton have found that members of Congress vote in a more extreme way than the median voter in their state or district.[67] Not surprisingly, however, activists and donors are more polarized than the average voter.[68] The missing moderates in Congress also cause problems for negotiation, which means that major legislation is passed without bipartisan or concomitant support among the public in the contemporary era.

BUDGETING AND APPROPRIATIONS

One of Congress's most important obligations is to pass twelve annual appropriations bills that the president signs into law to fund discretionary federal spending. Absent these bills, or a continuing resolution that keeps funding flowing at a specified level, the government shuts down on October 1, the start of the fiscal year. A historically bipartisan process has become mired in conflict in a polarized era,[69] particularly in the context of divided party control of government. The last two decades have seen a general trend toward late bills and packaging appropriations bills into omnibus spending bills, or combining appropriations bills with a continuing resolution or separate policy proposals.[70] When George W. Bush was president, for example, in six out of eight years, most bills passed as part of an omnibus bill. As mentioned above, in 2013, the government shut down for sixteen days when Congress failed to agree on a budget for the new fiscal year. The Republican majority in the House pushed to "defund" the Affordable Care Act, and Senate Democrats and the Obama administration rejected the proposals, leading to the shutdown that furloughed federal employees and closed nonessential departments. In December 2014 Congress passed a last-minute "cromnibus" bill, a trillion-dollar package that funded the government and included multiple provisions unrelated to budgeting, such as financial regulations that loosened the Dodd-Frank Wall Street rules enacted in 2010; $5 billion to fight Islamic terror; a 1 percent pay raise for federal workers; and a surprise increase in the limits on campaign contributions to the national political parties. In an era of gridlock, "must-pass" budget bills become the only moving vehicle in town. According to the Center for Responsive Politics, the "cromnibus" received more attention from lobbyists than any other piece of legislation in 2014, with spending by 852 clients who paid lobbying firms to represent them, including health insurers, labor unions, banks, and defense contractors.[71]

CONCLUSION

Congress has become mired in partisan conflict, which affects its ability to govern effectively, pass important legislation and budget bills, or respond to public mood. Members of Congress act as two competing teams vying for majority party control, and partisan ties have overwhelmed traditional means of linking members to the institution and to constituents. There is no doubt that the party's substantive disagreements over policy are real, but partisan conflict spills over into every step of the legislative process, hurting Congress's reputation and standing in our constitutional system along the way.

NOTES

1. See, for example, the American Political Science Association's 2013 Task Force on Negotiating Agreement in Politics Report, last accessed May 10, 2018, https:// scholar.harvard.edu/files/dtingley/files/negotiating_agreement_in_politics.pdf; and the Bipartisan Policy Center's Commission on Political Reform 2015 report, "Governing in a Polarized America: A Bipartisan Blueprint to Strengthen Our Democracy," last accessed May 10, 2018, https://bipartisanpolicy.org/library/governing-polarized -america-bipartisan-blueprint-strengthen-our-democracy.

2. James Madison, *Federalist* 10, in Alexander Hamilton, James Madison, and John Jay, *The Federalist Papers,* ed. Ian Shapiro (New Haven, CT: Yale University Press, 2009), 48.

3. Marjorie Hershey, *Party Politics in America,* 11th ed. (New York: Longman, 2005).

4. Senator's prerogative to engage in unlimited debate, or filibuster, is not written anywhere in the Constitution. Instead, the Framers anticipated that the Senate would operate under majority rule. Sarah A. Binder and Steven S. Smith, *Politics*

or Principle? Filibustering in the United States Senate (Washington, DC: The Brookings Institution, 1997).

5. E. E. Schattschneider, *Party Government* (New York: Holt, Rinehart and Winston, 1942).

6. American Political Science Association (APSA), *Toward a More Responsible Two-Party System, a Report* (Menasha, WI: American Political Science Association, 1950).

7. Austin Ranney, *Curing the Mischiefs of Faction: Party Reform in America* (Berkeley: University of California Press, 1975).

8. Michael Barber and Nolan McCarty, "Causes and Consequences of Polarization," in *American Political Science Association, Negotiating Agreement in Politics, Report of the Task Force on Negotiating Agreement in Politics,* ed. Jane Mansbridge and Cathie Jo Martin, (Washington, DC: American Political Science Association, 2013), 19–53.

9. See Nolan McCarty, Keith Poole, Howard Rosenthal, and Chris Hare, "Polarization Is Real (and Asymmetric)," *Voteview Blog* (2012), last accessed May 10, 2018, http://themonkeycage.org/2012/05/polarization-is-real-and-asymmetric/; Jacob S. Hacker and Paul Pierson, *Off Center* (New Haven, CT: Yale University Press, 2006); and Thomas E. Mann and Norman J. Ornstein, *It's Even Worse Than It Was* (New York: Basic Books, 2016).

10. Frances Lee, *Beyond Ideology: Politics, Principles, and Partisanship in the US Senate* (Chicago: University of Chicago Press, 2009).

11. Kenneth A. Shepsle, "The Changing Textbook Congress," in *Can the Government Govern?,* ed. John E. Chubb and Paul Peterson (Washington, DC: The Brookings Institution, 1989).

12. David R. Mayhew, *Congress: The Electoral Connection* (New Haven, CT: Yale University Press, 1974), 27.

13. David Mayhew, "Observations on Congress: The Electoral Connection a Quarter Century after Writing It," *PS: Political Science & Politics* 34, no. 2 (June 2001): 251–252.

14. David W. Rohde, *Parties and Leaders in the Postreform House* (Chicago: University of Chicago Press, 1991); John H. Aldrich, *Why Parties? The Origin and Transformation of Political Parties in America* (Chicago: University of Chicago Press, 1995); John H. Aldrich and David W. Rohde, "The Transition to Republican Rule in the House: Implications for Theories of Congressional Politics," *Political Science Quarterly* 112, no. 4 (Winter 1997–1998): 541–567; and John H. Aldrich and David W. Rohde, "The Consequences of Party Organization in the House: The Role of the Majority and Minority Parties in Conditional Party Government," in *Polarized Politics,* ed. Jon Bond and Richard Fleisher (Washington, DC: CQ Press, 2000).

15. Gary W. Cox and Mathew McCubbins, "Toward a Theory of Legislative Rules Change: Assessing Schickler and Rich's Evidence," *American Journal of Political Science* 41, no. 4 (October 1997): 1376–1386; Gary W. Cox and Mathew D. McCubbins, "Agenda Power in the US House of Representatives, 1877 to 1986," in *Party, Process, and Political Change in Congress,* ed. David W. Brady and Mathew D. McCubbins (Stanford, CA: Stanford University Press, 2002); and Gary W. Cox and Mathew D.

McCubbins, *Setting the Agenda: Responsible Party Government in the US House of Representatives* (Cambridge: Cambridge University Press, 2005).

16. David W. Rohde, *Parties and Leaders.*

17. Aldrich and Rohde, "Transition to Republican Rule," 565–566.

18. Gary W. Cox and Mathew D. McCubbins, *Legislative Leviathan: Party Government in the House,* 2nd ed. (New York: Cambridge University Press, 2007); Gary W. Cox and Mathew D. McCubbins, "Bonding, Structure, and the Stability of Political Parties: Party Government in the House," *Legislative Studies Quarterly* (1994): 215–231; and Cox and McCubbins, "Toward a Theory."

19. Cox and McCubbins, *Legislative Leviathan,* 278.

20. Keith Krehbiel, "Where's the Party?," *British Journal of Political Science* 23, no. 2 (April 1993): 235–266.

21. Keith Krehbiel, *Information and Legislative Organization* (Ann Arbor: University of Michigan Press, 1991); Keith Krehbiel, *Pivotal Politics: A Theory of US Lawmaking* (Chicago: University of Chicago Press, 1998); and Keith Krehbiel, "Party Discipline and Measures of Partisanship," *American Journal of Political Science* 44, no. 2 (April 2000): 212–227.

22. Nolan McCarty, Keith T. Poole, and Howard Rosenthal, "The Hunt for Party Discipline in Congress," *American Political Science Review* 95, no. 3 (September 2001): 673–687.

23. See for example, Aldrich and Rohde, "Transition to Republican Rule"; Aldrich and Rohde, "Consequences of Party Organization"; Sarah A. Binder, Eric D. Lawrence, and Forrest Maltzman, "Uncovering the Hidden Effect of Party," *Journal of Politics* 61, no. 3 (August 1999): 815–831; and Barbara Sinclair, *Legislators, Leaders, and Lawmaking: The US House of Representatives in the Postreform Era* (Baltimore: Johns Hopkins University Press, 1995).

24. Binder and Maltzman, "Uncovering the Hidden Effect"; James Snyder and Timothy Groseclose, "Estimating Party Influence in Congressional Roll-Call Voting," *American Journal of Political Science* 44, no. 2 (April 2000): 193–211; and McCarty, Poole, and Rosenthal, "Hunt for Party Discipline."

25. Snyder and Gloseclose, "Estimating Party Influence."

26. Kathryn Pearson, *Party Discipline in the House of Representatives* (Ann Arbor: University of Michigan Press, 2015).

27. Frances Lee, *Beyond Ideology.*

28. David W. Brady and Charles Bullock III, "Is There a Conservative Coalition in the House?," *Journal of Politics* 42, no. 2 (May 1980): 549–559; Richard Bolling, *House Out of Order* (New York: Dutton, 1965); Joseph Cooper and David W. Brady, "Institutional Context and Leadership Style," *American Political Science Review* 75, no. 2 (June 1981): 411–425; Charles O. Jones, "Joseph G. Cannon and Howard W. Smith: An Essay on the Limits of Leadership in the House of Representatives," *Journal of Politics* 30, no. 3 (August 1968): 617–646; Nelson W. Polsby, *How Congress Evolves: Social Bases of Institutional Change* (New York: Oxford University Press, 2003); Eric Schickler and Kathryn Pearson, "Agenda Control, Majority Party Power, and the House Committee on Rules,

1937–65," *Legislative Studies Quarterly* 34, no. 4 (November 2009): 455–491; and Kenneth A. Shepsle, "The Changing Textbook Congress," in *Can the Government Govern?*, ed. John E. Chubb and Paul Peterson (Washington, DC: The Brookings Institution, 1989).

29. Polsby, *How Congress Evolves*.

30. Jones, "Joseph G. Cannon," 617–646.

31. Rohde, *Parties and Leaders*; and Polsby, *How Congress Evolves*.

32. Rohde, *Party Government*; and Polsby, *How Congress Evolves*.

33. Rohde, *Parties and Leaders*; and Eric Schickler, Eric McGhee, and John Sides, "Remaking the House and Senate: Personal Power, Ideology, and the 1970s Reforms," *Legislative Studies Quarterly* 28, no. 3 (2003): 297–331.

34. Charles Jones, "Joseph G. Cannon and Howard W. Smith"; Rohde, *Parties and Leaders*; and Eric Schickler, *Disjointed Pluralism: Institutional Innovation and the Development of the US Congress* (Princeton, NJ: Princeton University Press, 2001).

35. William Connelly and John J. Pitney Jr., *Congress' Permanent Minority? Republicans in the US House* (Lanham, MD: Rowman and Littlefield, 1994); and Rohde, *Parties and Leaders*.

36. Connelly and Pitney, *Congress' Permanent Minority?*

37. Matthew N. Green, *The Speaker of the House: A Study of Leadership* (New Haven, CT: Yale University Press, 2010).

38. Connelly and Pitney, *Congress' Permanent Minority?*, 27.

39. Connelly and Pitney, *Congress' Permanent Minority?*; and Sean M. Theriault, *The Gingrich Senators: The Roots of Partisan Warfare in Congress* (Oxford: Oxford University Press, 2013).

40. Connelly and Pitney, *Congress' Permanent Minority?*

41. Barbara Sinclair, *Unorthodox Lawmaking: New Legislative Processes in the US Congress* (Washington, DC: CQ Press, 2012); Juliet Eilperin, *Fight Club Politics: How Partisanship Is Poisoning the U.S. House of Representatives* (Lanham, MD: Rowman Littlefield, 2006); and Thomas E. Mann and Norman J. Ornstein, *The Broken Branch: How Congress Is Failing America and How to Get It Back on Track* (New York: Oxford University Press, 2006).

42. Eric Schickler and Kathryn Pearson, "The House Leadership in an Era of Partisan Warfare," in *Congress Reconsidered*, 8th ed. (Washington, DC: CQ Press, 2005); and Mann and Ornstein, *The Broken Branch*.

43. Dennis J. Hastert, "Reflections on the Role of the Speaker in the Modern Day House of Representatives," Library of Congress Address, November 12, 2003, reprinted in *Roll Call*, November 17, 2003, 4.

44. *CQ Weekly*, 2015 Vote Studies: Presidential Support Hits Low for Obama, February 18, 2016.

45. Pearson, *Party Discipline*, 2015.

46. Jonathan Strong, "Speak Softly or Carry a Big Stick," *CQ Weekly*, January 14, 2013, 62–64.

47. *CQ Almanac* 2014, 69th ed., Jan Austin, ed. (Washington, DC: CQ-Roll Call Group, 2014); and Gallup, "Congress and the Public," last accessed May 10, 2018, http://www.gallup.com/poll/1600/congress-public.aspx.

48. Barbara Sinclair, *Unorthodox Lawmaking: New Legislative Process in the US Congress*, 5th ed. (Washington, DC: CQ Press, 2017).

49. Stanley Bach and Steven S. Smith, *Managing Uncertainty in the House of Representatives: Adaptation and Innovation in Special Rules* (Washington, DC: The Brookings Institution, 1988); Bruce I. Oppenheimer, "The Rules Committee: New Arm of the Leadership in a Decentralized House," in *Congress Reconsidered*, ed. Lawrence C. Dodd and Bruce I. Oppenheimer (New York: Praeger, 1977); Rohde, *Parties and Leaders*; Schickler, *Disjointed Pluralism*; and Barbara Sinclair, *Party Wars: Polarization and the Politics of National Policy Making* (Norman: University of Oklahoma Press, 2006).

50. Bach and Smith, *Managing Uncertainty*; and Sinclair, *Party Wars*.

51. Donald R. Wolfensberger, "Getting Back to Legislating: Reflections of a Congressional Working Group," Bipartisan Policy Center, November 12, 2012, last accessed May 10, 2018, https://www.democracyfund.org/media/uploaded/Culture_Congress_Report.pdf.

52. Pearson, *Party Discipline*.

53. Sinclair, *Unorthodox Lawmaking*.

54. Sinclair, *Unorthodox Lawmaking*.

55. Sinclair, *Unorthodox Lawmaking*.

56. Sinclair, *Unorthodox Lawmaking*, 147.

57. Sinclair, *Unorthodox Lawmaking*.

58. James M. Curry, *Legislating in the Dark* (Chicago: Chicago University Press, 2015).

59. Mann and Ornstein, *The Broken Branch*.

60. David Mayhew, *Divided We Govern: Party Control, Lawmaking, and Investigations, 1946–1990* (New Haven, CT: Yale University Press, 1991).

61. John J. Coleman, "Unified Government, Divided Government, and Party Responsiveness," *American Political Science Review* 93, no. 4 (December 1999): 821–835.

62. Sarah A. Binder, "The Dynamics of Legislative Gridlock, 1947–96," *American Political Science Review* 93, no. 3 (September 1999): 519–533; and Sarah A. Binder, *Stalemate: Causes and Consequences of Legislative Gridlock* (Washington, DC: The Brookings Institution, 2003).

63. Eliza Newlin Carney, "Standing Together against Any Action," *CQ Weekly*, March 16, 2016, 37.

64. *CQ Weekly*, "2015 Vote Studies: Presidential Support Hits Low for Obama," February 8, 2016.

65. *CQ Weekly*, "2015 Vote Studies."

66. *CQ Weekly*, "2015 Vote Studies."

67. Joseph Bafumi and Michael C. Herron, "Leapfrog Representation and Extremism: A Study of American Voters and Their Members in Congress," *American Political Science Review* 104, no. 3 (2010): 519–542; and Joshua D. Clinton, "Representation in Congress: Constituents and Roll Calls in the 106th House," *Journal of Politics* 68, no. 2 (2006): 397–409.

68. Alan I. Abramowitz, *The Disappearing Center: Engaged Citizens, Polarization, and American Democracy* (New Haven, CT: Yale University Press, 2010).

69. John H. Aldrich and David W. Rohde, "The Transition to Republican Rule in the House: Implications for Theories of Congressional Politics," *Political Science Quarterly* 112, no. 4 (Winter 1997–1998): 541–567.

70. Sinclair, *Unorthodox Lawmaking*.

71. Clark Mindock, "Crowding in on Cromnibus, Most Heavily Lobbied Bill of '14," Center for Responsive Politics, February 5, 2015, last accessed May 10, 2018, https://www.opensecrets.org/news/2015/02/crowding-in-on-cromnibus-most-heavily-lobbied-bill-of-14/.

CHAPTER 4

Governing by Dividing: How the Legislative Executive Drives Polarization

Benjamin Kleinerman

Though polarization is an intrinsic element of democratic politics, in recent decades extreme political polarization has become the norm in the United States. Indeed, this polarization has caused such profound dysfunction that the government has frequently teetered on the edge of catastrophic shutdowns. The election of Donald Trump to the presidency in 2016 only exacerbated the tensions in the system. A self-consciously polarizing figure, Trump engendered a "resistance" to his governing by many on the left that included opposition in states and cities to the enforcement of national immigration law and a concerted and long-lasting effort by Senate Democrats to stall the staffing of his administration.

Although the two sides in American politics have previously endured periods of discord and disagreement, the animosity did not impede the government from working, even if it made it less efficient. However, in a separation-of-powers system characterized by checks and balances, the object of government is not legislative efficiency but rather the sort of conflict that fosters reasonable deliberation among the branches.[1] The polarization that threatens to bring government to a halt ought to trouble us much more than the usual divisions of normal politics that slow down the legislative process. Though the effects of excessive polarization often manifest themselves in congressional dysfunction, much of the cause of our present ills stems from transformations in the presidency, especially the creation of the modern partisan legislative presidency.

In the modern era, partisan presidents have become the vehicle with which to ram through the congressional gridlock in pursuit of ideological policy goals. Instead of fulfilling its independent legislative authority, Congress now primarily exists to frame the next election and either to contest or support the president's control over policy. Consequently, each party focuses on its candidates winning the "prize" of the presidency. In this process, Congress's independent authority over legislation has dissipated in favor of quasi-parliamentary partisan executive authority. The problem is that there is a fundamental mismatch between this idea of a quasi-parliamentary president and the separation-of-powers system in which Congress and the president actually still function. With closely contested elections, high levels of partisanship, and universal acceptance of the president's legislative authority, real bipartisanship has become essentially impossible, and high levels of partisan polarization almost inevitable. These factors have combined to make the inherently partisan nature of presidential legislative authority deeply problematic and divisive. Whereas the separation-of-powers Constitution encourages presidents to govern by unifying, these legislative presidents now govern by dividing.

THE CONSTITUTIONAL ORDER AND ITS TRANSFORMATION

The Constitution creates institutions that are internally strong and functional, even as they are in potential external conflict with each other. Thus, for instance, the presidency is unified so that it can act with the energy necessary to maintain healthy government—especially in crisis situations but also in ordinary times. As Hamilton writes in *Federalist* 70: "Energy in the Executive is a leading character in the definition of good government."[2] Among several of the executive functions listed by Hamilton, two in particular illustrate the president's primarily preservative character: "It is essential to the protection of the community against foreign attacks; it is not less essential to the steady administration of the laws."[3] Although the president has a role in shaping legislation through his responsibility to recommend measures, he is also empowered through his veto to prevent legislative malfeasance and misconduct: "The protection of property against those irregular and high-handed combinations which sometimes interrupt the ordinary course of justice."[4] Accordingly, if the legislature planned to use its power to take people's property tyrannically, the president's same preservative authority could step in to prevent it.

As long as the conflicts among the branches arise primarily from disputes about their respective ranges of influence, each branch remains sufficiently independent to fulfill its necessary function. Although the branches would come into conflict around the edges of their authority, their differences prevent them only from ranging too far into another's sphere. It is the Progressives rather than the Founders who thought that the system of checks and balances was created not to preserve the separation of powers and to promote deliberative lawmaking, but—as Woodrow Wilson put it—to tie the government into an "inactive equilibrium."[5] Wilson and other Progressives who followed him argued that the separate branches existed not because there are independent spheres of power and function but rather to create the balancing forces between these separate branches.[6] Whereas the Founders created the system of "checks and balances" in order to preserve the separation of powers, Wilson seemed to think the Founders created the separation in order to make the checks possible.

Given their belief that the Founders misguidedly tied government up into a hopeless knot, the Progressives, especially Woodrow Wilson, aimed to invest the presidency with a great deal more authority. Instead of energetically preserving and guiding the government, the president would take the country in a specific direction by coming into office with a clear legislative agenda. Yet as I will show by examining Lincoln's critique of the Jacksonians, although the Progressives were not the first to conceive of this kind of presidential authority, they were the ones who developed it most fully. Thus, the polarization problems that arise from this sort of presidency emerged most dramatically once the Progressive agenda for the presidency had succeeded in the twentieth century.

More generally, much of the mismatch between the quasi-parliamentary political parties we have now and the separation-of-powers system in which they operate arose out of the Progressive agenda. Frustrated with the limitations on democratic government imposed by the separation of powers, Wilson and others thought they could work around the system by investing the president with the same legislative authority that parliamentary parties enjoy when they win an election. If presidents were elected on the basis of a set of announced principles, then a mandate for change in the direction of those principles would follow from their election. Whereas the pre-Progressive constitutional order had maintained some notion of independent legislative authority within Congress, the Progressives essentially wanted to transfer that authority to the president.[7]

Although it had always existed to a certain degree, polarization between the parties became deeper and more indelible once the president became the primary agent of legislative change. Precisely because the system of the separation of powers was set up to preserve the boundaries between the spheres of authority, this presidential foray into the authority of the legislature—a foray that the legislature not only accepts but even encourages—throws a wrench into the system that exacerbates polarization and produces profound dysfunction. Instead of creating a secure framework within which Congress can pass deliberative legislation, the legislative presidency becomes the "prize" that both parties use the other institutions to seek.

Despite the expectations created by the legislative presidency, the Constitution expects Congress to legislate largely on its own (subject, of course, to the presidential veto). In the American separation-of-powers system, the process of passing legislation necessarily involves compromise and inclusivity across ideological divides. By contrast, the parliamentary system that the Progressives so admired involves no compromise between the parties: the winning party gets to pass independently its legislative policies. Insofar as the presidency is currently framed around the ideal of parliamentary government, the same partisan ethic has taken over. Just as the losing parliamentary party thinks only about how to win the next election, so too the losing presidential party thinks almost entirely in terms of the next election. Both parties want to win the "prize" of the presidency—and all that comes with it—and obtaining this prize does not involve compromising with the other side.

THE ADMINISTRATIVE STATE AND THE PRESIDENCY

The administrative state then ingrains this unfortunate dynamic. Working within the administrative state, presidents can achieve much of the partisan change on which they campaigned. The president is now free to shape the "legislation" of the nation while not passing any actual legislation. This explains, for example, why conservatives, initially quite suspicious of Donald Trump, were so pleased at his domestic Cabinet appointments; they knew that much modern governing occurs through administrative and bureaucratic decisions. Thus, whereas presidents previously had to work with the other side to achieve their legislative ambitions, the prize has become that much more valuable insofar as it is untainted by the need to compromise. At the same time, the political environment's systematic discouragement of compromise affords the president that much more authority to work around the divisiveness of Congress. The politics of prize seeking makes the prize itself that much more valuable.

The Obama presidency illustrated well this uncompromising dynamic and its dilemmas. Consider two of the administration's major achievements: health care reform and immigration reform. In passing health care reform, former president Obama did not seek meaningful compromise with the Republican Party just as the Republican Party refused to compromise with him. While the president wanted his legislation passed on his terms, the Republican Party wanted his legislation to fail so that it could frame the next election around that failure. Without real deliberative compromise between the two sides, the resultant legislation looked like an incoherent partisan power grab. Whereas parliamentary parties are formidable enough to form a coherent bill and then expect their members to coalesce around that bill, even when presidents can marshal their party behind their specific bills, many compromises remain necessary. Instead of a piece of legislation forged from compromises on policy in its crafting, most bills end up looking more like a bundle of benefits for individual constituencies and the special interests about whom members of Congress always worry. As a result, the bill itself ends up being incoherent.[8] In a parliamentary government legislative coherence arises from the internal unity of the party; in a separation-of-powers system, legislative coherence arises from mutual deliberation among various independent players in both the legislature and the executive office. If the president thinks in parliamentary terms, and if his party is a majority in Congress, he will expect that he can move a coherent legislative agenda through Congress. But to achieve this ambition he will have to make all kinds of vote-trading compromises with the members of Congress and the special interests that are so powerful there, thereby eviscerating the internal coherence of the law. The passage of the health care law is the example par excellence of this problem.

On the other policy—immigration reform—Obama was unable to persuade Congress to enact any significant legislation and instead turned to unilateral administrative action. For the first two years of the Obama administration, Democrats held unified control of the government but did not advance immigration reform. After 2010, the Republican-controlled Congress took up immigration reform on several occasions but did not pass a bill. Consequently, Obama turned to the tools of the presidency to achieve limited reforms. When the DREAM Act, which would give legal status to children brought into the country illegally by their parents, failed in Congress, Obama achieved the same results by simply enacting the program administratively as Deferred Action for Childhood Arrivals (DACA). When Congress failed to pass broader immigration reform, Obama extended temporary lawful status and indefinite reprieve from deportation to the parents of these children, again administratively, through Deferred Action for Parents of Americans and Lawful Permanent Residents (DAPA). The administration estimated that between five and six million of the nation's eleven million illegal immigrants would be affected by these two programs. DAPA was tied up by court challenges during the last two years of the Obama administration. In June 2017, six months after taking office, the Trump administration rescinded the program. Later that year, the Trump administration announced plans to end DACA. That decision was challenged in court, and federal judges ordered that the program remain largely in place while the litigation proceeded. The history of DAPA and DACA show that although presidents have power to take administrative actions with broad legislative effect, those actions are vulnerable to challenge in the courts. Moreover, even when a unilateral executive action survives legal challenge, a future administration can reverse course just as unilaterally.

PRESIDENTIAL AUTHORITY BOTH AT THE FOUNDING AND IN THE PRESENT

In the Constitution, the Founders—to the extent that they agreed on the question of presidential authority—intended that the president embody the energy necessary to keep the ship of state from sinking while guiding it into calmer waters. The presidential oath most clearly indicates this preservative expectation. Although officers in every other institution are required by the Constitution to swear only "to support" it, the president swears to do more: to "preserve, protect and defend" it. In the first place, presidents follow the Constitution by defending it.[9] Within the political order created by the Constitution, presidential authority is greatest when presidents can claim that their powers and actions are essentially preservative. In this way, at least at its founding, the constitutional presidency seems almost nonpartisan. Indeed, the nation's first president, George Washington, went out of his way to steer clear of the partisan battles that were beginning to roil during his time in office.

Although it might seem obvious that partisan presidents like Bush and Obama would be affected more by polarization than a relatively nonpartisan president like George Washington, the causal relationship actually runs in the other direction. When they aim to transform their authority into a partisan mandate to seek change, presidents inevitably polarize our politics. Or perhaps it would be better to say that in a political environment such as our present one, which has the potential to be polarized, partisan presidents solidify and exacerbate the problem.

The Constitution expects Congress to insist on its legislative authority even if presidents intrude on it. In so doing, Congress takes those steps necessary to legislate. The members of Congress have to work with their political opponents through a process of reasonable compromise. The expectation of some at the founding of the United States was that presidents would intervene in the legislative process only so as to protect their own executive power. In this constitutional order, presidents provide Congress with the room to compromise and legislate on their own. Once presidents intrude more into the legislative sphere, the politics of congressional compromise is transformed into a politics of either obstruction or acquiescence.

Given that Woodrow Wilson initiated this new type of presidential authority, the question becomes, however, why the legislative presidency, or what Jeffrey Tulis called "the rhetorical presidency," did not generate the extreme partisanship and polarization that it has more recently. For much of the twentieth century, both parties were characterized by significant internal divisions. The presence of both conservative southern Democrats and liberal northern Republicans engendered bipartisanship. The parties were too weak and divided to insist on the kind of ideological uniformity we see now.[10] By contrast, with stronger, more unified, and more partisan parties, our modern partisan presidents both cause and deepen polarization because their power systematically discourages congressional bipartisanship. Instead of trying to pass legislation—a process that necessarily requires cooperation across party lines—members of Congress line up for or against the president, thinking always about the next national election.

To some degree, the problem of presidential polarization arises from the Constitution itself. Because the authors of the Constitution envisioned elected officials as partisans of their institution rather than as partisans of a legislative program, they failed to appreciate fully the nature of presidential representation in relation to Congress. The Framers of the Constitution assumed that Congress would be the representative body and that the president's representative authority would derive mostly from his oath of preservation. Legislation would then necessarily arise from the deliberation among different and opposing interests within Congress. But when the president exercises his authority to recommend measures and to veto proposed legislation, he necessarily becomes a major player in the legislative process and therefore a potentially polarizing partisan.

If, however, the legislative presidency as a source of polarization is rooted in the Constitution itself, why is extreme polarization that threatens the very functioning of our institutions a particularly modern problem? Lincoln's speech to the House of Representatives in 1848, which I will examine for its illuminating insights into the results of presidential partisanship, also points toward an explanation for the recent rise in polarization. Before the 1980s, there had always been a political party in the United States that represented something closer to the "Whig" view of presidential power and authority.

These "Whiggish" presidents interpreted their legislative authority narrowly (except when Congress attempted to infringe on the executive sphere), thus permitting the normal legislative processes to take place. And because they did not believe that it was the job of the president to embrace and drive forward the congressional party's legislative ambitions, neither they nor their party colleagues in Congress used the legislative process mainly to frame the next presidential election for the party's benefit. In other words, presidents could only fully polarize once both parties had fully embraced the very notion of a robust and partisan presidency.

THE POLITICS OF PRESIDENTIAL AUTHORITY IN THE EARLY NINETEENTH CENTURY

Although, as noted earlier, former President Washington tried to steer clear of partisan battles, the same cannot be said for his secretary of the Treasury, Alexander Hamilton. Hamilton had written in *Federalist* 72, "The administration of government, in its largest sense, comprehends all the operations of the body politic, whether legislative, executive, or judiciary; but in its most usual, and perhaps its most precise signification, it is limited to executive details, and falls peculiarly within the province of the executive department."[11] Besides foreign policy matters and the command and direction of the military, which very obviously fall under executive authority, Hamilton lists among those details "the preparatory plans of finance" and "the application and disbursement of the public moneys."[12] Though Washington himself was nonpartisan and "above the battle," his administration very much took an active role in domestic policy, especially in economic and financial matters.[13]

The differences between Washington's presidency and the "modern" presidency stem not from the president's legislative role but from his relation to the American people. The architects of the presidency saw the officeholder as only in a certain sense the representative of the people. Although presidents would represent the people insofar as they sought their interests, they were considered unbound to the people's misguided inclinations. Hamilton writes: "When occasions present themselves, in which the interests of the people are at variance with their inclinations, it is the duty of the persons whom they have appointed to be the guardians of those interests, to withstand the temporary delusion."[14] For this reason, in the Framers' understanding, presidential authority stems from the Constitution, not from the president's direct connection to the people. By including people as diverse as Hamilton and Jefferson in his administration, Washington signaled that he was governing in a manner that only sought to address the people's interests. Unlike a parliamentary government or the presidential version of it, Washington's presidency governed by uniting rather than by dividing.

Of course, this nonpartisan governing style was not always successful even under Washington—and it became impossible under Adams, as a partisan division arose between the Federalists and the Jeffersonian Republicans. By the end of the Adams administration, the partisanship became as vitriolic as anything the United States has seen since. After the flare-up between the Federalists and the Jeffersonian Republicans, however, the complete defeat and disappearance of the Federalists allowed the Jeffersonians to return to a mode of presidential nonpartisanship. Unlike Adams and even Jefferson, Madison and Monroe really only faced disunion within their administrations, rather than from opposing partisans. Because they did not have to contend much with a unified and strong opposition, they could assume the same nonpartisan posture as Washington.[15]

As the Jeffersonian party was fracturing from the inside, a new type of presidential candidate emerged: Andrew Jackson. Unlike his predecessors, he stood for something more than good government, broadly understood. The Democratic Party that he and Martin Van Buren fashioned stood against the national bank, against internal reforms, and for states' rights in a very well-defined way. Nonetheless, Jackson emerged as a president who sought the people's support not only in order to have the authority to govern them well but also to represent them. Before Jackson, presidents deferred to Congress as the primary representative of the people. Jackson, however, insisted that he was the direct representative of the American people and that he governed on their behalf. As president, he assumed the leadership of the Democratic Party. The combination of his personal political appeal, his party leadership, and his presidential authority made him the primary representative of the people.

Jackson's representation is not, however, entirely equivalent to presidential representation as we understand it now. As we will see, Lincoln's response to Jackson's presidential representation looks much like the presidential representation we experience in the present: this is why Lincoln's argument is so useful in thinking through today's partisan presidency. Sidney Milkis suggests, however, that the "partisan organizations that arose during the Jacksonian era—the Democratic and Whig parties—assumed a form that centered partisan responsibility and practices in the Congress and state governments." Although current presidential candidates essentially capture their party, the institution of the Democratic Party could still exercise control over Jackson.[16] The primary characteristics of Jacksonian politics were "decentralized organization" and "hostility to administrative centralization"; these "restrained rather than facilitated executive power."[17] In other words, although Jackson seems like today's partisan president, and Lincoln reacted to him as though he were, he did not have the same effect as today's president because not only did he not have an administrative state on which to exercise his singular authority but also his principles themselves were hostile to the centralized authority of the national government. The Jacksonians were attracted to the centralized representative capability of the nation's president insofar as that president could represent their hostility to the centralizing forces of the national government. To a certain extent, Jackson illustrates the particular contemporary dangers of presidential power by standing against the type of government in which presidents would become dangerous.

LINCOLN'S ARGUMENT AGAINST PRESIDENTIAL REPRESENTATION

In direct contrast to the Jacksonians, the Whigs were in favor of more centralization and more national power but opposed to the notion of the president as the primary representative of the people.[18] In a speech delivered as a Whig member of the House of Representatives on July 27, 1848, Lincoln argued against this Jacksonian notion of presidential leadership, suggesting that it leads to both the collapse of Congress and an unhealthy bipolarized partisanship. In this speech, Lincoln addressed the upcoming presidential election between Whig Zachary Taylor and Democrat Lewis Cass. First, he responded to the charge that the Democrats are in "utter darkness as to his opinions on any of the questions of policy which occupy the public attention."[19] Lincoln defended Taylor against this charge by admitting its truth. Taylor had not taken any positions because he would defer "'to the will of the people, as expressed through their Representatives in Congress.'" The legislative will "ought to be respected and carried out by the Executive."[20]

Lincoln argued that Taylor did have a principle: that the executive ought to defer to and carry out the will of the legislative branch. This principle was rooted in the theory that Congress will represent the will of the people, taken as a whole, better than the president ever can. Because of the transition since the founding of the country to the notion that the national government should respond to the will of the people rather than governing for them, the key political question has become which branch will better accomplish this. Because this question is still up for grabs at this time, Lincoln's speech captures well the argument against presidential representation and for Congress. The representative principle underlying the presidency is, Lincoln argues, far inferior to that of Congress. Lincoln says: "I understand your idea, that if a Presidential candidate avows his opinion on a given question, or rather upon all questions, and the people, with full knowledge of this, elect him, they thereby approve all those opinions." The president's election would represent what the people want on a given set of questions as a national constituency. Lincoln, however, calls this view a "most pernicious deception." He continues, "By means of it measures are adopted or rejected, contrary to the wishes of the whole of one party, and often nearly half of the other."[21]

Lincoln points to a fundamental contradiction in the notion of the president as representative of "the people." If the victory of a president is understood as conferring authority for an entire legislative agenda, then that agenda could represent not the people or even the majority; it merely represents the majority of people within the president's majority party who supported him on all of his measures. Indeed, there is no assurance that even a majority of his own party agrees with the presidential candidate on every position he espouses. Thus, the entire notion of the president as a representative of what the people want is theoretically insensible.

In Lincoln's view, Congress was the closest thing the national government had to an approximation of the "people." Since it represents a necessarily wide diversity of constituencies and opinions, it does not suffer from the same one-sided focus on a single set of issues from a single perspective as does a nationally representative president. Insofar as Taylor refused to take a position on the wide variety of principles that his opponent did, he has "the best sort of principle . . . the principle of allowing the people to do as they please with their own business." It is, Lincoln says, the "true Republican position."[22] The people cannot speak through a single man except in a voice that is one-sided and ill-fitting. It is the nature of congressional representation to allow many more voices to be heard and for legislative majorities to form and re-form depending on the issue at hand, thus making it more likely that a majority vote in Congress will accurately reflect majority opinion in the nation on that particular issue. Congress, then, has the potential to achieve something closer to a voice that speaks for the people as a whole.

Lincoln and his fellow Whigs shared a fundamentally different understanding of the purpose and meaning of elections than did the Jacksonian Democrats. The Jacksonians wanted elections to represent a ratification of a "set of party principles," whereas the Whigs were "in favor of making Presidential elections and the legislation of the country distinct matters."[23] If presidential elections were not mainly about legislation, the people through their representatives in Congress could "legislate as they please, without any hindrance."[24] Legislating through Congress in a manner that is independent of presidential framing allows measures to receive that consideration and attention necessary both to be fully representative and as reasonable as possible.

The difference between presidential and congressional representation has important consequences for the politics of polarization. The translation of presidential representation into a legislative agenda comes from the top. Legislative representation, by contrast, begins from the bottom. When Congress legislates, the various parts of the population represented by the various members of Congress expect only that their particular interests and desires find their way into congressional measures. The incentive is then for compromise among these interests in order to arrive at legislation that can garner a majority of votes. Although parties still matter in accumulating and consolidating support, it is the legislation itself that is likely to matter more. Although the two sides compete, there will be significant areas where members of one party can forge alliances with members of the other in order to get legislation passed. These alliances depend, however, on cross-cutting cleavages between the two parties that allow members to forge compromises with one another across the aisle.

Of course, in much less polarized environments, presidents have used their authority to help forge partnerships between the sides; nevertheless, insofar as presidential representation is top-down, it always points to the possibility of thinking only in terms of the victory of one party over the other. It makes vote trading across issues much more difficult. Lincoln says that although "almost half the Democrats here are for [internal] improvements [such as roads and canals] . . . they will vote for Cass. . . . If he succeeds, their votes will have aided in closing the doors against improvements."[25] If legislation originates in Congress and arises from the principle that the individual members of Congress best represent what the people want, then it would permit the internal-improvement Democrats to ally with pro-improvement Whigs to achieve their measures. Presidential representation points toward increased polarization because these internal-improvement Democrats would be likely to migrate to the other side if this is the issue about which they care most. If their only chance of winning on this issue lies in the presidency, then they will join the side on which they can win. Thus it is that the principle of presidential representation has the tendency to increase polarization.

Yet history shows that it does not always do so. There have been periods in American history where presidents have embraced a legislative role without this resulting in the kind of extreme polarization we see today. Lincoln's argument means, however, that when politics becomes more polarized, the representative/legislative presidency will often exacerbate that polarization. There might be no better example of this than Lincoln's own election before the Civil War. Despite the overheated rhetoric by some about the present day, political polarization was never more divisive than in the 1850s. In that environment, the election of Lincoln in 1860 meant the complete victory of one side. Having lost the election, the South appeared to be defeated. Southerners left the Union because Lincoln's election meant, they thought, their defeat within the Union. Lincoln's electoral victory polarized the nation insofar as it seemed to mean the triumph of the northern idea that the spread of slavery must be arrested and that the nation must recommit itself to the founding principle of freedom for all.

PARLIAMENTARY VERSUS
SEPARATION-OF-POWERS SYSTEMS

Followed all the way through, the logic of the position that Lincoln attacked would lead to something that looks like a parliamentary system, with the president setting the legislative agenda for Congress. In a true parliamentary system, the majority party, as represented by the prime minister, pursues its agenda with a free hand, unencumbered by the minority party because it does not have the votes to stand in the way. So, too, if presidents have a majority in both houses of Congress, they presumably would be able to pursue their legislative agenda with the same freedom. As already discussed, frustrated with the gridlock and inefficiency of Congress, and the American government more generally, Woodrow Wilson explicitly aimed to reframe the American system so that it resembled a parliamentary system. As Jeffrey Tulis effectively shows, Wilson's project aimed to create a president who would set out a much more extensive agenda than did the Jacksonians.[26] The Progressives wanted to consolidate power in the national government, whereas the Jacksonians were trying to accomplish the opposite. The post–Civil War presidents, especially the Republicans, were primarily still "Whiggish" in their conceptions of presidential authority, even as the congressional Republicans aimed to nationalize power. Thus, Wilson's theory was the first argument for a president who would both consolidate power at the national level and promote a national legislative agenda. The policy of the country would be determined by the results of elections. In the nineteenth century, the argument for a powerful national government was consistently decoupled from the argument for a legislative presidency, and vice versa. Woodrow Wilson's argument ushered in an alliance between a legislative president and a consolidated and powerful national government. Although the Republicans resisted the coupling well into the twentieth century, the presidency of Ronald Reagan marked their final concession to a president who represented and attempted to achieve a specific legislative agenda—a concession perhaps made easier by Reagan's promise to return power to the states. At least since the 1980s, Americans across the political spectrum have embraced the legitimacy of the legislative (and quasi-parliamentary) presidency. Once both sides fully accepted its legitimacy, presidential representation of legislative programs could blossom into its full form. In its full form, it pretends to be almost entirely parliamentary. In its full form, it both creates and exacerbates partisan polarization.

Nonetheless, as much as presidential authority over legislation might resemble a parliamentary system, the separation of powers means that it cannot become one. Presidential authority over legislation always rests uneasily within a system that expects Congress to legislate and that, after all, vests formal legislative authority in that body. As votes in the US Senate in the summer of 2017 on President Trump's call to "repeal and replace" Obamacare reminded us, even the members of Congress who belong to the president's party often resist the president's legislative plans. Because the members of the House and Senate are independently elected and have different constituencies and thus potentially different political and policy interests than do presidents, whatever their party affiliation, they cannot be compelled to vote as the president wishes.

In his classic book on Congress, David Mayhew shows that the party system in a country like Great Britain will always be stronger than in the United States. He suggests that whereas the American system provides the opportunity and incentive to resist the president, "the [British] arrangement of incentives and resources elevates parties over politicians."[27] Moreover, as has been said already, in the period after World War II, the parties were much more divided and, as a result, much too weak to exert any effective control over their members. Now, American parties are more unified and thus strong enough to exert a great deal of control over Congress and effectively prevent Congress from legislating in any meaningful way. But they are not strong enough to govern. Thus, Lincoln's worry about unfettered presidential rule has not quite materialized.

But something worse has developed instead. It is not just that the expectations of presidential rule look like a parliamentary party system while the separation of powers stands in the way. The combination itself creates more profound problems, including extreme polarization and governmental dysfunction. In their recent biting critique of Congress, Mann and Ornstein identify this mismatch as one of the fundamental dysfunctions of our current system. They write: "These parties have become as virulently adversarial as parliamentary parties but operate in a constitutional system that makes it extremely difficult for majorities to act. . . . Parliamentary-style parties in a separation-of-powers government are a formula for willful obstructionism and policy avoidance."[28]

The problems arise because of the difficulties of governance in this in-compatible system. The "parliamentary" party in control of Congress can never get its way if the president belongs to the other party. And even if Congress and the president belong to the same party, the margins between the two parties in Congress tend to be so small that the minority party can use processes like the filibuster to obstruct majority rule. Whereas Congress had an incentive to legislate by crossing party lines in the days before the leg-islative/rhetorical presidency, the centrality of the president's agenda makes that mutual legislation impossible, or close to it. On most issues, real biparti-sanship can no longer exist in the era of presidential rule. Since elections are so closely contested, and both sides work within a perpetual campaign, the incentive has become to frame the next election rather than to compromise with the other side. The question now is only whether the president's party, if a majority in Congress, can enforce sufficient discipline among its members or can pick off enough members from the opposition party to get the presi-dent's legislation passed. The two sides are not deliberating together to form legislation on which they might agree; the one-sidedness of the president's partisan agenda makes that impossible. The question is not: Can we get rea-sonable legislation passed? The question has instead become: Will Congress pass the president's agenda?

THE NEW CONGRESSIONAL OBSTRUCTIONISM

Lincoln was wrong to worry that Congress would become nothing more than a vehicle for passing the president's agenda, as Congress still plays an impor-tant role in our system. However, his deeper systemic worry about the effect of this legislative/representative president has come true. Only Congress can represent the people in the broadest sense and legislate with a view to the minutia only it can understand. Rather than acting as a forum for legislation, Congress has become little more than a forum for debate about the president's agenda. Moreover, those in Congress who care about the institution's consti-tutional role have a powerful incentive to resist what the president wants lest the institution become a rubber stamp undoing the constitutional balance. Thus, it can seem that obstructionism has become Congress's primary role, especially under divided government.

The behavior of Republican lawmakers during the Obama administration illustrates this obstructionist dynamic exceedingly well. In 2010, in an inter-view in the *National Journal*, then Senate minority leader Mitch McConnell, the long-standing senator from Kentucky, said: "The single most important thing we want to achieve is for President Obama to be a one-term president." This meant that McConnell stood in the way of the president's agenda not just because he was in the opposing party; he also wanted to deny the president any legislative victories that he would otherwise be able to claim in the next election cycle.[29] To achieve the prize of the presidency in the next election, the Republicans did everything they could to generate a narrative of a failed Obama presidency. For this reason, Republicans opposed any legislation that the Obama administration wanted even if there might have been commonalities on which they could agree. Republican representative Michael Castle of Delaware said: "We are just into a mode where there is a lot of Republican resistance to voting for anything the Democrats are for or the White House is for."[30] The Republicans were more interested in affecting the next national election than they were in stopping any specific legislation that came from the other side.

The Republicans' behavior arose more from a long-term strategy to win the presidency than it did from the depths of their ideological disputes with the Democrats. But the framing goes in both directions. Just as the Republicans could only claim success if they "stopped" the president, the Democrats could only claim success if they broke their way through the Republican opposition. During the Obama administration's attempt to pass its health care bill, the Republican leadership tried to persuade and coercively prevent moderate Republicans from compromising with the president's legislation. Similarly, the Democratic leadership accepted only limited compromises with the Republicans. Both sides were in a "winner-take-all" struggle—a struggle that only makes sense given the prize of the presidency. Edwards writes: "Senators Max Baucus (Democrat) and Charles Grassley (Republican), the leaders of the Senate Finance Committee's negotiations over health care reform, both confronted whispers that they might lose their leadership positions if they conceded too much to the other side."[31] Edwards also highlights Arlen Specter's comment that "Republican Senate leader Mitch McConnell put heavy pressure on Republicans like himself, Olympia Snowe, Susan Collins, George Voinovich, Lisa Murkowski, and Mel Martinez not to cooperate with the White House."[32] To win the game, you have to keep all your players on the same side, though, as Senate Republican defections on Obamacare showed in 2017, this is not always possible.

PRESIDENTIAL ACTION AND ITS LIMITS

As Congress has become more dysfunctional, presidents have assumed an ever-increasing amount of power in the vacuum left by congressional inaction. Thus, in 2011, after a frustrating first two years of his presidency, Obama said to a crowd in Las Vegas: "I'm here to say . . . to the people of Nevada and the people of Las Vegas—we can't wait for an increasingly dysfunctional Congress to do its job."[33] In a somewhat similar vein, George W. Bush pushed his "faith-based initiative" using the tools of the administration rather than legislation. Speaking to a group of faith-based leaders, Bush said: "Congress wouldn't act . . . so I signed an executive order—that means I did it on my own."[34] Although some executive orders and administrative directives merely implement congressional legislation, others are effectively indistinguishable from legislation.[35] Presidents have used the administrative state to achieve their partisan objectives. As Lowande and Milkis write: "Modern presidents have attempted to strengthen their capacity to achieve political and policy objectives by wielding administrative powers through the bureaucracy rather than navigating a complex system of separated powers."[36]

As party polarization and obstructionism have seemingly paralyzed Congress, the presidential assumption of power has become both more widespread and, to many more, legitimate. Presidents now routinely misinterpret prior legislation in relatively obvious ways in order to serve partisan objectives. In his 2014 State of the Union Address, former president Obama boldly proclaimed to Congress that, although he was "eager to work with all of you . . . America does not stand still—and neither will I. So wherever and whenever I can take steps without legislation to expand opportunity for more American families, that's what I'm going to do."[37] Of course, the existing legislation might actually have allowed the president to take the executive actions he promised in these speeches and interviews.[38] But the truth of the matter is, in a certain way, beside the point; the striking thing is that the president was so brazen in his assertion of legislative power. Although within the system of the separation of powers the people should view these assertions themselves as an abuse of power, the people are now so comfortable with them that presidents make these assertions in order to please the people by looking like they will be tough and active.

Presidents are not, however, as strong as they pretend to be. For instance, blocked by Congress, Obama acted unilaterally to push for policy change in both immigration and gun control. Earlier we saw the limits on Obama's efforts to change immigration policy through executive action: his far-reaching DAPA program was first stymied by the courts and then simply ended by the Trump administration. Likewise, Obama's executive actions in 2016 to reform gun control policy amounted to no more than a memorandum "promoting smart gun technology" and a "fact sheet" that announced a series of actions that the president would attempt to take on the issue of gun violence.[39]

The promise of substantive reform through unilateral presidential action was mostly smoke and mirrors. Although Obama might have bragged about the ability of his pen and his phone to enact the equivalent of major legislation, they actually seemed to have been able to do little more than allow him to direct various agencies to do their jobs and to announce major reforms that he was going *to seek*. While unilateral executive action—trumpeted as though it is the solution to legislative dysfunction—might win public opinion points, it does little to solve the deeper problem. Obama's presidency revealed both the power and the limits of the legislative presidency. While no one disputes that the presidency is the greatest prize in the American political system, it is, perhaps, not quite as valuable as it seems.

PRESIDENTIAL AUTHORITY, THE PARTISAN AGENDA, AND THE ADMINISTRATIVE STATE

Presidential authority in the system of the separation of powers is greatest when presidents are acting with energy to execute the laws, conduct foreign policy, and preserve peace and order. As Charles Thach shows, the Founders learned their lessons about executive power from Shays's Rebellion and the state governmental experience more generally.[40] The democratic regime needed an energetic force capable of preserving it against its worst impulses. The Founders thought of the presidency mostly in terms of the problems it would solve and not as an institution that would direct national domestic policymaking.

The Constitution does not, however, make the president a merely preservationist force. The president has the power to veto, to issue a State of the Union message, and to recommend "measures as he shall judge necessary and expedient." In other words, the Constitution indicates that the president will be both political and nonpolitical at one and the same time. George Washington solved this problem by emphasizing the dignity and nonpartisanship of the office while allowing his cabinet to pursue a legislative program in tandem with Congress. Although there were partisan disagreements below the level of the president, Washington could still remain above the fray. In doing so, he preserved the role of Congress as *the* representative institution.

Over the course of American history, however, with some fits and starts, the presidency has increasingly rivaled Congress as the representative institution. Perhaps the Founders failed fully to foresee or appreciate this development. As long as a president like Washington was merely an indirect representative of a more abstract notion of the people—more on the model of a king than a democratic executive—he could engage in the politics surrounding the State of the Union address without becoming a partisan. He was more like a stately wise man who simply guided the ship of state in a certain general direction while allowing the rest to do the real work of legislating down below.

Once presidents became representatives of the people, defined only by the majority who elected them, partisan politics inevitably ensued. If the winning candidates command the authority to pursue their legislative agendas, who wins the election is tremendously important. And because it is tremendously important who wins the election, Congress is now more of a framing mechanism than a meaningful representative institution. If the partisan president represents the people, then the president's partisans in Congress do everything they can to assure victory for their team.

When most major policies required positive congressional assent, Congress retained a meaningful role in the system. Winning presidents had no choice but to pursue their agendas through Congress and the deliberation and compromise made necessary by Congress's lawmaking role curtailed and moderated polarization within Congress. But the growth of the administrative state and the president's role as head of that state have opened up new avenues for presidents to make policy, thus end-running Congress, and they can do so with very little compromise. Because they are elected as though they are the head of a parliamentary majority, the logic of partisanship in relation to a prize like the presidency requires commitment without compromise. That same logic of partisanship permits a great deal of presidential legislative authority over the administration. If the partisans have won the ultimate prize, why shouldn't they be able to exercise all the power associated with that prize? And so, the polarization continues until the next election. Just as Lincoln thought, the partisan presidency short-circuits deliberative democratic politics, as it was framed by the separation-of-powers Constitution.

NOTES

1. See, for instance, Mariah Zeisberg, "Constitutional Fidelity and Interbranch Conflict," *Good Society* 13, no. 3 (2004): 24–30. Zeisberg effectively explicates the extent to which the system of the separation of powers exists as much, if not more, to foster deliberation between the branches about legislation and other government activity than to control power. George Thomas also develops this argument, although he emphasizes more the agonistic relation between the branches fostered by checks and balances, and the ways in which that conflict itself can generate good government. George Thomas, *The Madisonian Constitution* (Baltimore, MD: Johns Hopkins University Press, 2008).

2. Alexander Hamilton, *Federalist* 70 in Alexander Hamilton, James Madison, and John Jay, *The Federalist Papers,* ed. Clinton Rossiter (New York: Mentor, 1999), 391.

3. Hamilton, *Federalist* 70.

4. Hamilton, *Federalist* 70.

5. Woodrow Wilson, *Constitutional Government in the United States* (New York: Columbia University Press, 1908), 56, 199–200.

6. For a later appropriation of Wilson by one of the most prominent scholars of the presidency, see Richard Neustadt, *Presidential Power* (New York: A Signet Book, 1964). He writes: "The constitutional convention of 1787 is supposed to have created a government of 'separated powers.' It did nothing of the sort. Rather, it created a government of separated institutions sharing powers" (42).

7. For a neo-Progressive critique of the Constitution and accompanying call for a president with more obvious and automatic legislative power, see Will Howell and Terry M. Moe, *Relic: How Our Constitution Undermines Effective Government and Why We Need a More Powerful Presidency* (New York: Basic Books, 2016).

8. Howell and Moe are very good on the problem of incoherent legislation. It is the one way in which their book *Relic* offers more than just a restatement of the Progressive critique of Congress and the Constitution.

9. See, for instance, my argument on this point: Benjamin A. Kleinerman, *The Discretionary President: The Promise and Peril of Executive Power* (Lawrence: University Press of Kansas, 2009).

10. For the conception of a rhetorical presidency, see Jeffrey Tulis, *The Rhetorical Presidency* (Princeton, NJ: Princeton University Press, 1987). For a discussion of the ideological convergence between the parties during much of the twentieth century, see Sean M. Theriault, *Party Polarization in Congress* (New York: Cambridge University Press, 2008), 23–27.

11. Hamilton, *Federalist* 72, 403.

12. *Federalist* 72, 403–404. For an excellent description of the extensive domestic administration envisioned by Hamilton, see John C. Koritansky, "Alexander Hamilton and the Presidency," in *Inventing the American Presidency,* ed. Thomas E. Cronin (Lawrence: University Press of Kansas, 1989). See also, David Nichols, *The Myth of the Modern Presidency* (University Park: Pennsylvania State University Press, 1994).

13. See, for instance, the description of the Founders' presidential power in Louis Fisher, *Presidential War Power* (Lawrence: University Press of Kansas, 1995).

14. *Federalist* 71, 400.

15. Ralph Ketcham has the best treatment of the nonpartisan nature of the early presidency; see Ralph Ketcham, *Presidents above Party: The First American Presidency, 1789–1829* (Chapel Hill: University of North Carolina Press, 1984).

16. Kenneth Lowande and Sidney Milkis claim that we have seen "the rise of an executive centered party-system, which relies on presidential candidates and presidents to pronounce party doctrine . . . and advance party programs." "'We Can't Wait': Barack Obama, Partisan Polarization and the Administrative Presidency," *The Forum* 12, no. 1 (April 2014): 4. James W. Ceaser makes the compelling case that this

new theory of the president in relation to political parties came primarily from Martin Van Buren. Van Buren used Jackson to instantiate the theory. James W. Ceaser, *Presidential Selection: Theory and Development* (Princeton, NJ: Princeton University Press, 1979), 123–169.

17. Sidney M. Milkis, *The President and the Parties: The Transformation of the American Party System Since the New Deal* (New York: Oxford University Press, 1993), 6–7.

18. For a full development of Whig philosophy, including its opposition to a legislative president, see Daniel Walker Howe, *The Political Culture of the American Whigs* (Chicago: University of Chicago Press, 1979).

19. Abraham Lincoln, *Abraham Lincoln: His Speeches and Writings*, ed. Roy P. Basler (Cleveland: Da Capo, 1946), 235.

20. Lincoln, *His Speeches and Writings*.

21. Lincoln, *His Speeches and Writings*, 236.

22. Lincoln, *His Speeches and Writings*, 236.

23. Lincoln, *His Speeches and Writings*, 238.

24. Lincoln, *His Speeches and Writings*, 238.

25. Lincoln, *His Speeches and Writings*, 237.

26. Jeffrey Tulis, *The Rhetorical Presidency* (Princeton, NJ: Princeton University Press, 1988).

27. David Mayhew, *Congress: The Electoral Connection*, 2nd ed. (New Haven, CT: Yale University Press, 1974), 22.

28. Thomas E. Mann and Norman J. Ornstein, *It's Even Worse Than It Was* (New York: Basic Books, 2012), xiv–xv.

29. See the quotation from McConnell and the discussion of the aim to deny legislative victories in Robert G. Kaiser, *Act of Congress: How America's Essential Institution Works, and How It Doesn't* (New York: Vintage Books, 2013), 273.

30. Quoted in George C. Edwards III, *Overreach: Leadership in the Obama Presidency* (Princeton, NJ: Princeton University Press, 2012), 126.

31. Edwards, *Overreach*, 124.

32. Edwards, *Overreach*, 124.

33. Quoted in Lowande and Milkis, "'We Can't Wait,'" 3.

34. Anne Farris, Richard P. Nathan, and David J. Wright, "The Expanding Administrative Presidency: George W. Bush and the Faith-Based Initiative," The Roundtable on Religion and Social Policy, Rockefeller Institute of Government, 2004, 4–5, last accessed December 28, 2016, http://www.rockinst.org/pdf/federalism/2004–08-the_expanding_administrative_presidency_george_w_bush_and_the_faith-based_initiative.pdf.

35. For the classic statement on both the administrative state and Congress's failure to provide meaningful legislation to regulate it, see Theodore J. Lowi, *The End of Liberalism: The Second Republic of the United States*, 2nd ed., 40th anniversary ed. (repr. New York: W. W. Norton, 2009).

36. Lowande and Milkis, "'We Can't Wait,'" 5.

37. See Peter Baker, "In State of the Union Address, Obama Vows to Act Alone on the Economy," the *New York Times* online, January 28, 2014, last accessed December 31, 2016, http://www.nytimes.com/2014/01/29/us/politics/obama-state-of-the-union.html.

38. For a complete study of presidents' use of executive orders, see Kenneth R. Mayer, *With the Stroke of a Pen: Executive Orders and Presidential Power* (Princeton, NJ: Princeton University Press, 2001).

39. "Memorandum," The White House, last accessed December 28, 2016, https://www.whitehouse.gov/the-press-office/2016/01/05/memorandum-promoting-smart-gun-technology; and "Fact Sheet," The White House, last accessed December 28, 2016, https://www.whitehouse.gov/the-press-office/2016/01/04/fact-sheet-new-executive-actions-reduce-gun-violence-and-make-our.

40. Charles C. Thach, *The Creation of the Presidency, 1775–1789: A Study in Constitutional History* (repr. Indianapolis: Liberty Fund, 1969).

CHAPTER 5

An Activist's Court: Political Polarization and the Roberts Court

Amanda Hollis-Brusky

In the 1830s Alexis de Tocqueville observed, "Scarcely any political question arises in the United States that is not resolved, sooner or later, into a judicial question."[1] Almost two centuries later, this observation rings truer than ever. With polarization and gridlock in Congress, individuals and organized interest groups are increasingly looking to the judicial branch to carry out their policy agendas. The Supreme Court, itself intensely divided along partisan lines, has demonstrated a willingness to play a more active, hands-on role in politics. In the last decade, for example, the High Court has issued divided and divisive rulings on voting rights, campaign finance, gun rights, contraception, marriage equality, environmental regulation, and health care.[2]

A far cry from the run-of-the-mill judicial activism of decades past, this pattern of judicial intervention into politics is the product of deeper structural changes in our politics that have enabled and encouraged the judiciary to play an unprecedented role in policymaking. We have entered a new era of judicial receptivity to activists and activism—a phenomenon being encouraged and even celebrated by party activists, interest groups, and legislators on both sides of the political aisle. It is not an understatement to characterize the Roberts Court (since 2005) as an "activist's court."

This chapter provides an overview of the "causes, contours, and consequences"[3] of this new norm of judicial engagement. First I identify a few of its primary causes, highlighting specific developments in our politics and our political culture that have enabled and encouraged this new pattern of judicial intervention. I then turn to discuss the contours and consequences of this era of heightened judicial involvement for democratic politics and policy development, illustrating its vices as well as its virtues.

AN ACTIVIST'S COURT: CAUSES

As Tocqueville and political scientists since him have observed, certain underlying features of our political system and our political culture invite lawyers and judges to play a significant role in policymaking in the United States. These features include a mismatch between our inherited political institutions and our political culture and a politically selected, independent federal judiciary with the power of judicial review.

That our political institutions reflect a profound distrust and skepticism of concentrated power has been an implicit feature of our political culture. As James Madison famously wrote in *Federalist* 51: "In framing a government which is to be administered by men over men, the great difficulty lies in this: you must first enable the government to control the governed; and in the next place oblige it to control itself."[4] Dividing and fragmenting power through federalism and the separation of powers, our Madisonian system of government was designed to rein in and prevent an overly active or energetic government.[5] On the other hand, and in tension with this set of inherited political and constitutional structures, we have a political culture that increasingly seeks out and demands "total justice"[6]—that is, a set of attitudes that "expects and demands comprehensive governmental protections from serious harm, injustice and environmental dangers."[7] In short, Americans increasingly want the government to protect them from harm   to ensure their airplanes and vehicles are safe, their food and water are not poisoned, their toys are not harmful to children[8]—but the fragmented political institutions we have inherited on top of our lingering skepticism of "Big Government" make courts, not legislatures or bureaucracies, a much more appealing option for satisfying these demands.

Thomas Burke, building on the work of Robert A. Kagan, explains how and why this mismatch between our political structures and our political culture invites and encourages policymaking through litigation and courts: "First, courts offer activists a way to address social problems without seeming to augment the power of the state. . . . Second, [policymaking through litigation] offer[s] a means of overcoming the barriers to activist government posed by the structures of the Constitution . . . activists [can] surmount the fragmented, decentralized structure of American government, which (as its creators intended and James Madison famously boasted) makes activist government difficult."[9] An independent and politically selected judiciary makes litigation even more attractive to policy entrepreneurs, especially to those on the losing end of the political process. Political losers and political minorities turn to the independent, that is, unelected and unaccountable, judiciary in the hopes of persuading judges of claims that fail to command a majority in the legislature. Because federal courts have the power of judicial review, interest groups and policy entrepreneurs routinely ask them to strike down federal and state statutes, or to overturn the rulings of administrative agencies. Additionally, the decentralized structure of the American judiciary actively encourages forum shopping, that is, policy entrepreneurs with resources testing their claims in multiple courts in the hope of finding a sympathetic judge who is willing to creatively interpret existing statutory or constitutional language to advance their policy agenda—or to thwart the policy agenda of their political opponents.[10]

The underlying structural and cultural features that have long invited judges and lawyers to play a role in American politics have been amplified over the past twenty years by political polarization in Congress, the rise of divided government, and alternating and uncertain party control of government. These developments in our legislative politics have further incentivized groups or movements seeking policy change to opt for a strategy of litigation over legislation.

Since 1980, the ideological distance between the Democrat and Republican elites has grown at a remarkable rate.[11] Before Ronald Reagan's rise to power, there was "no meaningful gap in the median liberal-conservative scores of the two parties," with both Democrats and Republicans in Congress occupying "every ideological niche."[12] Fast-forward a quarter of a century, and there is currently no ideological overlap between the two parties in Congress. The most liberal Republican is still to the right of the most conservative Democrat, and vice-versa. This phenomenon of political polarization affects the judiciary in two important ways. First, because "the Supreme Court follows the election returns," our polarized politics have produced a polarized, ideologically divided judiciary. As regime politics theory details, because we have a politically selected judiciary, over time the courts will tend to reflect the values of the electoral coalition that dominates.[13] As Cornell Clayton and Michael Salamone write, "During the past 40 years, American politics has been dominated by a partisan regime that is at once more conservative than the New Deal regime it replaced, but also more closely divided and polarized than any in more than a century."[14] Control of the White House and control of the Senate has vacillated between Republicans and Democrats since the late

1980s, when the most senior associate justice was appointed to the Supreme Court. This pattern of alternating party dominance in national electoral politics, coupled with the rise of strategic retirements by judges and justices since former president Clinton (that is, retiring under an ideologically compatible or same-party president),[15] has left us with a correspondingly divided and polarized Supreme Court.

Since 2010, for example, the Supreme Court has been strictly divided along partisan lines, with every justice appointed by a Democratic president voting more liberally than every justice appointed by a Republican president.[16] Far from being the historical norm, this partisan divide is out of step with traditional patterns of voting and alignment on the Court.[17] For example, the Roberts Court has split or "sharply divided" (5–4, 4–4, 4–3, or 3–2) on nearly one of every five decisions it has rendered, which is the highest rate of division of any court since the New Deal.[18] This partisan split on the Court has produced divided and divisive 5–4 rulings on major issues such as gun control, health care, voting rights, campaign finance, and fair housing. As Brandon Bartels noted in 2016, a "vicious circle" exists between polarization on the Supreme Court and the nomination process, "with just one swing justice (Kennedy) on the current Court, whoever is president has the chance to create the first ideologically homogenous majority voting bloc since the Warren Court of the 1960s."[19] Moreover, this polarization on the Supreme Court has invited politicians, scholars, and commentators to attack and attempt to delegitimize judicial rulings by noting that the judiciary is doing nothing more than enacting its preferred policy and voting on strictly partisan lines.[20]

The rise of divided government and alternating party control has also resulted in increasing gridlock and obstructionism in the federal government, which has further encouraged policy entrepreneurs to use the courts rather than legislatures to advance their own policy agendas. Though pursuing a legal strategy to advance a policy agenda can be risky due to the unpredictable nature of judicial rulings and the various constraints[21] that inhibit courts from easily enforcing broad and sweeping changes in policy, groups are more attracted to litigation as a strategy under two primary conditions: when significant political and institutional barriers make litigation the only realistic option, and when policy entrepreneurs want to insulate their policy gains[22] from shifting and uncertain electoral fortunes. Both conditions currently exist.

Divided government, which occurs when one political party controls the presidency while the opposition controls at least one branch of Congress—the norm in American politics since 1989—erects barriers to policymaking through legislative channels.[23] This is because divided government, particularly when coupled with ideologically distant parties, increases the number of

potential veto points in the policymaking process, often requiring supermajorities to pass legislation. As Thomas Keck writes, "On both the left and the
right, legislative losers turn to the courts as a matter of course."[24] More veto
points and more gridlock make virtually every group a "legislative loser" and
make the courts a more attractive venue. Instead of having to win the votes
of majorities or supermajorities in the legislature, at the Supreme Court, one
only needs to secure five votes.[25]

Pursuing policy through the courts also allows policy entrepreneurs to "insulate" their victories from political enemies.[26] This is a particularly attractive option when partisan control of the legislature and the executive is in
near-constant flux and turnover, as it has been since the 1980s. In the period
from 1980–2017, for example, control of the presidency alternated between
Democrats and Republicans five times; the Senate changed hands seven times;
and the House of Representatives three times. And, as detailed earlier, for the
majority of this period, neither party had control of both houses of Congress
and the presidency, making policy gains through the federal legislature a risky
and uncertain bet. Because courts are relatively independent from the rest
of the political system, they can provide a "seemingly safer route" for policymaking and implementation than the political branches.[27] Moreover, because
judges serve longer terms and create legal precedent with their rulings, judicial decisions tend to be stickier, or more "path-dependent," than conclusions
formed in the political branches.[28]

These recent developments in our politics—political polarization, divided
government, gridlock, alternating party control—have created an open invitation for courts to take a more active, engaged role in policymaking. And, as
detailed in the next section, courts have accepted the invitation.

AN ACTIVIST'S COURT: CONTOURS

The new norm of active judicial engagement on the Supreme Court, encouraged and enabled by these recent political developments, has two principal
contours: the kinds of issues the justices are "deciding to decide,"[29] and the
scope and sweep of those decisions. Taking the first contour, this new era of
judicial engagement is characterized by an increased willingness of the justices
to wade into "the political thicket."[30] No case more clearly exemplifies the justices wading into the "political thicket" than *Bush v. Gore*—the 2000 decision in
which the Supreme Court, by a 5–4 vote, split along ideological lines, stopped
the ballot recount in Florida, and effectively resolved the 2000 presidential
election in favor of George W. Bush.[31] Since then, the Supreme Court has
"decided to decide" cases at the heart of politics and the political process. The

justices have issued divided and divisive rulings dismantling legislation dealing with campaign finance, voting rights, and even the conduct of war[32]—an issue that was once at the very heart of what the Supreme Court considered off limits due to it being a "political question."[33]

To be sure, sometimes cases and issues are thrust upon the justices, and the Supreme Court cannot avoid deciding deeply divisive political issues. This happens, for example, when the lower federal courts disagree on how the Constitution applies to a particular set of issues and hand down split or contradictory rulings, as they did when reviewing marriage bans in the states before *Obergefell v. Hodges.*[34] It also happens when the lower courts disagree about the scope or applicability of a particular statute—as was the case when the Supreme Court intervened to determine whether federal health insurance exchanges established through the Affordable Care Act were entitled to the same subsidies as those "established by the State" in *King v. Burwell.*[35]

But, in other cases, the justices have actively invited political controversy. For example, recent scholarship has documented how rather than waiting passively for issues to reach the High Court, the justices have started to "signal"[36] to activists that they are interested in considering specific kinds of political issues. The most striking recent example of how Supreme Court signaling resulted in a future revolutionary ruling involves Justice Clarence Thomas's concurrence in *Printz v. United States,* a Tenth Amendment case involving the implementation of certain provisions of the Brady Bill.[37] In that case, Justice Thomas signaled intense interest in hearing a case that would challenge the long-settled "collective rights" understanding of the Second Amendment, writing, "Perhaps, at some future date, this Court will have the opportunity to determine whether Justice Story was correct when he wrote that the right to bear arms 'has justly been considered as the palladium of the liberties of a republic.'" Thomas supported this claim by way of reference to a "growing body of scholarly commentary" that has indicated the right to bear arms was an individual, not a collective right.[38] Within a few years of issuing that "signal," activists initiated and successfully brought a well-framed case to the Supreme Court, challenging the long-settled collective rights view of the Second Amendment. And in *District of Columbia v. Heller,* a five-justice majority announced for the first time ever that the Second Amendment protected an individual, not a collective, right to bear arms.[39]

Moving on to the second contour of this period of heightened judicial engagement in politics, when deciding these deeply political issues, the Supreme Court justices have abandoned the notion of "judicial restraint."[40] An old term, "judicial restraint" simply restates what is implicit from our system of separated federal powers: that as an unelected minority of the federal government, the justices should be extremely cautious when striking down democratically enacted legislation. This concept also counsels justices to avoid issuing sweeping rulings that move the law too far, too fast or unsettle long-standing doctrines and judicial precedent. On this first dimension of "judicial restraint"—preserving the democratic will whenever possible—the Roberts Court scores low. The current Supreme Court's approach "reflects a combination of institutional distrust—the Court is better at determining constitutional meaning—and substantive distrust—congressional power must be held in check."[41] In other words, the elected branches should be innocent until proven guilty. Under the current regime, the legislative majorities seem to be guilty until proven innocent. In recent cases such as *Citizens United v. FEC*[42] and *Shelby County v. Holder*,[43] for example, a five-justice majority on the Supreme Court seemed eager to strike down provisions of key bipartisan congressional regulation on questionable constitutional authority. This heightened skepticism of the democratic process is dangerous, not just from a judicial supremacy and separation-of-powers standpoint, but also for the ripple effects it might have in the public's trust of the democratic process and of the Supreme Court. As Pamela Karlan writes, "The Court's dismissive treatment of politics raises the question whether, and for how long, the people will maintain their confidence in a Court that has lost its confidence in them and their leaders."[44]

On the other dimensions of "judicial restraint"—being mindful not to upset long-settled areas of law and not to push the law too far too fast—the current Supreme Court does not score much better. Similar to the role of the justices in reaching out to hear *District of Columbia v. Heller*, the case that radically reinterpreted the right to bear arms and unsettled the long-held "collective rights" view of the Second Amendment, Chief Justice John Roberts did something similar—but arguably even more "activist"—in the litigation that resulted in the landmark case *Citizens United v. FEC*. This case interpreted the First Amendment's free speech guarantee as a license for corporations and unions to spend unlimited amounts of money on elections from their general treasuries. To quote legislator Jerrold Nadler (D-NY), who chaired a series of hearings in the wake of the Supreme Court's decision in *Citizens United*: "One of the things that strikes me . . . is the extent to which an extraordinarily activist Court reached out to issue this decision. The justices answered a question they weren't asked in order to overturn a century of precedent which they had reaffirmed only recently."[45] Nadler's assessment is accurate. *Citizens United* was initially argued to the Supreme Court in a very narrow way, and the litigants were not asking the Supreme Court to revisit or overturn any previous precedent. But after an in-chambers drama among the conservative justices, Chief Justice Roberts agreed to order a new round of arguments for the case, and asked the parties to file new briefs directly addressing whether two previous Supreme Court decisions ought to be overruled.[46] In short, the justices had the case they wanted in order to make a radical change in the law, but not the right questions. So, in a move entirely at odds with any traditional notion of "judicial restraint," the conservative majority asked for the question they wanted to answer so they could overrule and unsettle an area of law that they disliked.

Together, these two contours give shape to the ideal "activist's court"—a court that is ready and willing to hear cases that implicate deeply political questions, and to resolve these cases in a manner that enacts fundamental, sweeping change.

AN ACTIVIST'S COURT: CONSEQUENCES

When courts become deeply involved in politics and policymaking, they run the risk of provoking some of the more pernicious features of our constitutional design. Policymaking through courts can invite elite capture or minority tyranny and weaken the checks and balances built into the constitution. Additionally, when policy becomes "juridified"[47]—that is, when it becomes legalized and enshrined in judicial precedent—it can have adverse and unintended consequences for policy development and political advocacy down the road. On the other hand, in our current political system—characterized as it is by political polarization and gridlock—policymaking through courts might be the only viable and realistic option.

Policymaking through courts invites a handful of elite, unelected lawyers and judges to craft and shape policy, which in turn facilitates the kind of minority capture our Constitution was designed to guard against. When policy entrepreneurs turn to courts instead of legislatures, they can effectively circumvent the various safeguards and constitutional veto points built into the legislative process, such as congressional committees, majority requirements, supermajority requirements, and the presidential veto. These veto points are designed to decelerate the legislative process, to ensure broad coalitions for governing, and to prevent smaller, energetic "factions" from capturing and dominating the process. As Madison wrote in *Federalist* 10, among the "numerous advantages" of this model of government is its ability to "break and control the violence of faction" by "extending the sphere" and multiplying the number of competing voices and distinct interests involved in the process.[48] These multiple veto points "foster more pluralistic legislative inputs and outputs" and prevent legislatures from acting swiftly and energetically.[49]

Policymaking by lawyers and judges circumvents these checks, leaving policy in the hands of the few, unelected elite, which, if we follow Madison's analysis in *Federalist* 10, facilitates tyranny of the minority, or elite capture: "The smaller the society, the fewer probably will be the distinct parties and interests composing it; the fewer the distinct parties and interests, the more frequently will a majority be found of the same party; and the smaller the number of individuals composing a majority, and the smaller the compass within which they are placed, the more easily will they concert and execute their plans of oppression." When it comes to judicial policymaking, the number of individuals with access to power and the "compass" within which they are placed are both incredibly small. To make policy through the Supreme Court, for example, policy entrepreneurs simply need to secure five votes. And, while historically the justices of the Supreme Court have come from diverse backgrounds, education, and careers, we currently have a Supreme Court that is composed entirely of Ivy League educated lawyers with no political or legislative experience.[50] As Mark Graber writes, the Supreme Court "Justices tend to act on elite values because justices are almost always selected from the most affluent and highly educated stratum of Americans."[51] In other words, Madison's recipe for elite capture in *Federalist* 10—a small number of people with uniform interests and backgrounds who can readily and easily concert to execute their plans—reads like a template for our current Supreme Court.

Moreover, because judicial policymaking requires lawyers to argue and bring cases to the courts (judges and justices cannot simply make cases and questions appear before them "as if by magic"),[52] the policymaking process is de facto captured and controlled by this unelected, elite group. This capture by lawyers has become even more pronounced over the past two decades, with the rise of two organized and ideologically opposed "factions" or interest groups in the law: the Federalist Society on the right and the American Constitution Society on the left.[53] These two groups of lawyers are actively working to shape both the "supply side" of judicial policymaking—bringing cases, organizing litigation campaigns, providing intellectual support for judicial decisions—as well as the "demand side"—working to get particular kinds of judges and justices nominated and confirmed. In doing so, the Federalist Society and the American Constitution Society are trying to create a de facto monopoly on the "training, promotion and disciplining of lawyers and judges"[54] on the right and the left, respectively. While normatively this effort raises the same kinds of concerns addressed earlier about minority capture of the policymaking process, it also stirs doubt about the vicious cycle of polarization of the judiciary. If a young, ambitious law student needs to pledge allegiance to one or the other of these ideologically charged organizations in order to be credentialed and considered for a future judgeship, then the farm team for future judgeships will reflect the same ideological divisions that plague our current politics and our current judiciary.

Perhaps even more perniciously for our constitutional design, political polarization in Congress effectively weakens the checks and balances built into the Constitution by empowering judges to have the final say in the interpretation and implementation of policy. When political scientists discuss the checks and balances between the courts and Congress, they often point out that the courts do not necessarily have the final say in matters of statutory and constitutional interpretation.[55] "The governing model of congressional–Supreme Court relations," Richard Hasen writes, "is that the branches are in dialogue on statutory interpretation: Congress writes federal statutes, the Court interprets them, and Congress has the power to overrule the Court's interpretations."[56] If for instance the courts interpret a federal statute in a way Congress does not like or agree with, the latter can pass an override that revises or fixes the statute, which is what happened in 2007 when the Supreme Court narrowly interpreted the statute of limitations for filing an equal pay lawsuit regarding pay discrimination under the Civil Rights Act of 1964.[57]

Congress responded by passing the Lilly Ledbetter Fair Pay Act of 2009, which clarified that the statute of limitations resets with every paycheck affected by discriminatory action.[58] If the courts strike down part of a statute as unconstitutional, Congress can propose a constitutional amendment to address it, as it did with the Twenty-Sixth Amendment, which overrode the Supreme Court's decision regarding lowering the voting age in *Oregon v. Mitchell* (1970). Alternatively, Congress can rewrite the statute or part of the statute so that it aligns with the court's understanding of the Constitution.

But when political polarization results in gridlock and paralysis in Congress, its ability to "counteract" the "ambition" of the courts is severely compromised. Two different scholars, using different methodologies, studied congressional overrides of Supreme Court decisions and reached the same conclusion: the number of congressional overrides of court decisions has dramatically declined since 1998.[59] This means that, for all intents and purposes, the Court has the final say in matters of statutory and constitutional interpretation, which has real, practical consequences for the checks and balances between the branches. As Hasen concludes, "In a highly polarized atmosphere and with Senate rules usually requiring sixty votes to change the status quo, the Court's word on the meaning of statutes is now final almost as often as its word on constitutional interpretation."[60] When the Supreme Court, by a 5–4 vote, struck down Section 4 (the coverage formula) of the Voting Rights Act in *Shelby County v. Holder* (2013), Chief Justice John Roberts suggested in his opinion that Congress could simply update the coverage formula and make the statute constitutional: "Congress may draft another formula based on current conditions. . . . Our country has changed, and while any racial discrimination in voting is too much, Congress must ensure that the legislation it passes to remedy that problem speaks to current conditions."[61]

But, as all astute political observers at the time recognized, this invitation to Congress to simply "draft another formula" would not be taken up. In the dialogue that has traditionally characterized Court-Congress relations, Congress has effectively silenced itself through polarization and gridlock and has, as a consequence, shifted the balance of power to the courts.

Finally, when social and economic policies become legalized; that is, when judicial decisions supplant ordinary politics, this process can have unintended and sometimes adverse long-term consequences for policy development and advocacy. As Gordon Silverstein describes in *Law's Allure*, "Turning to the courts, relying on judicial decision making . . . as substitutes or replacements for the traditional methods of politics . . . can shape, frame, and constrain policy choices and politics itself."[62] Once judges intervene in a policy area, their written opinions can limit or open up avenues for future policymaking in interesting ways. Moreover, because judicial policy becomes legal precedent, and because the norm of stare decisis tends to discourage overturning precedent, juridified policies tend to be more "path dependent," more difficult to change, unstick, or overturn than their legislative counterparts.[63]

While this new norm of judicial activism raises several concerns—an increased risk of minority tyranny and elite capture, creating an imbalance of power, and irrationally and adversely shaping and constraining long-term policy development—it is not without its virtues. There are defensible reasons on both the left and the right for a more activist court and for heightened judicial engagement in politics. Scholars and legal theorists on the left, for example, have long embraced a theory of judicial review that defers to elected majorities on most economic issues but demands judicial intervention on social issues, especially when majority legislation seems to be unfairly targeting and restricting the rights of minorities and politically vulnerable populations.[64] This theory has been deployed, traditionally, to defend the judicial activism of the Warren Court in the areas of voting rights, criminal defense, due process, and desegregation. More recently, this defense has been deployed to defend the Supreme Court's judicial activism in *Obergefell v. Hodges* (2015), the landmark 5–4 ruling legalizing gay marriage nationwide.

On the right, conservatives and libertarians who once advocated "judicial restraint" and deference to elected majorities are now openly calling for judicial activism or, as they have rebranded it, "judicial engagement." This is especially true in areas where business interests, economic liberties, states' rights, right to contract, and gun rights are concerned. The proponents of "judicial engagement" see an opportunity to realign the Constitution with its fundamental purposes and its original meaning; to remedy the judicial excesses and liberal interpretation of constitutional provisions that have resulted in—as they argue—the fetishizing of democracy at the expense of liberty. For this group, an activist court is the only way to restore the Constitution, even if in doing so they upend precedent, disregard stare decisis, overturn the majority will, and unsettle entire areas of constitutional law.

But aside from these theoretical or ideological justifications and defenses of judicial activism, there is a practical defense of it. Because of political polarization, judicial activism is now an integral and indispensable feature of our current political and constitutional order. Our "polarized political order" has produced a constitutional politics of aggressive judicial intervention and engagement.[65] It has done so by affecting the kind of judges we have on the Supreme Court through polarized and politicized judicial selection, and by empowering judges to have more of a say in policymaking as policy entrepreneurs are increasingly looking to courts to circumvent gridlocked legislatures. Our "polarized political order" has also invited courts and judges to have more of a final say in statutory and constitutional interpretation by silencing Congress's voice in the interbranch dialogue, and neutering its ability to override judicial decisions.

CONCLUSION: "FOLLOW[ING] THE ELECTION RETURNS"

As this chapter has attempted to show, our current Supreme Court can and should be understood as an "activist's court." But rather than characterizing this new receptivity to activism and activist's issues as being at odds with our political and constitutional order as traditionally understood—that is, passing normative judgment on whether the Supreme Court ought or ought not to be engaged in politics in this way—we must understand this behavior as a result of our new political order and, as such, an integral part of contemporary American governance.

First, as scholars have documented, our polarized politics have led to more ideologically motivated and partisan appointments to the Supreme Court. Whereas the elected branches have historically considered multiple factors when making a nomination to the High Court—geography, patronage, professional experience, ideological compatibility—given the high-stakes nature of appointments and the fact that judges and justices are serving longer and longer terms, there is now a "near-exclusive focus on ideological compatibility and reliability" when making judicial appointments.[66] Thus, it should come as no surprise that the justices themselves, a product of this appointment process, represent these polarized divisions. Secondly, gridlock in Congress and uncertainty in the political realm created the political opportunity structure for the Supreme Court to play a heightened role in policymaking. Of course the Supreme Court is not without agency here. It might have demurred and refused to seize these opportunities for policymaking, professing instead a position of "judicial restraint" and opting to avoid political questions. However, beginning with the appointment of Samuel Alito to replace Sandra Day O'Connor, the Supreme Court opted to become deeply involved in politics—overturning precedent and abandoning stare decisis in the realm of campaign finance, reconstructing long-settled constitutional frameworks in the First and Second Amendments, creating new rights in the area of marriage equality, and dismantling parts of landmark legislation such as the Voting Rights Act and the Affordable Care Act.

While the judiciary can and does shape and structure our politics, our judiciary is first and foremost the product of our politics. As Pamela Karlan writes (and political scientists are fond of reminding people), "The composition of the Supreme Court is itself the consequence of our political choices. The Court follows the election returns . . . in the more fundamental sense that its composition is a product of who wins elections and what the winners do about judicial nominations."[67] We cannot change the Supreme Court without first changing our politics. This new norm of judicial intervention into politics, itself a product of our divided and divisive politics, is now an integral feature of our polarized political order—and will continue to be so into the foreseeable future.

NOTES

1. Alexis de Tocqueville, *Democracy in America*, Phillips Bradley, ed., Book I, Chapter XVI (New York: Knopf, 1945), 280.

2. Shelby County v. Holder, 570 U.S. 2 (2013); Citizens United v. FEC, 558 U.S. 310 (2010); McCutcheon v. FEC, 572 U.S. ___ (2014); District of Columbia v. Heller, 554 U.S. 570 (2008); McDonald v. City of Chicago, 561 U.S. 742 (2010); Burwell v. Hobby Lobby, 573 U.S. ___ (2014); Obergefell v. Hodges, 576 U.S. ___ (2015); Massachusetts v. EPA, 549 U.S. 497 (2007); NFIB v. Sebelius, 567 U.S. 519 (2012); and King v. Burwell, 576 U.S. ___ (2015).

3. Robert A. Kagan, *Adversarial Legalism* (Cambridge, MA: Harvard University Press, 2001).

4. James Madison, *Federalist* 51, in Alexander Hamilton, James Madison, and John Jay, *The Federalist Papers*, ed. Clinton Rossiter (New York: Mentor, 1999), 290.

5. Kagan, *Adversarial Legalism*, 13–14. See also Thomas F. Burke, *Lawyers, Lawsuits, and Litigation* (Berkeley: University of California Press, 2004), 7.

6. See generally, Lawrence Friedman, *Total Justice* (New York: Russell Sage, 1994).

7. Kagan, *Adversarial Legalism*, 15.

8. Lawrence Friedman, *Law in America: A Short History* (New York: Modern Library, 2004), 6–7.

9. Thomas F. Burke, *Lawyers, Lawsuits, and Legal Rights: The Battle over Litigation in American Society* (Berkeley: University of California Press, 2004), 7.

10. See Kagan, *Adversarial Legalism*, 16.

11. Neal Devins and Lawrence Baum, "Split Definitive: How Party Polarization Turned the Supreme Court into a Partisan Court," *William & Mary Law School Research Paper* No. 9–276 (2016): 28.

12. Devins and Baum, "Split Definitive," 29.

13. Robert A. Dahl, "Decision Making and Democracy: The Supreme Court as a National Policy Maker," *Journal of Public Law* 6 (1957): 279; Howard Gillman, "Courts and the Politics of Partisan Coalitions," in *The Oxford Handbook of Law and Politics*, ed. Gregory A. Caldeira, Daniel Keleman, and Keith Whittington (New York: Oxford University Press, 2008); and Cornell W. Clayton and J. Mitchell Pickerill, "The Politics of Criminal Justice: How the New Right Regime Shaped the Rehnquist Court's Criminal Justice Jurisprudence," *Georgetown Law Journal* 94, no. 5 (June 2006): 1385.

14. Cornell W. Clayton and Michael S. Salamone, "Still Crazy after All These Years: The Polarized Politics of the Roberts Court Continue," *The Forum* 12, no. 4 (2015): 740.

15. See Brandon L. Bartels, "The Sources and Consequences of Polarization in the US Supreme Court," in *American Gridlock: The Sources, Character and Impact of Political Polarization*, ed. James A. Thurber and Antoine Yoshinaka (New York: Cambridge University Press, 2016).

16. Devins and Baum, "Split Definitive," 7.

17. As Lawrence Baum and Neal Devins document, between 1937 and 2010, there was no clear partisan divide on the Court. Devins and Baum, "Split Definitive," 22–24.

18. Clayton and Salamone, "Still Crazy," 745.

19. Bartels, "Sources and Consequences," 172.

20. See, for example, James L. Gibson, "The Legitimacy of the US Supreme Court in a Polarized Polity," *Journal of Empirical Legal Studies* 4, no. 3 (November 2007): 50; and Bartels, "Sources and Consequences," 9.

21. See generally, Kagan, *Adversarial Legalism*; and Gerald N. Rosenberg, *The Hollow Hope* (Chicago: University of Chicago Press, 1991).

22. See Gordon Silverstein, *Law's Allure: How Law Shapes, Constrains, Saves, and Kills Politics* (New York: Cambridge University Press, 2009). See generally, Burke, *Lawyers, Lawsuits, and Legal Rights*.

23. Tyler Hughes and Deven Carlson, "Divided Government and Delay in the Legislative Process: Evidence from Important Bills, 1949–2010," *American Politics Research* 43, no. 5 (2015): 771–792.

24. Thomas Keck, *Judicial Politics in Polarized Times* (Chicago: University of Chicago Press, 2014), 20.

25. It is illustrative here to cite the late Associate Justice William Brennan's famous Rule of Five: "Brennan liked to greet his new clerks each fall by asking them what they thought was the most important thing they needed to know as they began their work in his chambers. The pair of stumped novices would watch quizzically as Brennan held up five fingers. Brennan then explained that with five votes, you could accomplish anything." See Dawn Johnsen, "Justice Brennan: Legacy of a Champion," *Michigan Law Review* 111, no. 6 (2013): 1159.

26. Burke, *Lawyers, Lawsuits, and Legal Rights*, 14–15.

27. Burke, *Lawyers, Lawsuits, and Legal Rights*, 15.

28. Silverstein, *Law's Allure*, 63–70. See also Amanda Hollis-Brusky, *Ideas with Consequences* (New York: Oxford University Press, 2015), 149–151.

29. The Supreme Court has virtually complete discretion over which cases it hears and which it does not. This is called docket control. With close to 8,000 petitions to consider every term, the Supreme Court decides only about 1 percent of those cases each term, averaging seventy to eighty issued opinions each term. For more on how the justices "decide what to decide," see John Paul Stevens, "Deciding What to Decide: The Docket and the Rule of Four," in *Judges on Judging*, ed. David M. O'Brien (Washington, DC: Sage, 2012).

30. Justice Felix Frankfurter famously used this term in Colegrove v. Green, 328 U.S. 549, 556 (1946) to warn against the Supreme Court meddling in what he believed should be purely political or legislative issues (such as voting, legislative apportionment, etc.).

31. Bush v. Gore, 531 U.S. 98 (2000); this was a 5–4 per curiam decision holding that the standards by which different counties were counting ballots in Florida violated the Fourteenth Amendment's Equal Protection Clause. The decision effectively resolved the disputed 2000 election in favor of George W. Bush.

32. Wisconsin Right to Life v. FEC, 551 U.S. 449 (2007); Citizens United v. FEC, 558 U.S. 310 (2010); McCutcheon v. FEC, 572 U.S. ___ (2014); Northwest Austin Municipal Utility District No. 1 v. Holder, 557 U.S. 193 (2009); and Shelby County v. Holder, 570 U.S. ___ (2013). See for example, Rasul v. Bush, 542 U.S. 466 (2004); Hamdi v. Rumsfeld, 542 U.S. 507 (2004); Hamdan v. Rumsfeld, 548 U.S. 557 (2006); and Boumediene v. Bush, 553 U.S. 723 (2008).

33. The "political question doctrine" can be traced to former Chief Justice John Marshall's opinion in Marbury v. Madison. In that opinion he wrote, "The province of the court is, solely, to decide on the rights of individuals, not to inquire how the executive, or executive officers, perform duties in which they have discretion. Questions in their nature political, or which are, by the constitution and laws, submitted to the executive can never be made in this court." Some see the political question doctrine as encompassing constitutional grants of authority to the coordinate branches, whereas others see it as a tool for courts to avoid adjudicating an issue best resolved outside the judicial branch. It has been invoked with most frequency in foreign policy cases. See generally, Jared P. Cole, "The Political Question Doctrine: Justiciability and the Separation of Powers," *Congressional Research Service*, December 23, 2014.

34. Obergefell v. Hodges, 576 U.S. ___ (2015) was the landmark ruling in which the Supreme Court, by a 5–4 vote, found a fundamental right to same-sex marriage under the Fourteenth Amendment and struck down every single marriage ban in the United States.

35. King v. Burwell, 576 U.S. ___ (2015) involved interpreting Section 36B of the Affordable Care Act, which provided tax credits to individuals who purchase insurance through a health insurance exchange "established by the State." The question was whether exchanges established by the federal government were eligible for the same subsidies. The Supreme Court, by a 6–3 vote, held that they were entitled to the same subsidies.

36. For more on judicial "signaling," see generally, Vanessa Baird, *Answering the Call of the Court* (Charlottesville: University of Virginia Press, 2007). See also, Hollis-Brusky, *Ideas with Consequences*, 157–158.

37. Printz v. United States, 521 U.S. 898 (1997); this case struck down interim provisions of the Brady Handgun Violence Prevention Act as inconsistent with the Tenth Amendment and principle of "anti-commandeering."

38. Hollis-Brusky, *Ideas with Consequences*, 131.

39. District of Columbia v. Heller, 554 U.S. 570 (2008).

40. See Hollis-Brusky, *Ideas with Consequences*, 6–8, 16, 18, 147–164.

41. Pamela S. Karlan, "Forward: Democracy and Disdain," *Harvard Law Review* 126, no. 1 (2011): 2.

42. Citizens United v. FEC, 558 U.S. 310 (2010); this held by a 5–4 vote that the First Amendment prohibited government from restricting independent political expenditures by for-profit corporations and labor unions. In doing so, it struck down key provisions of the Bipartisan Campaign Reform Act.

43. Shelby County v. Holder, 570 U.S. 2 (2013); this held by a 5–4 vote that Section 4(b) of the Voting Rights Act of 1965, which was used to determine coverage for Section 5 preclearance, was unconstitutional because it violated principles of federalism and equal sovereignty of the states.

44. Karlan, "Democracy and Disdain," 13.

45. Hollis-Brusky, *Ideas with Consequences*, 62.

46. Hollis-Brusky, *Ideas with Consequences*, 83.

47. See generally, Silverstein, *Law's Allure*.

48. Madison, *Federalist* 10, 45.

49. Mark A. Graber, "Belling the Partisan Cats: Preliminary Thoughts on Identifying and Mending a Dysfunctional Constitutional Order," *Boston University Law Review* 94, no. 3 (2014): 643.

50. Michael McGough, "How to Diversify the Ivy League Club That Is the Supreme Court," *Los Angeles Times*, October 28, 2014, http://www.latimes.com/opinion/opinion-la/la-ol-supreme-court-diversity-ivy-league-20141028-story.html.

51. Mark A. Graber, "The Coming Constitutional Yo-Yo? Elite Opinion, Polarization, and the Direction of Judicial Decision Making," *Howard Law Journal* 56, no. 3 (Spring 2013): 661, 664.

52. See Charles R. Epp, *The Rights Revolution* (Chicago: University of Chicago Press, 1998). See also Hollis-Brusky, *Ideas with Consequences*.

53. See Hollis-Brusky, *Ideas with Consequences*, 165–175.

54. See Hollis-Brusky, *Ideas with Consequences*, 174.

55. Neal Baum and Lori Hausegger, "The Supreme Court and Congress: Reconsidering the Relationship," in *Making Policy, Making Law*, ed. Mark C. Miller and Jeb Barnes (Washington, DC: Georgetown University Press, 2004), 107.

56. Richard L. Hasen, "End of the Dialogue?," *Southern California Law Review* 86, no. 2 (January 2013): 205–261.

57. Ledbetter v. Goodyear Tire and Rubber Co., 550 U.S. 618 (2007).

58. Lilly Ledbetter Fair Pay Act of 2009, Public Law 111-2, S. 181.

59. See Hasen, "End of the Dialogue?"; and Matthew R. Christiansen and William N. Eskridge Jr., "Congressional Overrides of Supreme Court Statutory Interpretation Decisions, 1967–2011," *Texas Law Review* 92 (2014): 1318–1541.

60. Hasen, "End of the Dialogue?," 105.

61. Shelby County v. Holder, ___ Roberts, C. J. Majority, at 24.

62. Silverstein, *Law's Allure*, 15.

63. Silverstein, *Law's Allure*, 69–70.

64. John Hart Ely, *Democracy and Distrust: A Theory of Judicial Review* (Boston: Harvard University Press, 1980).

65. Graber, "Belling the Partisan Cats," 611, 617.

66. See Bartels, "Sources and Consequences," 177.

67. Karlan, "Democracy and Disdain."

CHAPTER 6

Polarization and the Administrative State

Eric Helland and Kenneth P. Miller

For the first century under the Constitution, the United States maintained a lean executive branch with few agencies and limited administrative powers. By the late nineteenth century, this approach to governance faced growing criticism. Reformers claimed that the federal government was ill-equipped to meet the proliferating needs of a modernizing society, and urged the nation to embrace a larger, more powerful central government staffed by specialized, professionalized, expert administrators. As these ideas took hold, Congress established and expanded what is now known as the "administrative state"—a complex bureaucratic system with broad rulemaking, enforcement, and other powers. The term "administrative state" is another way of describing the modern federal bureaucracy, and we use the terms interchangeably in this chapter. Today, the federal bureaucracy consists of hundreds of departments, commissions, boards, offices, agencies, and subagencies (440 agencies were listed in the Federal Register in 2018), staffed by nearly 2.7 million federal civilian employees collectively wielding vast programmatic and regulatory authority.[1] In addition to powers exercised by its own employees, the federal government extends its reach by administering many programs through state and local governments as well as networks of private contractors. The sprawling administrative state now reaches into most corners of American life and bears responsibilities unimaginable at the time of the nation's founding. As Chief Justice John Roberts has observed: "The Framers could hardly have envisioned today's vast and varied Federal bureaucracy and the authority administrative agencies now hold over our economic, social, and political activities."[2]

Disagreement over the proper size, powers, functions, and limits of the administrative state has helped differentiate the two major parties and, increasingly, has contributed to the polarization of American politics. As Democrats have more firmly committed to expanding the federal government to address social needs, the Republican Party's conservative base—exemplified by the Tea Party movement and the Freedom Caucus—redoubled its commitment to limited government. Although one can cite exceptions, such as Republican support for expanding Medicare under former president George W. Bush, the dominant pattern has been for Democrats to embrace the growth of the administrative state and Republicans to resist.

The Obama years reinforced this divide. Former president Obama and congressional Democrats sought to extend federal responsibilities in areas ranging from universal health care to environmental protection to financial regulation—all in the face of determined Republican opposition. In the most prominent example, a Democratic-controlled Congress enacted the Patient Protection and Affordable Care Act (ACA), or "Obamacare," in 2010 with overwhelming Democratic support, including unanimous Democratic support in the Senate, but no Republican votes for final passage in either the Senate or the House. After Republicans wrested control of Congress from the Democrats in 2010, the Obama administration increasingly gave up trying to achieve its policy goals through the legislative process and instead pursued its agenda through administrative action, over sharp Republican opposition.

The election of an unconventional, disruptive Republican to the presidency in 2016 introduced new complexities, yet, on balance, has reinforced the partisan divide over the administrative state. During the 2016 campaign, Donald J. Trump did not fully embrace the orthodox Republican commitment to limited government; instead, he promoted a populist vision of "America First" nationalism. Many observers thought a Trump presidency would blur left-right categories, in part by asserting a robust role for the federal government. When Trump assumed office, however, his initial actions strongly aligned with the conservative goal of limiting the size and reach of the administrative state. The new president issued a hiring freeze on agency employees; proposed a budget that sought to eliminate or reduce a long list of federal programs; issued executive orders overturning many Obama-era regulations and limiting the regulatory reach of federal agencies; and filled his cabinet with ideological conservatives committed to cutting federal regulatory powers. Within weeks of Trump's inauguration, then senior strategist Steve Bannon explained these moves to a Conservative Political Action Conference as part of the "deconstruction of the administrative state." Bannon called this "deconstruction" one of the Trump administration's top priorities, one of its three "verticals" along with economic nationalism and national security and sovereignty. "If you look at these cabinet appointees," Bannon said, "they were selected for a reason, and that is deconstruction." In his view, "the way the progressive left runs is that when they can't get something passed, they'll just put it into some regulation in some agency. That's all gonna be deconstructed."[3] At the same time that the Trump administration was plotting to deconstruct the administrative state, Republicans in Congress launched new efforts to repeal Obamacare and roll back a range of Obama-era federal regulations. These simultaneous moves by President Trump and congressional Republicans mobilized a strong Democratic reaction aimed at defending existing federal agencies and programs. Thus, at least initially, the disruptive election of 2016 reinforced the divide between the two parties over the proper scope and ends of federal administrative powers.

Meanwhile, the nation's polarized political environment has altered the operations of the administrative state. Although the architects of the modern administrative state sought to give agencies much independence from outside political control, they were forced to graft them into the Madisonian Constitution's checks-and-balances system, so that Congress, the president, and the courts exercise various levels of institutional control over agency actions. Polarization has shifted this balance based on such factors as whether the national government is unified or divided (that is, whether one party controls both the presidency and Congress) and the size of partisan margins in Congress, especially in the Senate. Under conditions of unified government and one-party domination of Congress, polarization facilitates shared control of the administrative state by the president and Congress. But the picture changes when the branches are divided between the parties—a frequent condition in recent decades.

First, in times of divided government, partisan polarization has weakened Congress's ability to control agencies.[4] Historically, Congress has influenced agency behavior by, among other means, establishing and amending agencies' governing statutes, controlling their budgets, and holding them to account through oversight hearings. In our polarized environment, however, members of Congress routinely show less loyalty to their branch than to their party,[5] and congressional control of agencies often bogs down in partisan conflict.[6] Second, polarization has helped presidents consolidate their influence over the administrative state. During recent Democratic and Republican administrations alike, presidents have used various means to assert greater control over agency actions and use those actions to their own ends. Especially in periods of divided government, polarization has created incentives for presidents to pursue their policy agendas directly through administrative action rather than through the legislative process.[7] The president's congressional opponents often object to this exercise of executive power, but, again, have difficulty mounting effective resistance. Third, as congressional control over the federal bureaucracy has eroded, the federal courts have begun to exercise a stronger check.[8] In recent high-stakes cases involving environmental policy, immigration, and other matters, the federal courts have reconsidered their historic deference to agency decision-making and exercised more aggressive review.[9] If this trend continues, courts will exert a more consequential institutional check on the administrative state.

This chapter explores these dynamics by examining how the modern administrative state was grafted into the original Madisonian Constitution, how it expanded over time, how it contributed to the nation's partisan divide, and how the combination of the Constitution's institutional design and the government's political polarization have affected its operation.

THE DEVELOPMENT OF THE ADMINISTRATIVE STATE

The original Madisonian Constitution created a federal government of limited powers, separated among three branches, and internally regulated by multiple systems of checks and balances. The Vesting Clauses allocated three forms of power—legislative, executive, and judicial—to the new government's three coordinate branches. Although the partition was not absolute—indeed, the Constitution provided for the interbranch sharing of certain powers—the principles of limitation and separation were among the system's defining features. The Founders designed the government this way to prevent the "accumulation of all powers legislative, executive, and judiciary in the same hands," which, according to Madison, "may justly be pronounced the very definition of tyranny."[10]

The constitutional text was virtually silent on the topic of administrative organization, an omission that has been called a "hole" in the Constitution.[11] Yet the Founders were acutely aware of the failures of governance under the Articles of Confederation and understood the importance of effective administration. The constitutional design anticipated that Congress would grant the executive branch sufficient resources and powers to carry out necessary administrative functions.[12] The First Congress quickly established new cabinet departments (Foreign Affairs, Treasury, and War), created the Office of Attorney General, and enacted legislation empowering the executive branch to perform functions such as administering customs tariffs and collecting duties.[13]

Over time, the federal government's administrative powers expanded, but as administrative law scholar Cass Sunstein observes, "The early United States, unlike European countries, lacked a well-defined bureaucratic apparatus."[14]

The federal government's modern administrative powers can be traced to the latter half of the nineteenth century. Two landmarks were the adoption in 1883 of the Pendleton Civil Service Reform Act, which sought to replace the spoils system with a professional civil service, and the creation in 1887 of the Interstate Commerce Commission (ICC), the federal government's first independent regulatory commission.[15] Soon, reformers such as Woodrow Wilson sought to move beyond these innovations to advocate more comprehensive change. In an 1887 essay titled "The Study of Administration," the future president laid out his vision for reinventing government.[16] To achieve efficiency and good government in an increasingly complex society, he argued, the constitutional system must incorporate new organizational forms that delegate power to professional policy experts—as he put it, "a body of thoroughly trained officials."[17] These ideas helped spur reforms that eventually created the modern administrative state.[18] The innovations included expanding the scope of federal regulatory powers; delegating powers to new administrative agencies; combining legislative, executive, and judicial functions in those agencies; and, to the extent possible, insulating the agencies from political control.

According to the Progressive vision, empowering administrative agencies in these ways would allow apolitical, specialized experts to make and enforce policy in the public interest. Congress would authorize agencies to implement new federal laws. By their nature, the enabling statutes would contain broad provisions; executing them would require agencies to make interpretive judgments that would have binding policy consequences. Accordingly, bureaucrats would not only interpret and implement the law but also, in a real sense, make it.

Reformers faced the challenge of establishing this scheme within the Madisonian constitutional structure of separation of powers and checks and balances. An important obstacle was the nondelegation doctrine, a principle derived from the separation of powers that limited the ability of one branch of government to cede power to another. By the 1930s, the forces driving the growth of the federal government overtook this doctrine, and the Supreme Court conceded to Congress near-total discretion in delegating powers to agencies.[19] The prevailing view was later summarized by Justice Harry Blackmun in *Mistretta v. United States* (1989): "Our jurisprudence has been driven by a practical understanding that in our increasingly complex society, replete with ever changing and more technical problems, Congress simply cannot do its job absent an ability to delegate power under broad general directives."[20] Congress thus established new agencies, and granted them a range of legislative, executive, and judicial powers.

The proliferation of federal agencies came in waves. The early twentieth-century organizations such as the Federal Reserve (1913) and the Federal Trade Commission (FTC) (1914) were followed by the "alphabet soup" agencies of the New Deal, such as the Securities and Exchange Commission (SEC) (1934) and the National Labor Relations Board (NLRB) (1935), which in turn were followed by more recent creations, such as the Environmental Protection Agency (EPA) (1970) and the Consumer Financial Protection Bureau (CFPB) (2010).

Congress granted these agencies varying responsibilities and degrees of independence. The most important conceptual distinction was between executive agencies and independent regulatory agencies. Executive agencies form the bulk of the federal bureaucracy. They include the fifteen cabinet departments (State, Defense, Treasury, and the like), as well as each cabinet department's organization chart of subagencies, bureaus, divisions, and offices, such as the Internal Revenue Service (IRS), under the Department of the Treasury, and the Federal Bureau of Investigation (FBI), under the Department of Justice. Some executive agencies, such as the EPA, are not situated within a Cabinet department yet are similarly responsible to the executive. The president selects the heads of the executive agencies—subject to Senate confirmation—and may remove these officials at will, as evidenced by President Trump's summary dismissal of former FBI director James Comey during the early days of his administration. By contrast, independent regulatory agencies are more formally insulated from the executive. These organizations often are headed by multimember boards rather than a single secretary or director. The board members are appointed by the president, subject to Senate confirmation, but have staggered terms. The boards must often be bipartisan. Moreover, generally Congress limits the president's ability to remove these officials by requiring good cause, such as corruption or incapacity. Examples of independent regulatory agencies include the Federal Reserve Board, the FTC, the NLRB, and the Federal Election Commission (FEC).[21]

In 1946 Congress adopted the Administrative Procedure Act (APA) to provide procedural standards for rulemaking by both executive and independent agencies. This act was designed to provide a framework for the administrative rulemaking powers introduced by the Progressives and expanded by the New Deal. The APA establishes the path administrative agencies must follow in order to adopt a new regulation. Essentially, the agency has two choices: conduct formal hearings on the regulation or, more commonly, establish a "notice and comment" period. The notice must provide the agency's rationale for why it has legal authority to adopt the rule and a detailed description of the rule. The APA's notice and comment process, combined with statutory right of affected parties to challenge the agency's action, are the main sources of judicial oversight of administrative agencies.

Through the mid-1970s, the growth of the administrative state generally enjoyed bipartisan support. After Republican Dwight Eisenhower won the presidency in 1952, for example, he did not seek to dismantle the New Deal's expansion of the federal government. Similarly, Richard Nixon's administration (1969–1974) accepted most elements of the 1960s Great Society programs and worked with Congress to extend federal regulatory authority into new areas, including environmental protection, worker safety, and affirmative action. Ronald Reagan's election, however, marked a breakdown in bipartisan support for the expansion of federal regulatory powers and, after 1980, the two parties became increasingly divided in their attitudes toward the administrative state. As Democrats continued to embrace a vision of strong, expansive federal action, Republicans increasingly advocated limits on federal administrative power.

The sorting of the national electorate—with conservatives increasingly identifying as Republicans and liberals as Democrats—has sharpened the partisan divide over the administrative state. Survey data obtained by several polling organizations and published by the Pew Research Center illustrate this gap. Between 1995 and 2015, survey respondents were asked whether they preferred a smaller government providing fewer services. Large and growing majorities of those who identified as Republicans or leaned Republican wanted government to shrink; those who identified as Democrats or leaned Democratic increasingly disagreed. By 2015, the partisan gap had grown to nearly 50 percentage points.[22] Similarly, a 2015 Pew Research Center survey asked respondents whether the government should do more to solve problems, or whether it is doing too many things better left to businesses and individuals. The question again revealed a sharp partisan divide. Sixty-six percent of those who identified as Democrats or leaned Democratic said the government should do more to solve problems, whereas only 26 percent of Republicans and Republican leaners shared that view.[23] Although these surveys are worded in general terms, they provide a glimpse of the partisan chasm over the proper size and role of the federal government and demonstrate the competing attitudes that have driven partisan efforts to gain control of the administrative state. Before we examine how polarization has both motivated and affected these efforts, we will first review the institutional powers the three branches of the federal government can assert over agencies.

EACH BRANCH'S INSTITUTIONAL CONTROL
OVER THE ADMINISTRATIVE STATE

Although it was designed to operate with varying degrees of independence from political control, the administrative state remains part of the Madisonian system of checks and balances. That is, Congress, the president, and the courts exercise various forms of power over agency behavior.[24] The branches have many and varied means to influence agencies, yet each branch also has limits to its ability to exert control.[25]

Congress

Congress is the body that creates agencies, establishes their scope of authority, and funds their activities. It can issue detailed mandates to agencies, hold them accountable through oversight hearings, and override their decisions through new legislation. Congress clearly has the institutional tools to exercise a high degree of control over agency behavior. And, indeed, a number of leading political scientists have advanced the theory of congressional dominance over agency behavior through application of principal-agent models. These models borrow heavily from theoretical work in economics, in which a single employee (the agent) negotiates a wage contract with an employer (the principal) in the presence of private information about the effort the employee has exerted on the principal's behalf. Although the principal and the agent have divergent interests, it is possible for the principal to write a contract that moves the agent's behavior in the principal's preferred direction.[26] More recently, scholars have focused on the so-called common agency model, which expands the principal-agent model to include two principals—Congress and the executive. Here, the result is coalition formation—one principal and the agent team-up at the expense of the other principal, for example. This approach is more consistent with the view that multiple principals control agencies.[27]

Scholars have analyzed the specific means by which Congress can control agencies, including legislative mandates, limits on appropriations, oversight investigations, decisions to confirm or deny confirmation to certain agency officials, and, in the extreme, passing new laws to change agency policy.[28]

As Congress delegated more authority to agencies during the twentieth century, it also sought additional means to exercise ex post control over agency behavior. From the 1930s to the 1980s, Congress exercised a check on agency behavior called the "legislative veto." Through this device, one or both houses of the Congress—or, sometimes, congressional committees—could negate, or veto, decisions made by agencies pursuant to a delegation of power. Over the course of six decades, Congress inserted various legislative veto provisions into more than two hundred laws.[29] In the 1983 case of *INS v. Chadha*, however, the Supreme Court declared that the legislative veto violated the Constitution's bicameralism principle as well as the Presentment Clause, which requires that all bills be presented to the president and subjected to the executive veto.[30] The Court's invalidation of the legislative veto, whether by one house or two, weakened Congress's power to control agencies.

In 1996, Congress attempted to reclaim some of the authority it lost in the *Chadha* case by enacting the Congressional Review Act (CRA). This act was designed to facilitate congressional review of new federal regulations by requiring agencies to submit new rules to Congress before they can take effect, and by giving Congress sixty calendar days after their submission to pass a "joint disapproval resolution" of "major" rules. A disapproval resolution must be endorsed by a majority vote in both houses (the resolution is not subject to a Senate filibuster) and presented to the president. If the president vetoes the resolution, a two-thirds vote is required in both houses to override the veto. If successful, a joint disapproval resolution blocks the rule from going into effect. The CRA procedure is a weaker congressional check on agencies than the legislative veto because, following *Chadha*, it has to conform to the constitutional requirements of normal legislation (two-house approval, presentment to the president) and it affects only newly promulgated agency rules. One can assume that a president will veto congressional attempts to override rules issuing from executive agencies within the president's own administration, but in times of transition, when both the Congress and a new president want to reverse an outgoing administration's last-minute regulations, the CRA offers an effective way to do so.[31]

For two decades after it was enacted in 1996, the CRA was successfully invoked only once, in 2001, during the transition between the Bill Clinton and George W. Bush administrations.[32] In 2000, the Clinton-era Occupational Safety and Health Administration (OSHA) proposed regulation of workplace ergonomics. The rule would have covered 102 million workers at six million work sites.[33] In early 2001, shortly after the inauguration of George W. Bush, the Republican 107th Congress passed and former president Bush approved a joint resolution disapproving the rule. For many years, this outcome was a solitary example. All subsequent attempts to invoke CRA failed, due to lack of two-house agreement or to presidential veto, until the 2017 transition from former president Obama to President Trump.

During the early months of 2017, the Republican Congress adopted and President Trump signed fourteen resolutions that overturned regulations promulgated at the end of the Obama administration by the Departments of

Labor, Education, Interior, Health and Human Services, and Defense, the SEC, the General Services Administration, the Federal Communications Commission (FCC), and NASA. Members of Congress voted on these resolutions along near-exact party lines; the resolutions succeeded because they did not need to meet a 60-vote threshold in the Senate. Delighted by these outcomes, some conservatives looked for ways to expand the CRA's reach, for example, by deeming older regulations subject to congressional disapproval if agencies failed to submit them to Congress in a timely way.[34]

The President

As the head of the executive branch, the president can exert considerable influence over agency behavior. The president's institutional resources include the power to appoint top agency officials, including the members of independent regulatory commissions when vacancies occur, the power to issue executive orders, signing statements, and presidential memoranda, as well as the power to grant conditional waivers from compliance with federal law.[35] As Michael S. Greve notes in the following chapter, states play an outsized role in implementing many federal policies, and the executive has repeatedly negotiated policy implementation state-by-state through use of waivers and other means. Further, the president can instruct heads of executive agencies to issue directives and guidance documents that outline how the agency will interpret its authority to enforce—or not enforce—statutes and regulations. Importantly, such changes in interpretation of enforcement authority are not covered by the Administrative Procedure Act's requirement that a new regulation go through the standard notice and comment period.[36]

To increase presidential control over the federal bureaucracy, the Reagan administration developed a concept known as "the unitary executive"—an idea Reagan's successors from both parties have embraced. Stated simply, the theory asserts that the president, as head of the executive branch, should be able to control agency decisions. Presidents have implemented the unitary executive concept in various ways, including through centralized oversight of agency rulemaking by the Office of Information and Regulatory Affairs (OIRA).[37]

Although presidents have adopted effective strategies to direct agency behavior, their power over agencies remains limited in various ways. First, the president's power to hire and fire agency officials is limited by law. Presidents can appoint and remove "political appointees," but those top-level officials constitute only a small fraction of the federal workforce, and, as noted above, Congress has enacted limits on the president's power to remove members of independent regulatory boards and commissions. Second, in some circumstances, the presidential will can be frustrated by bureaucratic inertia or outright opposition—that is, the president may order something to be done but face resistance at the agency level.[38] Third, as the transition from the Obama to Trump administrations clearly demonstrates, the president's ability to make policy unilaterally through executive agencies is vulnerable to override when administrations change. This is most evident with regard to executive orders, memoranda, and other guidance documents, which the incoming president can revoke with the stroke of a pen. Fourth, as noted above, Congress and a new president can invoke the CRA to override "midnight regulations" promulgated by agencies under the outgoing administration.

The Courts

The federal courts can assert power over some agency decisions through cases brought by affected individuals and organizations including, increasingly, state governments.[39] A court can overturn an agency rule if it finds that the rule violates the Constitution or otherwise is inconsistent with federal law.

Although courts exercise a constraint on agency action, this check is limited by various factors, including general limitations on judicial power such as the standing doctrine, as well as the Supreme Court's doctrine of deference to agency decisions, known as *Chevron* deference. Named for the landmark case *Chevron v. Natural Resources Defense Council* (1984),[40] the *Chevron* doctrine requires that a reviewing court defer to an agency's interpretation of the statute it administers if the agency's interpretation is "reasonable."[41] The reasonableness standard generally prevents a court from second-guessing an agency's interpretation of a statute even when the court believes there is a superior interpretation of congressional intent. By deferring to agencies when the interpretation deals with their enabling statutes, *Chevron* essentially acknowledges that agencies will have more information and expertise and are likely to be more accountable since they are responsible for making the policy work effectively.

Judges and scholars have debated whether this post-1984 deference violates the constitutional principle of checks and balances given that it grants authority to the executive branch and effectively removes the judiciary from administrative review.[42] Some administrative law scholars argue that *Chevron* is inconsistent with Chief Justice John Marshall's view, articulated in *Marbury v. Madison*, that the role of the courts is "to say what the law is."[43] Others, most notably the late Justice Scalia, have maintained that *Chevron* is consistent with the traditional approach and that the courts in the eighteenth and nineteenth centuries respected executive interpretations of the law.[44] Still others have asserted that while it might be a departure from the Madisonian system, *Chevron* still represents an improvement over the chaotic judicial rulings that preceded it.

Some signs suggest the Supreme Court is retreating from *Chevron*. In *King v. Burwell* (2015), for example, the Court chose not to defer to the IRS's interpretation of the ACA's tax provisions, stating that *Chevron* should not apply in cases of "deep economic and political significance."[45] Through this and other decisions, the Court has signaled that it plans to exercise a stronger check on the executive's use of agency decisions to make policies that arguably conflict with congressional intent. The prospects for such a change increased when Neil Gorsuch succeeded Justice Scalia on the Court. At his Senate confirmation hearings, Justice Gorsuch critiqued *Chevron* and suggested he favored less judicial deference to agency decisions.

The interbranch struggles for control of agencies are natural consequences of grafting the administrative state into the broader Madisonian checks-and-balances system. Has partisan political polarization appreciably changed these institutional dynamics? We now turn to that question.

HOW POLARIZATION HAS ALTERED INSTITUTIONAL CONTROL OF AGENCIES

In examining how partisan polarization has affected institutional control of agencies, we need to take into account whether one party controls both Congress and the presidency. The effects of polarization are quite different when government is unified than when control of the branches is divided between the two parties. Indeed, the effects are different even when the majority party in Congress holds a 60-vote supermajority in the Senate—and thus can overcome filibusters by the minority party—than when its Senate margin is narrower. The Obama and early Trump eras illustrate these dynamics.

Early Obama Years, 2009–2010

After the 2008 election, Democrats won the presidency and expanded their majorities in the House and the Senate, ushering in a period of unified government. During the 111th Congress (2009–2010), Democrats for a few months achieved a 60-vote Senate majority, including two independents who caucused with the Democrats; otherwise, they held cohesive but not overwhelming majorities in both houses of Congress during the first two years of the Obama administration. Throughout this period, the Democratic Congress and the president shared a desire to expand the federal government's powers and responsibilities. Because the two branches' "ideal points" were aligned, they coordinated in enacting major legislation that achieved their common ends. Two landmarks were the ACA, which massively reordered the American health care system and delegated new powers to agencies such as the Department of Health and Human Services (HHS), and the Dodd-Frank Act, which substantially increased federal regulation and oversight of the nation's financial services industry; gave new mandates to existing regulatory agencies; and established new regulatory bodies, including the CFPB and the Financial Stability Oversight Council.

Democrats were able to expand federal administrative powers in these and other areas because they controlled a unified government and maintained near-perfect party discipline. Under these conditions, Congress and the president worked cooperatively to direct the future course of the administrative state through landmark legislation. Because Democrats achieved these initiatives with virtually no Republican support, however, Republicans had nothing invested in them and looked for opportunities to roll them back.

Later Obama Years, 2011–2017

Mobilized by their opposition to the Democrats' progressive agenda, Republicans seized control of the House of Representatives in the 2010 midterm elections and the Senate in 2014. These Republican victories fractured the Democratic-controlled government of 2009–2010 and thus altered the relationship between Congress, the president, and the federal bureaucracy for the balance of the Obama administration. Under conditions of divided government, polarization produced gridlock. Starting in 2011, the Republican-controlled House was able to prevent further congressional expansion of the administrative state of the type enacted in 2009–2010. However, even after gaining control of the Senate in 2014, Republicans were unable to enact a conservative counter-agenda. As long as Obama remained in the White House and wielded a veto, he could block any efforts to reverse the Democrats' signature accomplishments from 2009–2010 or otherwise to reduce meaningfully the size and power of the administrative state. Moreover, because Democrats controlled the Senate until 2015 and retained enough votes to filibuster thereafter, they could generally spare Obama the effort of vetoing such bills by killing them before they could reach his desk.

As this condition of divided government persisted, the president faced a choice. He could follow Bill Clinton's example from the 1990s and look for ways to compromise with an opposition Congress—a "depolarizing" approach. Or he could dig in, hold fast to his ideological commitments, and look for ways to pursue his policy preferences outside the legislative process. Obama chose the second option. He increasingly turned away from Congress and pursued progressive ends unilaterally. He famously asserted that he wasn't "just going to be waiting for legislation," because "I've got a pen and I've got a phone. I can use that pen to sign executive orders and take executive actions and administrative actions that move the ball forward."[46] In a time of divided government, polarization encouraged executive unilateralism—the use of executive controls over the administrative state to achieve the president's preferred policy ends.

A notable example of executive unilateralism came in the area of immigration policy. Throughout the Obama years, most Americans believed the nation's immigration system was broken, yet disagreed on what was needed to fix the problem. Democrats increasingly sought expanded rights and benefits for undocumented immigrants, while Republicans generally opposed these moves and instead sought to tighten border security and, to varying degrees, step up deportation of those immigrants not legally in the country.

When Congress repeatedly failed to enact an immigration bill, Obama bypassed the legislative process and established new immigration policies through administrative action. In 2012, the president, with then Department of Homeland Security secretary Janet Napolitano, announced a policy of Deferred Action for Childhood Arrivals (DACA). Under DACA, the Department of Homeland Security (DHS) would grant "deferred action status," or temporary protection from deportation, to certain unauthorized immigrants who arrived in the United States as children. Although it did not grant permanent legal status to any unauthorized immigrants, DACA did provide them with temporary protection from deportation and eligibility for work authorization. At the time, government sources estimated that up to 1.7 million immigrants were eligible to apply for the program.[47] The following year, DHS announced that it would expand the DACA program by lifting the age cap and extending the protected period from two years to three. At the same time, DHS instituted a new policy called Deferred Action for Parents of Americans and Lawful Permanent Residents (DAPA). This policy provided eligibility for deferred action status to unauthorized immigrants whose children were lawful permanent residents or US citizens, and who met other requirements. Those who qualified under DAPA would also be eligible for work authorization and certain state and federal benefits. DAPA extended deferred action and its associated benefits to a much larger group of immigrants—approximately four million by some estimates.

Many congressional Republicans objected that both DACA and DAPA contravened existing immigration law and were an abuse of administrative authority. In response to these criticisms, Obama said: "When folks in Congress question my authority to make our immigration system work better, I've one answer: Pass a bill. Go ahead and pass a bill. . . . And the day I sign a comprehensive immigration bill into law, then the actions I take will no longer be necessary."[48]

The president's taunt highlighted a critical fact: Congress had no effective response to his unilateral action. Congress could not craft an immigration bill that would satisfy the Republican base and the president; it could not reverse, defund, or otherwise block DACA or DAPA. In a period of divided government, polarization had neutralized Congress's institutional check on administrative action.

A second leading example of this pattern was the fight over the regulation of greenhouse gasses. In 2013, Obama instructed the EPA to develop new regulatory standards for carbon emissions from plants that generate electrical power. In 2015, the president and the EPA formally announced the "Clean Power Plan"—a series of regulations that mandated reduction of carbon emissions on a state-by-state basis, with a goal of cutting such emissions nationally by 32 percent over 2005 levels by 2030. By all accounts, these regulations, if implemented, would have fundamentally transformed the nation's energy markets, causing renewable sources of energy to benefit; other sources, especially coal, to suffer. Indeed, some critics called the plan part of a "war on coal." The Obama administration argued that the EPA had authority to make this massive policy change through administrative action by virtue of powers delegated by Congress through amendments to the Clean Air Act of 1970. Congressional Republicans objected, arguing that the Clean Air Act provided the EPA no such authority.[49] In conditions of polarized divided government, however, Congress was unable to reverse the agency's decision. It passed a pair of resolutions under the CRA to overturn the Clean Power Plan regulations, but Obama vetoed them.

As Congress's check on the administrative state weakened during this period, the federal courts assumed a more central role. Congressional Republicans, attorneys general in Republican states, and allied interest groups sought to block Obama-era administrative actions through federal litigation— with considerable effect. Federal courts blocked implementation of several high-profile administrative actions, including the DAPA memorandum and the Clean Power Plan.[50] Many of these cases split the federal courts along ideological lines, with liberal justices siding with the agencies, and conservative justices siding with those challenging agency actions and showing less and less deference to Obama-era agency actions.[51]

Early Trump Administration

The 2016 election produced unified Republican government with relatively slim Republican majorities in Congress, especially in the Senate. By gaining control of both the presidency and Congress, Republicans had a window of opportunity to assert a measure of control over the federal bureaucracy through the CRA, the budget process, executive orders, new regulations, and more. President Trump's strategy for deconstructing the administrative state included issuing executive orders instructing the director of the Office of Management and Budget to develop a government reorganization plan to "eliminate unnecessary agencies, components of agencies, and agency programs"; another that required each agency to designate a regulatory reform officer to evaluate regulations with an eye to recommending some for repeal; and another that directed each agency to repeal two regulations for each new one it created. He also used executive orders to take aim at Obama-era administrative actions, directing agency officials to reverse, defer implementation of, or designate for review numerous Obama-era agency policies. Across the government, new agency officials took actions to reverse Obama-era administrative policies. In notable examples, Department of Homeland Security secretary John Kelly and Acting Secretary Elaine Duke rescinded the Obama administration's DAPA and DACA memoranda; EPA director Scott Pruitt issued a notice of rulemaking to overturn the Obama administration's Clean Power Plan; Undersecretary of State for Political Affairs Thomas Shannon Jr. issued a presidential permit for the Keystone-XL Pipeline, reversing the Obama administration's rejection of the project; the Federal Communications Commission, led by Trump-appointed chairman Ajit Pai, voted to overturn Obama-era net neutrality rules; Secretary of Education Betsy De Vos rescinded the Obama administration's "Dear Colleague" letter regarding procedural rules for campus sexual misconduct proceedings; the Departments of Health and Human Services, Treasury, and Labor issued rules expanding exemptions to the Obama-era HHS contraceptive mandate; and Attorney General Jeff Sessions rescinded Obama Justice Department policies limiting enforcement of federal restrictions on marijuana. As his administration was systematically reversing its predecessor's policies, President Trump was invoking the powers of the administrative state to pursue his own ends. An early example was his executive order temporarily limiting entry to the United States of certain foreign nationals from a list of Middle Eastern countries—a ban that Democrats attacked as a "Muslim ban."[52]

The Republican Congress was fully aligned with the Trump administration's efforts to reverse Obama-era administrative policies and, more ambitiously, to deconstruct the administrative state. As noted above, Congress was simultaneously pursuing similar objectives through its own powers, including the CRA. Unified government allowed Republicans in Congress and the White House to pursue their common cause. For their part, Democrats and their allies sought ways to resist, looking to the Senate filibuster and the federal courts to protect progressive policies and programs.

CONCLUSION

The administrative state has become one of the central battlegrounds of the nation's deepening partisan conflict. The Wilsonian ideal of "nonpolitical" administration, if it ever existed in practice, has been largely overwhelmed by partisan demands to exert control over the federal bureaucracy. Democrats seek to expand the bureaucracy's scope and powers and use it to achieve progressive policy goals, and Republicans want to "deconstruct" it—or at least limit its powers and redirect it to conservative ends. As the administrative state has grown in size and power, the stakes of these controversies have grown. Partisans on both sides have an intense desire to gain control of the presidency, the Congress, and the courts in large part because each of these institutions have some ability to control the federal bureaucracy's massive policymaking apparatus. In an era of political polarization, the ability of these institutions to control agencies increasingly depends on the level of one-party dominance. When government is unified, co-partisans in Congress and the White House can work together to direct administrative powers and decisions. When government is divided, however, the president has incentives to act unilaterally through agencies, and Congress has little ability to resist. In either circumstance, the courts present another potential check.

As institutional powers have shifted from one party to the other, the administrative state has been whip-sawed between the polarized objectives of the left and the right—between expansion and empowerment at one moment, and attempted deconstruction the next. In our present state of polarization, neither party has been able to sustain a dominant position over the long term, and it is an open question how far either side can move the administrative state before the other side counters. As president, Obama and congressional Democrats substantially expanded the powers of the federal bureaucracy, yet many

Eric Helland and Kenneth P. Miller

of their initiatives were either blocked by the courts or reversed once Republicans gained unified control of government. Conversely, when President Trump's advisors and other Republicans claimed they could "deconstruct" the administrative state, they were likely engaging in a fantasy. The modern federal bureaucracy is so deeply entrenched in our system of government and strongly defended by many constituencies that it could be truly "deconstructed" only after years or decades of concerted efforts by unified Republican government—an unlikely scenario in a closely divided nation. Instead, the more likely outcome is for long-term, nonconclusive, partisan struggle over the size, scope, powers, and policies of the administrative state.

NOTES

1. "Agencies," *Federal Register*, 2018, last accessed May 12, 2018, https://www.federalregister.gov/agencies.

2. City of Arlington, Texas v. FCC, 569 U.S. 290 (2013), Roberts, J., dissenting.

3. Philip Rucker, "Bannon: Trump Administration Is in Unending Battle for 'Deconstruction of the Administrative State,'" *The Washington Post*, February 23, 2017.

4. Nolan McCarty, "The Policy Effects of Political Polarization," in *The Transformation of American Politics: Activist Government and the Rise of Conservatism*, ed. Paul Pierson and Theda Skocpol (Princeton, NJ: Princeton University Press, 2007), 246; Miranda Elyse Yaver, "When Do Agencies Have Agency? Bureaucratic Noncompliance and Dynamic Lawmaking in United States Statutory Law, 1973–2010" (PhD diss., Columbia University, 2015); Gillian E. Metzger, "Agencies, Polarization, and the States," *Columbia Law Review* 115, no. 7 (November 2015): 1739; and Cynthia Farina, "Congressional Polarization: Terminal Constitutional Dysfunction?," *Columbia Law Review* 115, no. 7 (November 2015): 1689.

5. Daryl J. Levinson and Richard J. Pildes, "Separation of Parties, Not Powers," *Harvard Law Review* 119, no. 8 (June 2006): 2311–2386.

6. Metzger, "Agencies, Polarization, and the States," 1774–1775.

7. Kenneth S. Lowande and Sidney M. Milkis, "'We Can't Wait': Barack Obama, Partisan Polarization and the Administrative Presidency," *The Forum* 12, no. 1 (2014): 3–27.

8. Philip Hamburger, *Is Administrative Law Unlawful?* (Chicago: University of Chicago Press, 2014). In addition, polarization increases the ability of states to check federal agency power. As Jennifer Bulman-Pozen notes, the Madisonian design of "double protection" dampens the distorting impact of political conditions, such as partisan polarization, and that political polarization improves rather than hinders the states' ability to act as a check. Jessica Bulman-Pozen, "Federalism as a Safeguard of the Separation of Powers," *Columbia Law Review* 112, no. 3 (2012): 459–506.

9. Compare Chevron v. Natural Resources Defense Council, 467 U.S. 837 (1984) with, e.g., King v. Burwell, 576 U.S. __ (2015).

10. James Madison, *Federalist* 47 in Alexander Hamilton, James Madison, and John Jay, *The Federalist Papers*, ed. Clinton Rossiter (New York: Mentor, 1999).

11. Jerry L. Mashaw, *Creating the Administrative Constitution: The Lost One Hundred Years of Administrative Constitutional Law* (New Haven, CT: Yale University Press, 2012), 30.

12. Richard A. Epstein, *The Classical Liberal Constitution* (Cambridge, MA: Harvard University Press, 2014), 269.

13. Peter L. Strauss, "The Place of Agencies in Government: Separation of Powers and the Fourth Branch," *Columbia Law Review* 84, no. 3 (1984): 573, 601.

14. Cass R. Sunstein, *After the Rights Revolution: Reconceiving the Regulatory State* (Cambridge, MA: Harvard University Press, 1990), 18.

15. Robert L. Rabin, "Federal Regulation in Historical Perspective," *Stanford Law Review* 38, no. 5 (1986): 1189–1326.

16. Woodrow Wilson, "The Study of Administration," *Political Science Quarterly* 2, no. 2 (June 1887): 197–222.

17. Wilson, "Study of Administration."

18. Stephen Skowronek, *Building a New American State: The Expansion of National Administrative Capacities, 1877–1920* (New York: Cambridge University Press, 1982); James Q. Wilson, *Bureaucracy: What Government Agencies Do and Why They Do It* (New York: Basic Books, 1989), 45; and Marc T. Law and Sukkoo Kim, "The Rise of the American Regulatory State: A View from the Progressive Era," in *Handbook on the Politics of Regulation*, ed. David Levi-Faur (Cheltenham, UK: Edward Elgar Publishing, 2011), 113.

19. Rabin, "Federal Regulation," 1253–1262.

20. Mistretta v. United States, 488 U.S. 361 (1989).

21. Federal agencies can also take other organizational forms such as government corporations—stand-alone businesses that include the US Postal Service and Amtrak. See "Agencies," *Federal Register*, last accessed March 1, 2018, https://www.federal register.gov/agencies.

22. Pew Research Center, "Beyond Distrust: How Americans View Their Government," November 23, 2015, last accessed March 1, 2018, http://www.people-press.org/2015/11/23/2-general-opinions-about-the-federal-government/views-of-govt-9.

23. Pew Research Center, "Beyond Distrust."

24. Strauss, "The Place of Agencies," 600; and Keith E. Whittington and Daniel P. Carpenter, "Executive Power in American Institutional Development," *Perspectives on Politics* 1, no. 3 (September 2003): 495–513.

25. Barry R. Weingast, "Caught in the Middle: The President, Congress, and the Political-Bureaucratic System," in *The Institutions of American Democracy: The Executive Branch*, ed. Joel D. Aberbach and Mark A. Peterson (New York: Oxford University Press, 2005), 312–343.

26. Barry R. Weingast, "The Congressional-Bureaucratic System: A Principal Agent Perspective," *Public Choice* 44, no. 1 (1984): 147–192; and Barry R. Weingast and Mark J. Moran, "Bureaucracy Discretion or Congressional Control? Regulatory Policymaking by the Federal Trade Commission," *Journal of Political Economy* 91, no. 5 (October 1983): 765–800.

27. See Terry M. Moe, "An Assessment of the Positive Theory of Congressional Dominance," *Legislative Studies Quarterly* 12 (August 1987): 475–520.

28. For limits on appropriations, see Jason A. MacDonald, "Limitation Riders and Congressional Influence over Bureaucratic Policy Decisions," *American Political Science Review* 104, no. 4 (November 2010): 766–782. For oversight, see Richard J. Lazarus, "Congressional Descent: The Demise of Deliberative Democracy in Environmental Law," *Georgetown Law Journal* 94, no. 3 (2006): 619–682; and Douglas Kriner and Liam Schwartz, "Divided Government and Congressional Investigations," *Legislative Studies Quarterly* 33, no. 2 (May 2008): 295–321. For confirmations, see Anne Joseph O'Connell, "Shortening Agency and Judicial Vacancies through Filibuster Reform? An Examination of Confirmation Rates and Delays from 1981 to 2014," *Duke Law Journal* 64, no. 8 (2015): 1645–1716; and Dan B. Wood and Richard W. Waterman, "The Dynamics of Political Control of the Bureaucracy," *American Political Science Review* 85, no. 3 (September 1991): 801–828. For legislative override, see David R. Mayhew, *Divided We Govern: Party Control, Lawmaking, and Investigations, 1946–2002*, 2nd ed. (New Haven, CT: Yale University Press, 2005); and MacDonald, "Limitation Riders," 766–782.

29. Joseph Cooper, "The Legislative Veto in the 1980s," in *Congress Reconsidered*, 3rd ed., ed. Lawrence C. Dodd and Bruce I. Oppenheimer (Washington, DC: CQ Press, 1985), 364–389.

30. INS v. Chadha, 462 U.S. 919 (1983).

31. "Note: The Mysteries of the Congressional Review Act," *Harvard Law Review* 122, no. 8 (June 2009): 2162–2183.

32. See Julie A. Parks, "Lessons in Politics: Initial Use of the Congressional Review Act," *Administrative Law Review* 55, no. 1 (Winter 2003): 187–210; and Stuart Shapiro, "The Role of Procedural Controls in OSHA's Ergonomics Rulemaking," *Public Administration Review* 67, no. 4 (July–August 2007): 688–701.

33. Patrick J. Cleary, vice president of the National Association of Manufacturers, described it as the "largest regulation that OSHA has ever issued and probably more costly than anything else that the Federal government has done in the workplace." Steven Greenhouse, "Battle Lines Drawn over Ergonomic Rules; Business Pitted against Washington," the *New York Times* online, November 18, 2000, last accessed March 1, 2018, http://www.nytimes.com/2000/11/18/business/battle-lines-drawn-over-ergo nomic-rules-business-pitted-against-washington.html.

34. Jonathan Miller, "Congressional Review Act Gets a Workout," Roll Call, May 15, 2017, last accessed March 1, 2018, http://www.rollcall.com/news/politics /congressional-review-act-gets-a-workout.

35. For agency appointments, see Mathew D. McCubbins, Roger G. Noll, and Barry R. Weingast, "Structure and Process, Politics and Policy: Administrative Arrangements and the Political Control of Agencies," *Virginia Law Review* 75, no. 2 (March 1989): 431–482; and Michael A. Livermore, "Political Parties and Presidential Oversight," *Alabama Law Review* 67, no. 1 (2015): 45–134. For executive orders, see McCarty, "The Policy Effects," 224. For signing statements, see Neal Devins and David E. Lewis, "Not-So Independent Agencies: Party Polarization and the Limits of Institu-

tional Design," *Boston University Law Review* 88, no. 2 (April 2008): 459, 480; and Daniel B. Rodriguez, Edward H. Stiglitz, and Barry R. Weingast, "Executive Opportunism, Signing Statements, and the Separation of Powers," *Journal of Legal Analysis* 8, no. 1 (Spring 2016): 95–119. For presidential memoranda, see Kenneth S. Lowande and Sidney M. Milkis, "'We Can't Wait': Barack Obama, Partisan Polarization, and the Administrative Presidency," *The Forum* 12, no. 1 (2014): 3, 5–6. For waivers, see David J. Barron and Todd D. Rakoff, "In Defense of Big Waiver," *Columbia Law Review* 113, no. 2 (March 2013): 265–346; and Michael S. Greve and Ashley C. Parrish, "Administrative Law without Congress: Of Rewrites, Shell Games, and Big Waivers," *George Mason Law Review* 22, no. 3 (Spring 2015): 501–547.

36. Of course, the downside is that a future administration can reverse the interpretation without going through the notice and comment period, making it harder to "lock in" policy changes.

37. Elena Kagan, "Presidential Administration," *Harvard Law Review* 114, no. 8 (June 2001): 2245–2385; and Metzger, "Agencies, Polarization," 1753–1755.

38. Joshua B. Kennedy, "'Do This! Do That!' and Nothing Will Happen": Executive Orders and Bureaucratic Responsiveness," *American Politics Research* 43, no. 1 (January 2015): 59–82.

39. Sunstein, *After the Rights Revolution*.

40. Chevron v. Natural Resources Defense Council, 467 U.S. 837 (1984).

41. Aditya Bamzai, "The Origins of Judicial Deference to Executive Interpretation," *Yale Law Journal* 126, no. 4 (February 2017): 908, 912.

42. Moreover, it appears that Congress, through the Administrative Procedure Act (APA), expressed its desire for judicial review in that the APA attempted to codify the scope of judicial review of agency interpretations. Specifically, the APA states that a "reviewing court shall decide all relevant questions of law, interpret constitutional and statutory provisions, and determine the meaning or applicability of the terms of an agency action."

43. Richard A. Posner, "The Rise and Fall of Judicial Self-Restraint," *California Law Review* 100, no. 3 (June 2012): 519–556.

44. Antonin Scalia, "Judicial Deference to Administrative Interpretations of Law," *Duke Law Journal* 38, no. 3 (June 1989): 511–521. For a dissent from the view that *Chevron* is consistent with eighteenth- and nineteenth-century notions of judicial deference to executive decisions, see Bamzai, "Origins of Judicial Deference."

45. King v. Burwell, 576 U.S. __ (2015).

46. Rebecca Kaplan, "Obama: I Will Use My Pen and Phone to Take on Congress," *CBS News*, January 14, 2014, last accessed March 1, 2018, http://www.cbsnews.com /news/obama-i-will-use-my-pen-and-phone-to-take-on-congress.

47. Jeffery S. Passel and Mark Hugo Lopez, "Up to 1.7 Million Unauthorized Immigrant Youth May Benefit from New Deportation Rules," *Pew Research Center*, August 14, 2012, last accessed March 1, 2018, http://www.pewhispanic.org/2012/08/14 /up-to-1-7-million-unauthorized-immigrant-youth-may-benefit-from-new-deporta tion-rules.

48. Barack Obama, "Remarks by the President on Immigration—Chicago, IL," November 25, 2014, last accessed May 11, 2018, https://obamawhitehouse.archives .gov/the-press-office/2014/11/20/remarks-president-address-nation-immigration.

49. Barack Obama, "Remarks by the President in Announcing the Clean Power Plan," August 3, 2015, last accessed March 1, 2018, https://obamawhitehouse.archives .gov/the-press-office/2015/08/03/remarks-president-announcing-clean-power-plan; and National Conference of State Legislatures, "States Reaction to EPA Greenhouse Gas Emissions Standards," April 18, 2016, last accessed March 1, 2018, http://www .ncsl.org/research/energy/states-reactions-to-proposed-epa-greenhouse-gas -emissions-standards635333237.aspx.

50. United States v. Texas, 579 U.S. __ (2016), affirming by equally divided vote the decision of the Court of Appeals affirming the preliminary injunction in Texas v. United States, 809 F.3d 134 (5th Cir. 2015); and West Virginia v. EPA (In re Murray Energy Corp.), 788 F.3d 330 (D.C. Cir. 2015).

51. In one case overturning an EPA regulation, Justice Scalia wrote: "When an agency claims to discover in a long-extant statute an unheralded power to regulate a significant portion of the American economy, we typically greet its announcement with a measure of skepticism. We expect Congress to speak clearly if it wishes to assign to an agency decisions of vast economic and political significance." Utility Air Regulatory Group v. EPA, 573 U.S. __ (2014).

52. A later iteration of the travel ban also applied to North Korea and Venezuela. See "Presidential Proclamation Enhancing Vetting Capabilities and Processes for Detecting Attempted Entry into the United States by Terrorists or Other Public-Safety Threats," September 24, 2017, last accessed March 1, 2018, https://www.white house.gov/presidential-actions/presidential-proclamation-enhancing-vetting-capabil ities-processes-detecting-attempted-entry-united-states-terrorists-public-safety-threats.

CHAPTER 7

Federalism in a Polarized Age

Michael S. Greve

Two tendencies have shaped American federalism's development for the past four decades under widely varying economic conditions and political constellations: partisan-ideological polarization and the rise of executive government. On most accounts, the former has driven the latter. Polarization is naturally conducive to executive government, especially in a presidential system.[1] Institutional mechanisms that generate cooperation and exchange in a system of divided powers break down, and a deadlocked, "dysfunctional" legislature yields power to the executive.[2] And because most domestic policies are embedded in intergovernmental statutes and arrangements, polarization and the attendant rise of executive government have naturally shaped federalism's contours and operation. The legislative "cooperative" federalism of the post New Deal era has come to an end; an executive-dominated, harshly confrontational federalism has taken its place.[3]

While much can be said for this conventional, polarization-centered account, there are also reasons to consider it incomplete and perhaps a bit misleading. On one side, potent forces have pushed toward executive government wholly apart from increased partisan and ideological divisions. Foremost among those forces is a vast expansion of public expectations and political horizons, coupled with technological changes that have shaped both the demand for public policy and its supply in ways that naturally favor the executive. On the other side, the conventional story tends to underplay federalism's horizontal dimension and the significance of state-level polarization. An increasing number of states have become reliably "red" or "blue," and those blocs divide sharply over highly salient questions of public policy—from health care to climate change to immigration. Partisan, ideological polarization in this geographic, state-level dimension is a form of political sectionalism—that is, a divide among blocs of states that is too deep, on central issues of politics, to be bridged through ordinary transactional and coalitional politics.[4] Sectionalism in this sense accounts for some of the most conspicuous characteristics of contemporary federalism—such as sharply increased litigiousness and asymmetric, ad hoc federal-state bargains outside the bounds of statutory law and ordinary institutional channels.

While federalism has been sectional for much—and indeed most—of our history, the conjunction with executive federalism is something new in American politics. The origins, operation, contours, and prospects of that configuration are the subject of this chapter. The first part interprets the rise of executive federalism as a process of mutual reinforcement: while partisan polarization has clearly reinforced executive government, it is also the case that executive government has produced further polarization.[5] The second part describes the sectional features of contemporary federalism and the effects on federal-state bargaining, federal administration, and fiscal affairs. The third part attempts to put the two pieces together and to explain a seeming perplexity: while federalism has become executive across the board, it has become sectional only in some arenas, while remaining cooperative and bipartisan in others. The reasons have to do with political economy and, more specifically, interstate competition: federalism has turned sectional when, where, and because states can effectively compete for productive industries and citizens. The fourth part discusses the judiciary's capacity to organize and delimit executive, sectional federalism's metes and bounds, and finds it lacking. Last, the fifth part of this chapter offers a brief and necessarily tentative assessment of federalism's future. Federalism, I predict with the hesitation that accompanies all extrapolations from current trends, will remain increasingly executive, sectional, and constitutionally unconstrained.

EXECUTIVE FEDERALISM

Once upon a time, throughout the nineteenth century and beyond, federalism came from the Constitution and the federal courts. Its conventional moniker, "dual" federalism, captures the central features: limited federal powers; separate state and federal "spheres" of authority; and very limited intergovernmental arrangements, especially federal fiscal transfers to the states. After the demise of constitutional constraints in the New Deal and its aftermath, a new, "cooperative" federalism took hold. That federalism came from Congress, as the institutional forum where state and national leaders haggled out joint governance arrangements in a wide sphere of concurrent authority. Congress provided federal funding for intergovernmental programs, and it superintended them through committees and subcommittees. The number, scope, and scale of cooperative programs exploded in the Great Society era.

Today, federalism comes from the executive. Its contours are shaped by the Environmental Protection Agency (EPA), the Department of Health and Human Services (HHS), and the Department of Education and by agencies that until recently had little if any truck with federalism, such as the Internal Revenue Service[6]; by nominally private, quasi-governmental agencies[7]; and through legal settlements between federal regulators, state prosecutors, and private enterprises.[8] These law-making and policymaking initiatives have taken decidedly unorthodox forms. Federal agencies generate entire federalism programs from whole cloth, commandeer vast revenue streams to state and local governments at their discretion, and endeavor to entice or cajole ornery states into some form of cooperation with federal programs and ambitions. Initiatives of this description signal a migration from Congress to the executive as the key federalism actor. Moreover, they are exercises of presidential government. The federalism decisions that matter are not made by bureaucrats in the context of a routinized regulatory process; they are made by high-level political officials acting in close concert with the White House.[9]

Political science models that were once conventional suggest that this should not have happened. In the 1970s and 1980s, "executive federalism" was thought to be endemic to systems that combine federalism with parliamentary government, including Germany, Australia, and Canada.[10] Such systems tend to produce federal integration and coordination through intergovernmental bargains—typically among prime ministers or cabinet members and their provincial counterparts, often through formalized consultative processes, and almost always behind closed doors. Of course, America's "cooperative" federalism, too, was largely negotiated between the central and subordinate governments; however, the basic federalism bargains came from congressional committees and subcommittees. Executive-administrative negotiations within those confines took a much more improvised, particularistic, and lobby-driven form than is common in parliamentary systems. Thus, in comparative federalism studies, the United States often served as executive federalism's "legislative federalism" foil.

In retrospect, the association of executive federalism with parliamentary government looks spurious. The European Union (EU) is often described as an "executive federalism," chiefly because it lacks a parliament with full legislative powers. Presidential federal systems with weak or splintered parties, such as that of Argentina, have shown pronounced tendencies toward executive federalism.[11] And the United States has impressively moved in that direction. It has developed few, if any, of the institutional mechanisms that characterize executive federalism's parliamentary variant. It is not about to turn into the EU, and it has so far been spared most of the pathologies that afflict presidential federalisms in Latin America, such as massive state insolvencies and high levels of corruption. Very clearly, however, our federalism has become executive. How, and why? "In the last two decades," Thomas Gais and James Fossett wrote,

> the executive branch has used a growing range of administrative tools to negotiate directly with states over specific policies or to alter the context of state policy making without specific congressional approval. The federal executive branch and its interactions with the states have thus become a primary locus for producing major changes in domestic policies.[12]

The authors date executive federalism's emergence to the 1980s. The Reagan administration, they observe, was innovative in two respects: the formulation and implementation of major policy initiatives without Congress, and the centralization of those projects within the executive branch. Subsequent administrations have operated in the same fashion, except more so. The authors provide a survey of the executive's new tools: the aggressive use of discretionary authority under broad legislative waiver provisions; the expanded use of administrative rulemaking authority—as distinct from incentive-based instruments of shaping state policy; and management tools, such as the centralization of decision-making authority and the appointment of loyal, resolute administrators.

As Gais and Fossett acknowledge, the institutional change was a matter of degree. The New Deal's "legislative" federalism always demanded a great deal of executive discretion, improvisation, and negotiation with states and local governments. Still, no president, let alone some agency, could use that authority to "produce major changes in domestic policies" for fear of breaking the tenuous congressional compromises and coalitions that produced and sustained those policies. Executive federalism affords just that running room.

Perhaps the most obvious and instructive example is the use of "big," programmatic executive waivers under federal entitlement programs.[13] The use of such waivers was pioneered by the Reagan administration, under what was then Aid to Families with Dependent Children. The Clinton administration pursued that same course; by the time Congress enacted welfare reform in 1996, which was the hallmark federalism program of that decade, the president claimed with some justice that most of the envisioned programs had already been implemented through executive waiver and in cooperation with the states.[14] Most consequentially, administrations under presidents of both parties have routinely issued broad "Section 1115" waivers under Medicaid—which allow states great latitude to modify the program—to the point where none of the actual state programs has much to do with the statutory parameters. Fittingly, Medicaid has been identified as a pristine example of executive federalism.

By some measures, the Reagan era marks the beginning of a sustained increase in political polarization and congressional partisanship. Executive federalism may simply look like a by-product of that process. However, Gais's and Fossett's convincing account complicates that story. First, executive federalism emerged when "moderate Republicans" and "Boll Weevil" Democrats were not yet extinct. Second, a conspicuous number of laws that aggrandized executive federalism—including welfare reform, the No Child Left Behind Act, and several Medicaid expansions—were notable bipartisan achievements. Third, for most of the duration, executive federalism has been driven not only by congressional gridlock but also by deliberate legislative abdication, which has been practiced by both parties in Congress and under Republican and Democratic presidents alike. The executive for its part has responded in a highly partisan, political fashion. Beginning under the Reagan administration, presidents of both parties have promoted an executive-centered party system "that relies on presidential candidates and presidents to pronounce party doctrine, raise campaign funds, campaign on behalf of their partisan brethren, mobilize grass roots support and advance party programs."[15] Presidential unilateralism, exemplified by the Obama administration's "We Can't Wait (for Congress)" campaign and by some of the Trump administration's early initiatives,[16] has further exacerbated partisan polarization. It has been driven by electoral calculations and, at times, been deployed not to escape congressional "gridlock" but to preempt outbreaks of bipartisan compromise in Congress.[17] These observations suggest that executive government and its federalism partake of, or are driven by, forces that operate independently and at some remove from polarization.

In a powerful article, Christopher C. DeMuth has linked the rise of executive government and the corresponding decline of Congress to growing affluence and education and to advances in information and communication technologies.[18] He argues that these developments, by greatly increasing political participation and reducing political transactions costs, have transformed both sides of the market for government policy. On the demand side, an enormous array of interest groups can now organize effectively to lobby for government interventions on a limitless range of issues. These demands exceed the capacity of Congress. Legislatures and parties are fairly skilled at deciding who should get what, but they are not as skilled at arbitraging abstract values or superintending citizens' daily affairs. Politics becomes entrepreneurial and specialized: candidates, legislators, and officials work directly with interest and ideological support groups, bypassing the party and congressional hierarchies that previously controlled and limited the political agenda. Incapable of managing the resulting profusion of policies, Congress responds by delegating lawmaking to specialized agencies that can deploy modern technology much more efficiently in managing the "stakeholder communities" engaged in each policy field. Accordingly, Congress has evolved into an enabler of executive government. Its institutional function is to establish semi-autonomous special-purpose governments in response to political demands, while its individual members pursue their electoral careers.

DeMuth's account, wholly consistent with that presented by Gais and Fossett, suggests that tendencies toward executive government will operate with special virulence in the federalism arena, where specialized state- or local-based stakeholders are firmly organized, deeply entrenched, and—as governmental or quasi-governmental entities—in a position and often authorized to initiate or respond to political demands. At the same time, federalism-specific dynamics reinforce the drift toward executive government.

The central dynamic, Gais and Fossett argue persuasively, is a profound mismatch "between the federal government's authority and its fiscal and administrative powers."[19] The federal government has an enormous comparative advantage at raising money and cutting checks. Somewhat paradoxically, then, "assertions of federal authority over so many domestic policy areas through legislation" have entailed a greater role for state and local officials and a smaller role for Congress.

This interplay of delegation and devolution, too, is a matter of degree. The legislative federalism of the post–New Deal era consistently afforded state officials an important role in the implementation of nominally federal programs. Over the decades, the federal balance shifted in the states' favor, at least in some dimensions.[20] At some point, though, a difference in degree becomes a difference in kind. A delegated, executive federalism needs armies of servants, and as the national government's reach has expanded, so has the state servants' power to shirk or defect.[21] In many domains, federal agencies lack the capacity and expertise to monitor the state agents' conduct. At the same time, the national government's threats to protect against opportunistic stateside conduct through a withholding of funds or through conditional preemption have become less credible. State refusals to accept federal funds, virtually unknown until a decade ago, have become quite common, as have outright state refusals to administer federal programs.[22]

These centrifugal tendencies have in turn reinforced executive government. Only the executive, not Congress, can hope to cajole and rein in increasingly ornery states. It has many more tools at its disposal than the legislature; is relatively more nimble; can act on individual states; and can act strategically across program areas.[23] Intergovernmental relations on this model often require decisions that are too big and controversial to be made by mere administrators. They are made, as they must be, by political appointees. Importantly, the dynamic operates not only at the federal level but also stateside. Executive federalism is presidential federalism, and it is gubernatorial federalism.[24]

Clearly, partisan polarization has reinforced the tendencies just described. Once routine pork-barrel bills have often been stalled or blocked amid partisan strife, and partisan divisions have often prevented Congress from revising federal statutes when the underlying federalism bargains have become untenable, unworkable, or otherwise obsolete. Still, it appears that national level partisan polarization has gone hand-in-hand with secular forces that would generate executive federalism in any event.

SECTIONALISM: THE STATES OF POLARIZATION

States have followed the national pattern of high and growing partisan and ideological polarization.[25] By and large, the pattern has been one of increased partisan homogeneity within states and increased heterogeneity across and among states. States are reliably blue or red, with little in between. The number of states under one-party control has risen markedly: in over two-thirds of the states, one party governs the executive and both houses of the legislature.[26] Meanwhile, the ideological distance between and among states, and between "dissident" states and the federal government's agenda, has increased sharply. Red and blue states have formed and act as stable blocs over a wide range of issues, many of them of near existential interest to states on both sides. Environmental and energy policy, immigration, labor law, and of course the Affordable Care Act (ACA) provide ready examples. Two prominent federalism scholars have described changed pattern with admirable clarity:

> Unlike the previous era of cooperative federalism and national expansion, gridlock in Washington is now matched by equally trenchant conflicts among the states. Rather than respond to pent up policy demands for public action on broadly agreed goals and concerns, states instead have

cleaved to radically different policies and agendas mirroring the conflicts in Washington. Rather than acting as a relief valve for national policy paralysis, states have now tended collectively to ratify and intensify those conflicts.[27]

That assessment captures federalism's transformation especially over the past decade. In a longer-term perspective, though, the era of "cooperative federalism and national expansion" was an aberration from a pattern of conflictual politics and geographic polarization that, in varying shapes and with varying intensity, has been the rule in American politics.

Throughout the nineteenth century, American politics was intensely sectional. The central cleavage, of course, was slavery and, after the Civil War, its enduring legacy. Sectional politics was conducive to a "dual" federalism, characterized by limited federal authority and a low level of fiscal transfers. For example, there could be no encompassing federal commerce power that would have entailed federal authority to regulate slavery in the states. Similarly, fiscal transfers and other "cooperative" federalism arrangements could come about only rarely, due to intractable disagreements over the distribution of federal spending.

The Progressive and pre–New Deal eras—like ours, a time of high partisan polarization and sectional politics—did produce some "cooperative" federalism programs; in fact, the term dates back to that period. [28] It referred not so much to federal funding programs, which were few and far between, small, and often temporary. Rather, it referred primarily to federal statutes that "re-conveyed" to states authority over regulatory domains that, under the then-extant understanding of the Commerce Clause, otherwise would have fallen exclusively under Congress's authority as well as statutes that buttressed state authority by prohibiting interstate shipments of noxious goods. Such statutes were enacted in domains where states' interests were tolerably homogeneous or where Congress was able to compartmentalize political authority along state lines, as with liquor regulation. Throughout, however, Congress steered clear of enacting statutes that would have threatened the racial caste structure in the South.

Only the massive dislocations and the unusually high partisan consensus of the New Deal broke the sectional alignments and generated stable patterns of cooperative federalism.[29] Initially, that emergent federalism had a distinctly executive hue. The "emergency" programs of the early New Deal years conferred virtually unlimited spending discretion on the executive, and confidants of President Franklin Roosevelt, led by Harry Hopkins, roamed the country and sought to entice local politicians to adopt relief programs on a one-off basis.[30] Cooperative federal funding programs—called "entitlement programs" because they created legislative entitlements for the states—were enacted when and because Congress, the executive, and state and local politicians all shared an interest in greater regularity.[31] While those programs—for example, under the Social Security Act of 1935—left a great deal to administrative discretion, they established general funding formulas and, moreover, ensured legislative budget and program control through appropriations as well as continuous committee oversight.

The post–New Deal, postwar era was a time of high partisan consensus chiefly because southern whites ended up in the wrong party, but the sectional cleavage over race persisted. There could be no cooperative federalism in education or health care because for the South, there was nothing to negotiate. It took the Great Society, another episode of convulsion and single-party dominance, to break that pattern. The cooperative achievements of that period— the Elementary and Secondary Education Act of 1965, the accompanying civil rights mandates of Title VI, and Medicaid—reshaped the federalism landscape profoundly and with amazing speed.

The federalism literature of those decades—in political science, law, policy analysis, and economics—has a very confident, upbeat tone. Cooperative federalism, it suggests, would reduce the Founders' "new science of politics" to the study of intergovernmental relations. Federal courts would at long last bypass ideologically freighted first-order constitutional questions about the scope of congressional powers and instead attend to more nuanced problems of "process federalism's" proper operation. Fruitful collaboration among the levels of government would yield answers, not just to the horrid legacy of racial segregation but to a vast range of problems, from sexual harassment to environmental degradation that had theretofore seemed to elude an effective intergovernmental response. Fiscal transfers would remedy chronic revenue shortfalls at the state and local levels and, moreover, help to smooth out business cycles.

That perspective now looks sadly dated and perhaps shortsighted in its failure to anticipate cooperative federalism's near-tragic paradoxes. As explained earlier, the expansion of congressional ambitions, far from harmonizing national objectives with localist variegation, instead prompted the rise of executive government. More fatefully yet, the Great Society programs propelled the collapse of the New Deal coalition and over time produced partisan realignment and polarization that now dominates American politics at all levels.[32] In conjunction, those tendencies have fueled a federalism that is highly conflictual, asymmetric and extralegal, and increasingly expensive and fiscally unbalanced.

Bargaining and Litigation

Federal conditional funding and preemption programs, as noted earlier, reflect the mismatch between the federal government's expansive ambitions and its modest capacities. Under the Supreme Court's interpretation of the Constitution and as a practical matter, the federal government cannot compel a state to accept federal funds or to administer a federal program.[33] For this reason, federal programs aim to produce uniform state cooperation through some combination of (often fiscal) carrots and sticks, coupled with an assurance of state flexibility. The programs are structured to make it nearly impossible for any individual state to resist the federal "incentives." That form of federal integration is cooperative federalism's principal modus operandi. The system works, albeit not without friction and constant quarreling over the distribution of benefits and burdens, so long as states are tolerably homogeneous. The system breaks down when a substantial number of states, acting as a bloc, refuse cooperation or affirmatively work to thwart federal objectives. This is true even where the federal statute provides for a fallback in the form of direct federal regulation in noncompliant states: no federal agency is built to administer its programs directly in more than a handful of states. State-level polarization has produced noncooperative blocs and, consequently, a distinctive set of bargaining incentives and dynamics.

On the federal side, the attainment of national objectives under sectional conditions demands a strategy of picking off or subduing recalcitrant states one at a time, which is necessarily an executive undertaking. Congress can bargain with the states as long as they have a broadly consensual position—for instance, against federal preemption or for more generous funding and fewer "strings." By contrast, Congress cannot bargain with individual states whose interests run in opposite directions or with blocs of states whose demands are effectively nonnegotiable. To the extent that federalism's maintenance demands such negotiations, the executive's dominance increases. Stateside, the objective for dissident states becomes to hold and hang together—either by thwarting the central government's "divide and conquer" strategy ex ante (that is, by blocking the legislative or executive creation of "cooperative" programs), or by preventing defections after the fact.

With striking frequency, intergovernmental bargaining has broken down entirely and given way to litigation. The organization and coordination of state blocs in this domain is supplied by partisan associations, such as the Republican Attorneys General Association and the Democratic Attorneys General Association, or through more informal ad hoc arrangements. The long-running controversy over climate change policy, fought at shifting fronts for well over a decade, illustrates the partisan-sectional dynamics. The lawsuit that effectively compelled the EPA to regulate carbon dioxide as a "pollutant" under the Clean Air Act (1963), duly captioned *Massachusetts v. EPA*,[34] was brought by a coalition of liberal state attorneys general and environmental groups. Conservative attorneys general from energy-producing states were on the opposite side. The two blocs have opposed each other in numerous clean air and climate change controversies since. The most consequential engagement is the controversy over the Obama administration's "Clean Power Plan," an ambitious attempt to reconfigure the energy structure of all fifty states under a rarely used section of the Clean Air Act. Even before the plan was published in the Federal Register, the EPA sought to advance its objectives by promising compliant states and industries a great deal of flexibility, while at the same time signaling its resolute commitment to regulatory demands that would entail draconian impositions on the hold-outs.[35] A cohesive bloc of Republican states and energy industries, formed and battle-tested in earlier engagements over the administration's climate change initiatives, arrested the EPA's divide-and-conquer strategy by suing for a preliminary injunction against the EPA. While the litigation remained pending, Donald Trump took office as president. In October 2017, the EPA issued a Notice of Proposed Rulemaking, explaining its intent to repeal the Clean Power Plan on the grounds that it exceeds the agency's statutory authority.[36] Naturally, the state bloc that championed the Obama administration's plan threatened suit.

Bipartisan state litigation has not ceased entirely. For example, defenses against legal theories that would expose state and local governments to liability (for example, private rights of action implied under federal statutes or the Constitution) continue to enjoy near-unanimous state support. However, to an astounding extent and over a wide range of highly salient issues, state litigation has become partisan and sectional.[37] Bloc-driven litigation has accompanied the implementation of the ACA, immigration policies, labor regulation, and environmental and energy regulation on an ongoing basis. Under the Trump administration, such litigation has extended to questions that are far removed from the interests of states quo states, from the Federal Communications Commission's net neutrality policy to the president's alleged violations of the Constitution's Emoluments Clause.

Asymmetry and "Unorthodoxy"

Executive federalism is highly asymmetric: nominally federal policies take on entirely different contours in individual states. Medicaid is an oft-cited example. In an effort to expand Medicaid as envisioned under the ACA, the

Obama administration's Department of Health and Human Services (HHS) negotiated "Memoranda of Understanding" with individual states and extended funding for programs ranging from Vermont's single-payer system to quasi-privatized systems in Republican-led states.[38] The Trump administration changed the political but not the institutional dynamics: in 2018, HHS decided to grant waivers to states seeking to impose work requirements on Medicaid recipients.[39]

Even in legislative federalism's heyday, cooperative federalism programs occasionally contained statutory exemptions for individual states, and the interplay between federal law, agency discretion, and state and local administration produced a great deal of state-to-state variation. Especially over the past decade, however, the variance has become much greater. The use of executive waivers, as noted earlier, has increased greatly in scale and scope. In more than a few instances, moreover, explicit legislative delegations have proven insufficient to implement federal policy, necessitating a resort to decidedly "unorthodox" executive policymaking. Under the Obama administration, the implementation of the ACA, immigration reform, global warming programs, and labor regulation have all proceeded through presidential initiative, without and often in defiance of the authority of Congress. The early Trump administration reversed course on all those fronts, again—despite a GOP majority in both Houses of Congress—through unilateral administrative action.

Very often, those exertions have taken the form of extraordinary and extra-statutory accommodation: states have been granted asymmetric treatment by executive edict even where federal statutory law quite obviously forbids it or on conditions well outside the statutory parameters.[40] In some venues, executive federalism has created something resembling reverse preemption. For example, states that have legalized the use of marijuana have been granted a de facto exemption from the Controlled Substances Act and other federal regulatory statutes.[41] In this environment, federalism programs cease to be entitlement programs; they become policy and regulation by deal. Statutory constraints matter only at the outer margins; the principal policy instrument is "big waiver." Technically, the parties bargain in the shadow of the statutory default regime. However, in the increasingly common cases when neither the federal agency nor the individual state actually wants that regime to kick in, politicians and parties negotiate on an open field. Outcomes are contingent on partisan constellations including the individual parties' bargaining leverage, the states' ability to maintain sectional coalitions, and perceived political necessities.

Fiscal Effects

Each year, the US government transfers well in excess of $600 billion to state and local governments. Overwhelmingly, those payments finance social services and consumption, rather than investment (for, say, infrastructure); the largest share by far consists of Medicaid reimbursements. The transfer system is cooperative federalism's life blood, and its flow has been profoundly affected by the rise of executive government and sectional politics.

Quite probably, sectionalism has raised fiscal federalism's price. From their inception, cooperative fiscal federalism programs have been built for expansion and ever-increasing cash infusions.[42] Their point and effect is to increase the demand for government through fiscal illusion, by lowering the perceived tax price of public programs both at the federal and at the state level. When federally funded programs begin to crowd out non-funded or less-generously-funded programs, and state tax capacity reaches a limit, the cash must then come from the federal government. State-level polarization has likely exacerbated those inherently expansionist tendencies, as dissident states' reservation price goes up, and states whose preferences are aligned with the federal government's will ask why they should accept conditions less generous than those extended to renegade states. While it would be difficult to isolate the independent effect of partisan polarization, circumstantial evidence is highly suggestive. The ACA offered participating states a 100 percent reimbursement—declining in later years to 90 percent—for the cost of expanding Medicaid. Amazingly, about half the states responded to the ACA's unprecedented offer of full reimbursement—far and away the most generous bargain ever offered to the states under any major federal program—by suing.[43] To this day, many Republican-led states have declined to expand Medicaid—despite the short-term fiscal attractions, the federal government's exceptionally accommodating posture, and massive public and interest group pressures.[44] Non-ideological factors may explain some of the resistance. State politicians may have become more acutely aware of Medicaid's destructive long-term effects on state budgets, and especially in light of the federal government's indebtedness, they may have concluded that the ACA bargain is too good to be true and that the federal government will renege on its commitment. However, that hardly explains why those calculations should operate along sectional-partisan lines. Clearly, partisanship has contributed to the unprecedented display of state resistance to the ACA.[45]

Beyond their fiscal effects, sectional divisions tend to reinforce polarizing tendencies and executive government at the national level. The conventional prediction, amply supported by an impressive body of literature, is that executive-directed spending will disproportionately end up in "swing" states and districts, especially in years preceding a presidential election.[46] The United States experienced that pattern for a brief period in the early New Deal years, when funding under hastily created, broadly discretionary emergency programs disproportionately ended up in political swing states.[47] The experiment ended in 1935, with the Social Security Act and the creation of entitlement programs that constrained executive as well as congressional discretion.[48] It appears, however, that we are re-approximating a form of executive-dominated fiscal federalism on a far grander scale. The Obama administration's Medicaid expansion efforts, led by White House emissaries and conducted one state at a time, bore an uncanny resemblance to Harry Hopkins's relief efforts during the Roosevelt administration. And one could detect "telltale signs of an election-year strategy and partisan slant in the development of the [Obama administration's] We Can't Wait program": crucial initiatives were timed for the 2012 elections and disproportionately aimed at large swing states.[49]

One can confidently predict a further expansion and acceleration of these tendencies. State-level polarization both facilitates and exacerbates the executive manipulation of the transfer system for partisan, constituency-building ends: as the number of swing jurisdictions shrinks, the cost of identifying such jurisdictions decreases, and target accuracy increases. Moreover, executive dominance in this area may assume a new dimension. "Presidential pork"—an oft-used moniker for discretionary executive grant distribution—carries parochial localist connotations, and invites comparisons to congressional earmarks or appropriation riders. That picture may accurately describe the dynamics of executive grant-making for infrastructure, emergency relief, and similar discretionary programs. However, entitlement programs afford the executive far greater fiscal maneuvering room in the form of waiver authority and the manipulation of grant conditions under programs that are subject only to minimal or minimally effective congressional and judicial oversight.[50] The executive may come to use that discretionary authority not merely for electoral purposes but also for more systematic ends—at the extreme, the resolute fiscal repression of the opposing state bloc.

SECTIONAL FEDERALISM'S POLITICAL ECONOMY

In describing our federalism as executive and sectional, I have painted with a broad brush. The first part of the characterization seems reasonably accurate: legislative acquiescence to broad executive waiver and spending authority is pervasive, and it is hard to think of a policy domain in which Congress still insists on exercising its prerogatives. The second part is much more contestable: for all the sectional strife and partisan agitation over immigration, health care, and other salient issues, bipartisan and cooperative federalism arrangements have endured and at times flourished in education policy, financial regulation, and elsewhere. As a rough approximation, one can say that our federalism has become executive across the board. It has become sectional only in a handful of policy arenas, albeit highly salient ones.

The observation illustrates the hazards of extrapolating or generalizing from the federalism pattern in a few arenas—however central they may appear—to federalism at large. And especially when federalism's dynamics seem uniform in one dimension (executive federalism) and highly heterogeneous (sectional and conflictual versus bipartisan and cooperative) in another, the discontinuity calls for an explanation. I begin with some casual empirics and then present what seems to me the most plausible explanation of federalism's part-sectional, part-cooperative configuration: economic and policy competition between the blue- and red-state blocs.

Some Empirics

One can readily think of policy venues where federalism has remained non-sectional. For example, federal education policy under the No Child Left Behind Act (NCLB), enacted with bipartisan support, embodies a firm commitment to executive federalism. State resistance to the statute's commands also has been bipartisan. A "Common Core" reform initiative was a broad-based state effort, and legislative amendments enacted in 2015—amounting to a de facto repeal of core NCLB requirements—were supported by both blue and red states and by a somewhat odd coalition of Republican legislators and education unions. At times, executive federalism has not only failed to become polarized but actually produced new forms of federal-state cooperation across party lines. Asset forfeiture provides an example. Beginning in the 1970s, Congress, as well as state legislatures, incentivized public agencies to conduct the "war on drugs" by means of asset forfeiture, meaning the pretrial and pre-conviction seizure of assets from suspected violators. Initially limited to drugs and drug paraphernalia, the statutes soon came to cover the instruments and the proceeds of suspected drug trade, from cars to cash. In 1984, Congress authorized the Department of Justice to keep the proceeds of asset forfeiture for its own use.[51] Subsequently, Congress authorized the department to share the proceeds of asset forfeiture for federal crimes with the local authorities that made the seizure. This "fair share program" soon grew exponentially. It owes its creation and expansion to a sustained, bipartisan congressional strategy of executive empowerment.

Institutional path dependency has a great deal to do with these continuities. Federalism programs are embedded in a thicket of ancient statutes and regulations. They are administered by an entrenched intergovernmental machinery, and they have produced a vast ecology of supportive—and dependent— contractors, consultants, and constituencies.[52] None of that can be undone under normal political conditions. States that might oppose "cooperative" arrangements ex ante are locked into them, and political fights usually concern incremental adjustments in the vertical and horizontal distribution of benefits and burdens within those policy silos.[53] The intergovernmental machinery continues to grind, albeit under increased stress. Thus, one suspects that sectional conflicts are bound to arise primarily over new federal initiatives.

On inspection, that surmise also appears excessively general. As an initial matter, it is somewhat difficult to specify what constitutes a "new" federal policy. The Obama administration's immigration reforms, climate change initiatives, and even some core components of the ACA, especially its Medicaid expansion, all proceeded under existing statutes, and all were to be implemented through preexisting intergovernmental institutions. Even so, they produced intense partisan agitation and bloc-driven state litigation. More importantly, and conversely perhaps, some undoubtedly "new" federal initiatives have generated new forms of intergovernmental cooperation instead of sectional combat.

The most conspicuous example is the regulation of financial institutions. The 2010 Dodd-Frank Act, like the ACA, was crammed through Congress during a brief period of Democratic dominance over the House of Representatives and the Senate, and it enshrined the preferences of that temporary majority. The act rivals the ACA in its complexity, and it is a monument to executive government. It instructs regulatory agencies to conduct upward of 400 separate rulemaking proceedings; invests existing agencies and two newly created bodies, the Financial Stability Oversight Council and the Consumer Financial Protection Bureau (CFPB), with vast discretionary authority over the financial sector of the economy; and augments the enforcement powers of state as well as federal enforcers. Key provisions aim to protect these innovations not so much from the president but from any future Republican Congress. For example, Dodd-Frank made the CFPB self-funding and immunized it in other ways from effective congressional oversight.[54] Dodd-Frank has remained intensely controversial in the public debate and, in Congress, a target of unremitting GOP attacks. In sharp contrast, the actual operation of financial regulation—to the extent that it involves federalism and the states—has been thoroughly bipartisan.

At the time of enactment of the Dodd-Frank Act, state attorneys general were among the strongest supporters of an independent federal consumer financial protection agency. On a bipartisan basis and under the auspices of the National Association of Attorneys General, they lobbied aggressively for increased state authority to enforce federal consumer protection law and for a weakening of federal power to preempt state regulation and enforcement.[55] Ever since, broad, bipartisan coalitions of state attorneys general and financial regulators have cooperated closely with federal regulatory agencies and the Department of Justice.

Cooperation is particularly close and nonpartisan in the area of regulatory enforcement. In October 2010, all fifty state attorneys general announced a joint investigation of the mortgage servicing industry. That undertaking soon merged with a parallel investigation by the federal task force to investigate the subprime lending industry. In late 2012, the US Department of Justice, the US Department of Housing and Urban Development, and state attorneys general reached a $25 billion National Mortgage Settlement with the nation's five largest mortgage lenders over allegedly questionable mortgage loan servicing and foreclosure practices. In addition to mortgage relief for broad classes of borrowers, the settlement included approximately $2.25 billion distributed by the state attorneys general to hundreds of state and local agencies and nonprofit organizations.[56] It also contained mortgage-servicing standards that provided a template for a subsequent CFPB rulemaking finalized in January 2013.

The National Mortgage Settlement is the largest and best documented of numerous joint federal-state settlements concluded in the aftermath of the 2008–2009 financial crisis. The torrent of enforcement activity exemplifies executive federalism— an entire ecosystem of poorly supervised government agencies with overlapping authority, all exercising virtually unbounded discretion under state and federal law.[57] While the pattern is national in the sense that federal agencies are parties to nationwide settlements, it is also profoundly federal. States act as enforcement agents, parties to the agreements, co-recipients of the proceeds, and crafters and administrators of the nominally remedial, regulatory components of the agreements. And uniformly, the states have acted.

The pattern is perplexing in several ways. Historically, the divide between "Wall Street" and "Main Street," or between financial centers and agrarian states, has been among the most durable sectional cleavages in American politics (the antebellum era and the Gilded Age provide vivid illustrations), and it appears to have lost much of its force. Further, joint federal-state regulation is a marked departure from a system of regulation that traditionally has been characterized by separation rather than cooperation—a "dual" banking system; a quasi-constitutional "internal affairs" doctrine that a century ago established a division between state corporate law and federal antitrust law; an exclusively state-run system of insurance regulation; and a system of securities regulation that superimposed federal regulation under the auspices of the Securities Exchange Commission and the Commodities Futures Trade Commission on the states' "blue sky" and general consumer protection laws. Over a vast range, those dual arrangements have given way to institutional and functional interpenetration. Finally, the pattern just described stands in marked contrast to the sectional strife over climate change, health care, and immigration. In financial regulation, the rise of executive government has gone hand-in-hand with novel forms of bipartisan cooperation among states, and between states and the federal government.

State Competition

The most plausible explanation of our part-sectional, part-cooperative federalism begins with the economic dimension of the red state–blue state divide. As briefly suggested earlier, federally sponsored "cooperative" federalism has never and cannot come about under sectional conditions. Slavery and race have tragically marked the divide. In more recent decades, "social" issues such as the death penalty, abortion, or same-sex marriage have proven beyond the scope of monetized, legislative bargains.[58] Today the rift runs along lines of party and economic interest.

The partisan divide between red and blue states coincides with a deep ideological divide between rival commitments to very different business models. Blue states favor a quasi-European model, which reflects a high, authentic domestic demand for social services and environmental goods and a relatively high tolerance for accompanying tax payments. Red states are committed to a competitive model and production-oriented policies. As long as labor and capital remain highly mobile in the United States, the blue-state model is difficult to sustain. In fact, the rising polarization between state blocs has been accompanied by a migration of firms and individuals, especially high-income earners, from blue to red states. Arresting that dynamic requires two things. First, it requires cooperative federalism's perpetual fiscal illusions: very high federal transfer payments that appear to defray the full cost of providing the demanded services, even if those payments are disproportionately financed by the state's own taxpayers. Second, the blue-state model requires some means of raising red-state rivals' costs—that is, constraints and obstacles that reduce red states' ability to attract capital and labor.

Evidence of these dynamics is not hard to come by. Blue states such as New York, California, Connecticut, and Illinois have been consistent advocates and early adopters of expanded federal funding programs, foremost including the ACA's Medicaid expansion. They have pursued this course despite the fact that the costs are disproportionately paid by predominantly blue states with large numbers of high-income taxpayers, thus producing a negative "balance of payments" for blue states and a net subsidy for red states. Blue states tolerate the inequity because an attempt to finance the demanded services from own-source taxes would likely produce yet higher out-migration to states with a lower demand or willingness to pay.

Blue states' strategy to raise red state rivals' costs is best illustrated by their demands on climate change and energy policy.[59] Red states by and large house and welcome oil, natural gas, and other extractive industries; blue states generally do not. The blue-state bloc has sought to reduce red states' competitive and comparative advantages both unilaterally, through state regulations that raise the cost of energy production elsewhere, and more often by pushing for aggressive federal regulation.[60] Undoubtedly, such initiatives reflect genuine conviction as well as raw economic interest. Even so, the sectional political and economic implications have been obvious and politically salient especially in red states, where the Obama administration's environmental policies were widely perceived as a "war on energy."

What then of the more harmonious practices and arrangements in financial regulation? State competition—and thus sectional dynamics—can be thwarted even without central intervention when a single state's law has extraterritorial force across all jurisdictions. That, with few exceptions, is the general rule in financial regulation and other markets where producers cannot easily differentiate their product along state lines. The most restrictive state rule will dominate, thus obviating state competition and, along with it, sectional politics. Thus, while Texas and Oklahoma can, within the bounds of federal preemptive statutes, attract energy producers by offering favorable conditions for oil and gas extraction, they cannot offer any meaningful advantage to nationally operating banks or even manufacturers whose legal obligations will in all events be governed by the laws and enforcement practices of New York or California.

The prototype of such unilaterally induced "cooperation" is the 1998 Multistate Settlement Agreement (MSA) between the major tobacco manufacturers and the attorneys general of all fifty states. The agreement, purportedly a legal settlement of state damage claims against the producers, effectively imposed a nationwide excise tax—along with a detailed regulatory scheme—on the sale of tobacco products. The MSA then allocated the proceeds of the settlement among the fifty states, as well as the producers' and plaintiffs' lawyers. Some Republican state attorneys general vehemently resisted the litigation campaign and the settlement.[61] However, once the lead states and the producers had crafted a settlement that imposed the settlement costs on tobacco consumers across the country, dissident states were left with only one choice—leave the state's allocated settlement share on the table, or else take the money. Their eventually unanimous decision to participate reflects the MSA's extraterritorial dynamics and the red states' inability to differentiate their product, not the authentic preferences of those states or their political leaders.[62]

The analysis is supported by potent, if circumstantial, evidence. For example, multistate enforcement campaigns patterned after the MSA have all been led by attorneys general of blue states.[63] Red states have participated reluctantly and, on many occasions, at the insistence of corporate defendants who demand universal state participation as a condition of settlement. In short, sectionalism and state competition tend to dominate in arenas having to do with production, where states are able to offer and exploit comparative or competitive advantages. State-generated cooperation and uniformity persist in areas where legal doctrines facilitate cross-border rent extraction.

Executive Control

Suppose this rough-and-ready account captures federalism's sectional dynamics: What follows with respect to federalism's executive dimension? The most obvious implication is a further strengthening of executive dominance. Near-existential conflicts between state blocs cannot be resolved through compromise by a polarized Congress; thus, state blocs turn to the executive and the courts to protect or advance their interests. A second consequence is that the exercise of executive discretion will become yet more partisan and more firmly oriented toward strengthening the governing party's state bloc. As Sidney M. Milkis and Nicholas F. Jacobs have put it, the parties have ceased to fight over the size of government; instead, they fight over its control.[64]

As suggested earlier, regulatory as well as fiscal initiatives under both the Obama and the Trump administrations illustrate the executive's resolve to deploy the government's resources. If the Obama administration's energy and environmental policies benefited blue states, and imposed disproportionate costs on red, energy-producing states, the Trump administration effected a prompt, dramatic reversal, and undertook a raft of initiatives that benefit energy-producing and unfailingly red states, including a rescission of the Clean Power Plan and several additional EPA rules; the green-lighting of the Keystone and Dakota pipelines; and a substantial reduction of protected national monument areas in Utah. For good measure, the 2018 tax reform contained provisions to permit oil exploration and drilling in the Alaska wilderness.

Similarly, fiscal programs have become subject to much more intense partisan control and strategic use, especially under the Trump administration.[65] In 2017 Congress considered a Medicaid "block grant" reform that was plainly designed to benefit Republican states that had declined to accept the ACA Medicaid bargain.[66] While Congress eventually declined to enact that measure, the administration has the means and perhaps the will to accomplish a very similar objective by executive action.[67] Of potentially even greater consequence, Congress enacted a comprehensive tax reform that severely limits taxpayers' ability to deduct state and local taxes from their federal income tax. The curtailment of the SALT (state and local tax) deduction effectively terminates the somewhat uneasy but durable bipartisan consensus that sustained cooperative federalism: prosperous states—more precisely, states with disproportionate numbers of high-income taxpayers—supported poorer states. Net donor states such as New York, Connecticut, New Jersey, and California are uniformly and deeply blue; recipient states are overwhelmingly red. Net donor states, as noted, accepted the cross-subsidies as the price of financing, with the help of fiscal illusions and federal transfers, as well as expansive domestic service programs. But the arrangement was also stabilized through the SALT deduction, which disproportionately benefited taxpayers in high-income, high-tax, Democratic states. The repeal of the deduction strikes with near-surgical precision at blue states and their tax capacity. On most accounts, the effect was intended.

I do not mean to proffer the economic dynamics just sketched as a full or fully compelling explanation of federalism's part-sectional, part-cooperative pattern. In some venues that have become sectional, such as immigration and perhaps trade policy, considerations of relative state advantage are heavily overlaid with ideological commitments. In other venues, from transgender bathrooms to net neutrality, those commitments appear to dominate economic concerns. Nor do I mean to suggest that federal policies have been driven entirely by partisan, sectional calculations. But federalism maps those calculations, and illustrates, yet again, executive federalism's enormous capacity to mobilize the government's regulatory power and fiscal resources for the benefit of one state bloc to the detriment of the other. While presidents of both parties have increasingly availed themselves of that authority, it is likely that federalism's potential for unilateral partisan exploitation and constituency-building purposes has yet to be fully realized.

CONSTITUTIONALISM AND THE COURT

Executive federalism is litigious federalism. The executive as well as the states have tested the boundaries of lawful, constitutional government. Aggressive state attorneys general have flooded federal courts with legal objections against executive overreach. Many of those controversies have ended up in the Supreme Court, and the justices have been sharply split in those cases. A judicial divide once marked primarily by ideological rifts over abortion, gay rights, and other social issues has also come to characterize executive federalism questions, in cases over the ACA, energy and the environment, and immigration, and even in cases involving far more humdrum legalistic questions, such as the Federal Arbitration Act or federal preemption.[68]

Up to a point, of course, the constitutional system is designed that way: the delicate business of delineating federal and state powers must fall to the "impartial tribunal" of the Supreme Court.[69] Throughout our history, that has been among the judiciary's principal functions; and at crucial junctures, the Supreme Court's doctrines have been subject to intense ideological and partisan controversy. Present conditions, though, raise grave doubts about the judiciary's capacity to regularize executive federalism and to police its constitutional boundaries.

The judiciary's precarious ideological balance and the courts' central role at the executive federalism front have figured prominently in highly partisan, sharply polarized fights over judicial nominations. During the second Obama administration, then Senate majority leader Harry Reid undertook a dramatic and eventually successful campaign to appoint reliably liberal judges to the Court of Appeals for the District of Columbia Circuit, which hears most administrative law cases. The stated objective of the campaign was to clear the way for the executive's ambitious regulatory agenda;[70] it was accomplished by changing long-standing Senate rules to permit judicial appointments, except to the Supreme Court, by simple majority. Republicans repaid the favor by bottling up then president Obama's nomination of Judge Merrick Garland for the late Justice Scalia's seat on the Supreme Court. The open seat and, more broadly, political control over judicial appointments loomed large in the 2016 presidential campaign. Both sides warned in often apocalyptic tones that their opponents' victory would produce an executive-dominated judiciary, operating at the president's beck and call. The frightening prospect of a lasting executive-judicial alliance, with a jurisprudence to match, seems unlikely as long as the parties remain competitive. A more realistic apprehension is that the judiciary may entrench executive government and federalism by default, for want of institutional capacity and legitimacy.

Few if any legal scholars believe that the federal judiciary has the capacity to control administrative action in a systematic fashion: the administrative state is simply too big. Administrative agencies have any number of ways to evade judicial oversight. Instead of issuing formal rules, they can issue unreviewable guidelines or proceed through enforcement.[71] More aggressive judicial review, in cases that do reach the courts, increases agencies' incentives to pursue their objectives by informal means. An executive that has slipped the reins of Congress, it stands to reason, will also escape effective judicial control.

State litigation can do little in the overall scheme of things to enhance judicial control. To be sure, state-led litigation succeeded in derailing some of the Obama administration's policies, and the Trump administration will suffer the same fate. Such victories, however, come at a price. The partisan nature of state bloc litigation threatens to drag the judiciary into sectional trench warfare and to cast judges as one more set of combatants. The states' litigation tactics have done nothing to dispel that impression. Both state blocs have perfected a strategy of bringing multiple cases before district judges that are highly likely to rule in their favor. Thus, the defendant administration has to run the table in several hostile jurisdictions, while the plaintiff state bloc needs to win only once to obtain a nationwide injunction against the federal government. Whatever the merits of this or that lawsuit, there must be a better way of settling federalism disagreements.

Behind those tangible considerations lurks a more evanescent but potentially more consequential problem—the dearth of broadly accepted, constitutionally grounded doctrines that would provide judicial legitimacy and credibility. With respect to the separation of powers and to federalism, the Supreme Court has inherited doctrines and modes of thinking that are hopelessly out of sync with executive federalism's actual operation. Especially under polarized conditions it has no plausible means of adjusting those doctrines to current institutional realities.

Separation of powers doctrine paints a picture of rival, empire-building institutions: Congress versus the executive.[72] That conceptual framework is poorly matched to a separation of parties, not powers.[73] Moreover, governing doctrine treats Congress as a unitary, self-aggrandizing actor; thus, the pervasive phenomenon of congressional abdication finds no systematic recognition.[74] The lack of institutional realism extends to administrative law.[75] Its dogmatic premise is legislative supremacy: the will of Congress must prevail.

But Congress need not express that will with any kind of clarity or precision. The executive is permitted to exercise ample discretion as long as Congress has stated an "intelligible principle."[76] And while executive action remains subject to judicial review, the coin of that realm is judicial deference: when a statute is ambiguous, the Court presumes that Congress wanted the agency's judgment to carry the day. Such doctrines are hardly conducive to containing executive power, and recent cases have raised the specter of executive "rewrites" of entire federal statutes.[77] The pressing question of executive "underreach"—a wholesale dispensation or suspension of the law—is a matter of intense scholarly debate in a virtually doctrine-free environment.[78] In short, it is hard to think of a separation of powers doctrine that is calculated to contain executive power in any systematic fashion.

Federalism jurisprudence presents the same picture of doctrinal mismatch. The states appear as unitary actors with a set of uniform and symmetrical institutional interests; and those interests and the states' "dignity" are deemed to warrant judicial protection against congressional impositions. While the Supreme Court routinely invokes a wide range of federalism "values,"[79] virtually all federalism canons serve to protect states "as states"—that is, as quasi-sovereign political actors. Just as the Supreme Court has no separation of powers doctrine that accounts for congressional abdication, though, it simply assumes that states have empire-building motives and so fails to account for the pervasive state demand for federal intervention.

More fatefully, federalism jurisprudence misses entirely the starkly asymmetric and sectional features of contemporary federalism. Thus, the Supreme Court has described the ACA's Medicaid expansion as a "gun to the head"— without any evident recognition that numerous states nearly demanded the imposition.[80] In the same fashion, the Court speaks confidently of the authentic position and interests of "the states" even when many states oppose that position in that very case.[81] The sectional dynamics that drive such state disagreements should prompt systematic judicial attention to federalism's "horizontal," state-to-state dimension. Such doctrines, however, are virtually extinct, and the Court has shown little interest in reconstructing them.[82] Finally, federalism jurisprudence lacks a systematic comprehension of our federalism's executive nature. In administrative law cases, federalism canons come and go, usually without explanation.[83] Judicial opinions provide no framework and rarely even a hint that harmonizing administrative law and federalism canons—both very unsettled in their own right—demand sustained attention.[84]

The mismatch between judicial doctrine and institutional reality has worrisome implications, almost regardless of partisan constellations. A judicial attempt to develop doctrines commensurate with executive federalism in opposition to the government in power will look like a de facto coup: if no pre-existing, tolerably certain and settled doctrines govern the cases, the new ones must surely be made up. Conversely, executive federalism doctrines developed in harmony with the government in power will be perceived as a judicial surrender to the executive. The Supreme Court's predicament in the two ACA cases[85] was widely discussed in these terms, and its rulings were widely understood as maneuvering between the horns of the dilemma. Neither case has been viewed as a source of stable doctrine; overwhelmingly, the question has been whether the decisions are one-offs for the ACA train only or whether they further unsettle doctrines once thought to be tolerably well understood.

Under any interpretation, the cases illustrate the difficulty of developing a coherent set of executive federalism doctrines that would constitutionally constrain and regularize the system. Any attempt to do so would either mean a confrontation that the Supreme Court cannot hope to win or else an adjustment to the demands of executive government. Most likely, the Court will continue to muddle through; however, if it cannot speak with a clear voice for the Constitution, it will come to speak for the executive.

PROSPECTS

The rise of executive government, high levels of partisan-ideological polarization at the national and the state level, weak-to-nonexistent constitutional constraints, and an ideologically divided Court: we have never before encountered that confluence. There remains the question of federalism's future trajectory—and the question of whether and in what respects its central tendencies present a cause for concern.

Naturally, speculation about federalism's future trajectory is just that—speculation. Among countless other uncertainties, the electorate is not only polarized but also angry and fickle. While a competitive two-party system tends toward closely divided government, a single landslide election might produce lasting institutional change. At the state level, federalism's sectional dynamics would change dramatically and probably come to an end if Texas were to turn Democratic. Uncertainties of this sort should be recognized and borne in mind, even if one has to set them aside in attempting to discern trend lines and regularities.

It is exceedingly difficult to identify an institutional force or dynamic that might stem the rise of executive government and, hence, executive-dominated federalism. If the analysis above on executive federalism is approximately right, polarization and profound structural forces have interacted in ways that naturally favor the executive. A reversal of that dynamic presupposes a dramatic reduction of public demands on the national government—and more federalism in that elementary sense. That is not going to happen any time soon.

The sectional features of contemporary federalism call for a somewhat more nuanced assessment. As observed earlier, federalism has turned sectional only in some policy areas, albeit highly salient ones. Against the trajectory of American federalism over the past century, one might view executive federalism's "cooperative" manifestations as still dominant, and the bloc-driven contention over energy policy, health care, or immigration as the kind of resistance that has always accompanied our increasingly national federalism. The red-state bloc, anchored by Texas, is comprised of the states of the old Confederacy, along with newcomers like Utah. From the Progressive Era and the New Deal to the Great Society and beyond, that state bloc resisted and retarded cooperative federalism's expansion. One way or another, though, the center has always found ways to drag the recalcitrant South into modernity. That has usually taken decades of work. But the general tendency is clear enough, and it may well continue to unfold. Two reasons, however, counsel caution against that prediction.

First, unlike a century or a half-century ago, the sectional divide now maps partisan, ideological polarization. Under those conditions, broad-based, bipartisan policies to break a recalcitrant state bloc's resistance—akin to, say, the Elementary and Secondary Education Act—are very hard to imagine. Second, federalism's political economy differs greatly from its configuration in 1920, 1940, or 1960. The past unfolding of cooperative federalism was driven by a dominant center of modernizing industrial states, with the resources and the will to pull the backward periphery into its policies (for example, through federal transfer payments).[86] By contrast, many once-backward, mostly southern states are now among the most modern and competitive in the nation, whereas such once-dominant states as New York, New Jersey, Connecticut, California, and Illinois must contend with high out-migration and a high and perhaps unsustainable demand for social services and consumption. Contemporary sectionalism has no center that could integrate a backward periphery, only rival blocs whose fate depends in large measure on the occupant of the White House. One hesitates to call that constellation stable; but it may well continue to hold, albeit under shifting party alignments.

One additional factor merits consideration in assessing executive, sectional federalism's future trajectory: the rising level of public debt at all levels of government. With the exception of a few years in the 1990s, that trend has accompanied the rise of polarization, executive government, and sectionalism for the duration. At bottom it reflects a broad, politically stable consensus: a commitment to an expansive transfer state, coupled with a low willingness to pay. However, fiscal federalism's dynamics have quite clearly inflated the demand for a debt-financed government. In turn, acute fiscal pressures are bound to have profound effects on federalism both in its executive and its sectional dimension.

Fiscal federalism, especially in its executive forms and under sectional conditions, has been associated in many countries with high, often debt-financed fiscal imbalances, and at the state level, moral hazard in the form of excessive spending and bailout expectations.[87] Central governments' responses to state-level profligacy and insolvencies have often taken dramatic forms, including federal bailouts and takeovers of state governments. That has never happened in the United States—in part, on account of a credible commitment against bailouts; in another part, because our institutional framework provides few if any regularized mechanisms to provide targeted relief.[88] Instead, the common response to state-level fiscal distress has been "undercover" debt relief through expanded and more generous transfer programs for all states. This pattern began with the creation of large-scale fiscal transfer programs in the 1930s. It was repeated in the 1960s. And on all accounts, the trend has accelerated in recent years.[89] For a prominent example, the 2009 American Recovery and Reinvestment Act, though advertised as a "stimulus" response to the 2008–2009 financial crisis, was principally aimed at debt relief.[90] Tellingly, it contained a temporary increase of the federal funding formula for Medicaid—the most generous federal program, and on precisely that account the program most likely to induce overspending and to crowd out self-financed programs.

This strategy of fighting fire with gasoline—that is, of responding to the effects of state-level moral hazard with global undercover debt relief and programs that induce further overspending—has reached and perhaps exceeded its practical limits. Even during the Obama administration, many states began to question the federal government's will or ability to sustain long-term funding commitments, as evidenced by their refusal to accept grants for Medicaid expansion and various infrastructure projects. At the same time, the fiscal condition of many states, as well as local governments, has remained perilous. Detroit and several smaller cities have been rescued through a process that was conducted under, but in practice bore little resemblance to, the provisions of Chapter 9 of the US Bankruptcy Code.[91] The finances of the Commonwealth of Puerto Rico and its instrumentalities are being restructured by a supervisory board established by Congress.[92] And despite a booming stock market and a moderately but steadily growing economy, the pension systems of many states are more precariously underfunded now than they were a decade ago.[93] It is hardly premature to wonder and perhaps worry how another financial and public debt crisis might play out under conditions of executive dominance and state-level polarization. Under the Trump administration, all signs point to a more confrontational and less cooperative fiscal federalism—to fiscal repression of states on the tax side and retrenchment on the spending side. As noted earlier, those policies have sharply partisan, sectional connotations: disproportionately, they adversely affect blue states like Illinois, which also tend to have the largest unfunded pension obligations.[94]

If it is difficult to envision global federal relief for those mounting—and in some states unmanageable—obligations, constitutional and political considerations make it equally difficult to imagine more targeted measures. Insolvency mechanisms along the lines discussed in chapter 9 or those of the Puerto Rico oversight process are unlikely to pass constitutional muster when applied to an actual state, even when undertaken with that state's consent.[95] Perhaps, one can imagine a targeted federal relief program under executive auspices, akin to the Troubled Asset Relief Program (TARP) under which the US Treasury and the Federal Reserve Board salvaged financial institutions and car companies in the 2008–2009 financial crisis.[96] To suggest the option, though, is to highlight the dilemma. A TARP for states or their pension funds would make federalism yet more executive and asymmetric. It would amount to an undisguised transfer from primarily prosperous red states to blue states with high pension and bond obligations, thus throwing the sectional conflict and dynamics of our federalism into even sharper relief.[97]

Given the likelihood of continued government by executive and sustained sectional politics, the discussion so far is bound to reinforce pervasive concerns over the nation's polarized politics, a loss of political legitimacy, and policymaking at the outer limits of lawful government. Is there room for a more hopeful assessment? In full recognition and acknowledgment of popular and scholarly apprehensions, Jessica Bulman-Pozen has supplied a cautious, qualified defense of executive federalism.[98] In a polarized environment, she argues, executive federalism may provide a path to national policymaking and bipartisan cooperation, and a way of regaining the government legitimacy that comes from getting things done. While executive federalism's style of policymaking is often opaque, a lack of transparency creates much-needed space for bargaining and transactional politics. The process looks disorderly, but it draws in a wide range of contestants and can be called "representative" in a broad sense. While the outcomes rarely conform to the hopes or predictions of a rational policy planner, a high degree of improvisation and state-to-state variation is one of federalism's virtues. Moreover, executive federalism's inherently federal nature may help to dampen fears of autocracy that naturally attend a poorly constrained national executive. Its distinctly national and presidential coloration notwithstanding, federalism remains a two-way bargain. As the central government's demands on the states increase, so does the states' power to exact concessions.

Bulman-Pozen's account resonates with urgent calls to revive a more parochial and transactional style of politics at the national level,[99] and it has the virtue of searching for venues and resources that might facilitate such a politics outside the national arena and especially outside Congress. Federalism, a naturally parochial and transactional arena, may well be the right place to look. Even so, the rise of executive federalism also provides ample cause for concern.

While executive federalism may prompt bipartisan interaction, it may also have intensified ideological and partisan discord.[100] Sectional dynamics have exacerbated distressing tendencies: bargaining breakdowns; a migration of political authority from elected bodies into institutional back alleys; political bargains, waivers, and settlements well outside the shadow of any law; and hardball tactics that push fateful, intensely controversial decisions into an ideologically divided Supreme Court. In that light, it is difficult to see how executive federalism can enhance political legitimacy. Even the legitimacy that comes from "getting things done" depends on citizens' sense that government has done and is doing a tolerable job of doing things that, by and large, are worth doing and need doing. While a broad consensus of that kind might dampen the concerns that have accompanied the rise of executive government and executive federalism, there is little evidence to that effect. In the public's mind and the minds of sober, judicious political scientists, government fails consistently. Partisan polarization may be an effect rather than a cause of that pattern.[101] Far from offering a sensible accommodation between national objectives and local concerns, executive federalism may be part and parcel of a "kludgeocracy" that seems incapable of fashioning tolerably coherent responses to public concerns.[102]

A look abroad provides further cause for concern. Few countries feature all our central institutional arrangements: presidentialism, bicameralism, federalism, and a two-party system. Among them—until the disintegration of its party system—was Venezuela, which does not inspire a cheerful outlook. Other presidential and federal systems, such as Argentina's, feature weak parties and parliaments; they have not been models of democratic stability, either. The best explanation of why the United States has so far escaped a similar fate is the moderate nature of our party system.[103] Now that that moderation has given way to partisan-ideological polarization, a comparative perspective suggests grim scenarios commonly associated with presidential and federal systems especially in Latin America: highly personalized and plebiscitary leadership, extra-constitutional government, economic instability, and an oligarchic social structure. Scholars at considerable distance from partisan agitation and the Internet fever swamps have warned of signs of incipient Peronism in the contemporary political landscape.[104]

Scenarios of this sort converge on the specter of wholesale political corruption—not petty quid-pro-quo bargains and bribery, but rather the kind of "corruption" that the founding generation and its successors associated with party government: executive oppression, propaganda, lawlessness, and favoritism for purposes of comprehensive political, economic, and social control. Against that dystopian view stands the hope that our sectional federalism, far from collapsing into the center, remains vibrant and that states—unlike, perhaps, Congress and the judiciary—remain an effective check on the executive.[105] That dilemma, it turns out, is a very old one. It runs through Federalist and anti-Federalists' writings. It runs through the antebellum disputes over internal improvements, the banks of the United States, and national tariffs. Much has changed since then—too much to give much credit to facile historical comparisons. And still, we may be rehearsing yet again, and for good or ill, one of the oldest and most central questions of American politics.

NOTES

Great thanks to Jessica Bulman-Pozen, Chris DeMuth, Abbe Gluck, Eric Helland, Shep Melnick, Jeremy Rabkin, and Steve Williams for helpful comments on earlier drafts. Portions of the text have previously appeared under the title "Bloc Party Federalism" in volume 70 of the *Stanford Law Review*. Used by permission.

1. Daryl J. Levinson and Richard H. Pildes, "Separation of Parties, Not Powers," *Harvard Law Review* 119, no. 8 (June 2006): 2311, 2314–2315.

2. See, for example, Neal Devins, "Presidential Unilateralism and Political Polarization: Why Today's Congress Lacks the Will and the Way to Stop Presidential Initiatives," *Willamette Law Review* 45, no. 3 (Spring 2009): 395–397; Jack M. Balkin, "The Last Days of Disco: Why the American Political System Is Dysfunctional," *Boston University Law Review* 94, no. 3 (May 2014): 1159, 1165; and Sarah Binder, "The Dysfunctional Congress," *Annual Review of Political Science* 18 (May 2015): 85, 95.

3. "Executive federalism" has become a subject of entire volumes of scholarly inquiry. Contributions include Jessica Bulman-Pozen, "Executive Federalism Comes to America," *Virginia Law Review* 102, no. 4 (June 2016): 953; Jessica Bulman-Pozen and Gillian E. Metzger, "The President and the States: Patterns of Contestation and Collaboration under Obama," *Publius: The Journal of Federalism* 46, no, 3 (July 2016): 308–336; and Gillian E. Metzger, "Agencies, Polarization, and the States," *Columbia Law Review* 115, no. 7 (November 2015): 1739. An earlier, excellent, and remarkably

prescient contribution is Thomas Gais and James Fossett, "Federalism and the Executive Branch," in *Institutions of American Democracy: The Executive Branch*, ed. Joel D. Aberbach and Mark A. Peterson (New York: Oxford University Press, 2005), 486.

4. For a brief, instructive discussion of the voluminous literature, see Richard Franklin Bensel, *Sectionalism and American Political Development, 1880–1980* (Madison: University of Wisconsin Press, 1984), 3–4. In its strictest sense, "sectionalism" means a configuration of rival, contiguous state jurisdictions that divide along a political line of existential salience (exemplified, of course, by the Confederacy and the Union). Moreover, the term often implies secessionist tendencies. I use the term in a somewhat looser sense, meaning the presence of a cohesive state bloc that (1) is sufficiently large to thwart federal intervention and (2) has a reservation price on central issues of politics that exceeds the central government's willingness and ability to pay. I hope to show that the red state–blue state divide and its political dynamics fit this description.

5. Kenneth S. Lowande and Sidney M. Milkis, "'We Can't Wait': Barack Obama, Partisan Polarization and the Administrative Presidency," *The Forum* 12, no. 1 (2014): 3.

6. Hickman states: "[T]he IRS is now one of the government's principal welfare agencies, on par with the Department of Health and Human Services and the Social Security Administration." Kristin E. Hickman, "The (Perhaps) Unintended Consequences of *King v. Burwell*," *Pepperdine Law Review* 2015, no. 1 (2015): 56, 68–69.

7. Ann Joseph O'Connell, "Bureaucracy at the Boundary," *University of Pennsylvania Law Review* 162, no. 4 (March 2014): 841, 846–849.

8. Paul Nolette, *Federalism on Trial: State Attorneys General and National Policymaking in Contemporary America* (Lawrence: University Press of Kansas, 2015); and Christopher C. DeMuth Sr. and Michael S. Greve, "Agency Finance in the Age of Executive Government," *George Mason Law Review* 24, no. 2 (Winter 2017): 555.

9. "Polarized parties more closely link the President and agencies and offer the White House additional leverage over administration." Bulman-Pozen, "Executive Federalism," 962.

10. See Donald Smiley, *The Federal Condition in Canada* (Scarborough: McGraw-Hill Ryerson, 1987), 83; and David B. Walker, *The Rebirth of Federalism: Slouching Toward Washington*, 2nd ed. (Washington, DC: CQ Press, 1999), 24–25.

11. Mariano Tommasi, "Federalism in Argentina and the Reforms of the 1990s," in *Federalism and Economic Reform: International Perspectives*, ed. Jessica S. Wallack and T. N. Srinivasan (New York: Cambridge University Press, 2011), 25.

12. Gais and Fossett, "Federalism and the Executive Branch," 486–487.

13. See David J. Barron and Todd D. Rakoff, "In Defense of Big Waiver," *Columbia Law Review* 113, no. 2 (2013): 265.

14. Gais and Fossett, "Federalism and the Executive Branch," 508.

15. Lowande and Milkis, "We Can't Wait," 4; see also Sidney M. Milkis and Jesse H. Rhodes, "George W. Bush, the Republican Party and the 'New' Party System," *Perspectives on Politics* 5, no. 3 (September 2007): 461.

16. See Sidney M. Milkis and Nicholas Jacobs, "'I Alone Can Fix It': Donald Trump, the Administrative Presidency, and Hazards of Executive-Centered Partisan-

ship," *The Forum* 15, no. 3 (2017): 583; and Zachary Callen, "Repurposing the Administrative State," *The Forum* 15, no. 2 (2017): 379.

17. Some scholars argue that former president Obama delayed full implementation of health plan requirements to "preempt legislation that would gut health care reform." Lowande and Milkis, "We Can't Wait," 20; and R. Shep Melnick, "The Conventional Misdiagnosis: Why Gridlock Is Not Our Central Problem and Constitutional Revision Is Not the Solution," *Boston University Law Review* 94, no. 3 (May 2014): 767–769.

18. Christopher C. DeMuth, "Can the Administrative State Be Tamed?," *Journal of Legal Analysis* 8, no. 1 (2016): 121.

19. Gais and Fossett, "Federalism and the Executive Branch," 514.

20. See Miriam Seifter, "Further from the People? The Puzzle of State Administration," *New York University Law Review* 93, no. 1 (April 2018): 107. Seifter notes marked growth in states' expenditures, employment, and fiscal and institutional capacity after 1960. Despite—and in many ways because of—the enormous output of federal legislation and regulation the story of the growth of government is primarily the story of the growth of state and local government. See John J. DiIulio Jr., *Bring Back the Bureaucrats* (West Conshohocken, PA: Templeton Press, 2015), 16–17. See also Gais and Fossett, "Federalism and the Executive Branch," 95. To be sure, global assertions concerning a shifting federalism "balance" should be taken with a large dose of salt. No single vector exists to measure such a balance, and many plausible indicators are inherently ambiguous. For example, a growing fiscal imbalance, as measured by federal transfer payments to state and local governments, may signal increasing state dependency—or increasing state power to exact such transfers. For another example, state administration of federal programs may signal subjugation—or increased state power to shirk and oppose. See generally, Heather K. Gerken, "The Loyal Opposition," *Yale Law Journal* 123, no. 6 (April 2014): 1958.

21. Jessica Bulman-Pozen and Heather K. Gerken, "Uncooperative Federalism," *Yale Law Journal* 118, no. 7 (May 2009): 1256.

22. Austin Raynor, "The New State Sovereignty Movement," *Indiana Law Journal* 90, no. 2 (Spring 2015): 613; and Sean Nicholson-Crotty, "Leaving Money on the Table: Learning from Recent Refusals of Federal Grants in the American States," *Publius: The Journal of Federalism* 42, no. 3 (July 2012): 449.

23. Gais and Fossett, "Federalism and the Executive Branch," 507.

24. Depending on their design, cooperative federalism programs often have a centralizing effect on state administration. However, that intended effect has typically been accompanied by an equally intended effect of professionalization and specialization. Gubernatorial control, in contrast, is political control: "Governors leverage their control of state executive branches to shape *national* policy, mobilizing (or demobilizing) state agencies as a means of supporting or resisting federal action on immigration, environmental law, healthcare, and more." Miriam Seifter, "Gubernatorial Administration," *Harvard Law Review* 131, no. 2 (December 2017): 483, 486 (emphasis in origi-

nal). See also, "The partisan pathway has come to life in policy implementation, where elected officials have vaulted to the lead in determining intergovernmental positioning and bargaining strategies." Timothy J. Conlan and Paul L. Posner, "American Federalism in an Era of Partisan Polarization: The Intergovernmental Paradox of Obama's 'New Nationalism,'" *Publius: The Journal of Federalism* 46, no. 3 (2012): 301.

25. Boris Shor and and Nolan McCarty, "The Ideological Mapping of American Legislatures," *American Political Science Review* 105, no. 3 (2011): 530.

26. "Gubernatorial and Legislative Party Control of State Government," Ballotpedia, last accessed January 12, 2018, https://ballotpedia.org/Gubernatorial_and _legislative_party_control_of_state_government.

27. Conlan and Posner, "American Federalism," 299.

28. See Frank R. Strong, "Cooperative Federalism," *Iowa Law Review* 23 (1936): 459.

29. Jenna Bednar, William N. Eskridge Jr., and John Ferejohn, "A Political Theory of Federalism," in *Constitutional Culture and Democratic Rule*, ed. John Ferejohn, Jack N. Rakove, and Jonathan Riley (New York: Cambridge University Press, 2001), 223.

30. Jane Perry Clark, *The Rise of a New Federalism: Federal-State Cooperation in the United States* (New York: Columbia University Press, 1938); and James T. Patterson, *The New Deal and the States: Federalism in Transition* (New York: Praeger, 1981).

31. John Joseph Wallis, "The Political Economy of New Deal Fiscal Federalism," *Economic Inquiry* 29, no. 3 (1991): 510.

32. Matthew Levendusky, *The Partisan Sort: How Liberals Became Democrats and Conservatives Became Republicans* (Chicago: University of Chicago Press, 2009).

33. Printz v. United States, 521 U.S. 898 (1997); and New York v. United States, 505 U.S. 144 (1992).

34. Massachusetts v. EPA, 549 U.S. 497 (2007).

35. James W. Coleman, "Policymaking by Proposal: How Agencies Are Using Proposed Rules to Transform Industry Long before Final Rules Are Tested in Court," *George Mason Law Review* 24, no. 2 (Winter 2017): 500.

36. Repeal of Carbon Pollution Emission Guidelines for Existing Stationary Sources: Electric Utility Generating Units, 82 Fed. Reg. 198 (proposed October 16, 2017, to be codified at 40 C.F.R. pt. 60).

37. Paul Nolette, "State Litigation during the Obama Administration: Diverging Agendas in an Era of Polarized Politics," *Publius: The Journal of Federalism* 44, no. 3 (July 2014): 451.

38. Shihyun Noh and Dale Krane, "Implementing the Affordable Care Act Health Insurance Exchanges: State Government Choices and Policy Outcomes," *Publius: The Journal of Federalism* 46, no. 3 (July 2016): 416, 434.

39. Nicholas Bagley, "Are Medicaid Work Requirements Legal?," *Journal of the American Medical Association* 319, no. 8 (February 2018): 763–764.

40. Nicholas Bagley, "Legal Limits and the Implementation of the Affordable Care Act," *Pennsylvania Law Review* 164, no. 7 (2016): 1715; and Barron and Rakoff, "In Defense of Big Waiver," 297–299.

41. Bulman-Pozen, "Executive Federalism."

42. Aaron Wildavsky, "Double Security: Federalism as Competition," *Cato Journal* 10, no. 1 (Spring/Summer 1990): 39, 43–46.

43. By a 7–2 vote, the Supreme Court held in NFIB v. Sebelius, 132 S. Ct. 2566, 2604 (2012) that despite the terms of the statute, the government could not condition the states' receipt of "old" Medicaid funds on their participation in the ACA's expansion.

44. Metzger, "Agencies, Polarization, and the States," 1783.

45. This is true with respect to both the ACA's Medicaid expansion and its provisions for health care exchanges. John Dinan, "Implementing Health Reform: Intergovernmental Bargaining and the Affordable Care Act," *Publius: The Journal of Federalism* 44, no. 3 (July 2014): 399; and Noh and Krane, "Implementing the Affordable Care Act," 416.

46. The most thorough discussion is John Hudak, *Presidential Pork: White House Influence over the Distribution of Federal Grants* (Washington, DC: Brookings Institution Press, 2014).

47. Price V. Fishback and Valentina Kachanovskaya, "The New Deal and Executive Control of the Distribution of Federal Funds across States," *Defining Ideas* (June 19, 2016), last accessed February 28, 2018, http://www.hoover.org/research/politics-new-deal.

48. John J. Wallis, Price V. Fishback, and Shawn E. Kantor, "Politics, Relief, and Reform: Roosevelt's Efforts to Control Corruption and Manipulation during the New Deal," in *Corruption and Reform: Lessons from America's Economic History*, ed. Edward L. Glaeser and Claudia Goldin (Chicago: University of Chicago Press, 2006), 343, 355–357.

49. Lowande and Milkis, "We Can't Wait," 13.

50. Mila Sohoni, "On Dollars and Deference: Agencies, Spending, and Economic Rights," *Duke Law Journal* 66, no. 8 (May 2017): 1678.

51. Margaret H. Lemos and Max Minzner, "For-Profit Public Enforcement," *Harvard Law Review* 127, no. 3 (January 2014): 853, 868.

52. DiIulio, *Bring Back the Bureaucrats*.

53. Conlan and Posner, "American Federalism," 283.

54. Note, "Independence, Congressional Weakness, and the Importance of Appointment: The Impact of Combining Budgetary Autonomy with Removal Protection," *Harvard Law Review* 125, no. 7 (May 2012): 1822, 1823–1824.

55. Mark Totten, "The Enforcers and the Great Recession," *Cardozo Law Review* 36, no. 5 (June 2015): 1611, 1613.

56. For discussion, see DeMuth and Greve, "Agency Finance."

57. Lemos and Minzner, *"For-Profit Public Enforcement,"* 901–903; Margaret H. Lemos, "Aggregate Litigation Goes Public: Representative Suits by State Attorneys General," *Harvard Law Review* 126, no. 2 (December 2012): 486; and David Freeman Engstrom, "Public Regulation of Private Enforcement: Empirical Analysis of DOJ Oversight of Qui Tam Litigation under the False Claims Act," *Northwestern University Law Review* 107, no. 4 (2013): 1689.

58. For this reason, the Supreme Court—rather than Congress—undertook the enterprise of locking dissident states into a national, postmodern morals cartel. Michael S. Greve, *The Upside-Down Constitution* (Cambridge, MA: Harvard University Press, 2012), 268–272.

59. Jason Scott Johnston, "A Positive Political Economic Theory of Environmental Federalization," *Case Western Reserve Law Review* 64, no. 4 (2014): 1549, 1550–1551.

60. California and other consumption states have attempted to regulate the production of eggs, foie gras, and, much more importantly, energy produced in other states and even foreign countries. James W. Coleman, "Importing Energy, Exporting Regulation," *Fordham Law Review* 83, no. 3 (December 2014): 1357.

61. See William H. Pryor Jr., "A Comparison of Abuses and Reforms of Class Actions and Multigovernment Lawsuits," *Tulane Law Review* 74, no. 5/6 (2000): 1885. At the time of the MSA negotiations, Judge Pryor served as Alabama's attorney general.

62. Martha A. Derthick, *Up in Smoke: From Legislation to Litigation in Tobacco Politics*, 3rd ed. (Washington, DC: CQ Press, 2011); and Michael S. Greve, "Compacts, Cartels, and Congressional Consent," *Missouri Law Review* 68, no. 2 (Spring 2003): 285.

63. Nolette, *Federalism on Trial*, 11, 14–16; Derthick, *Up in Smoke*; and Totten, "The Enforcers," 1612–1614.

64. The authors argue that "with the development of executive-centered partisanship, political contestation in the United States is no longer a struggle over the size of the State; rather it is a struggle between liberals and conservatives, to seize and deploy the State and its resources." Milkis and Jacobs, "I Alone," 586.

65. Executive fiscal repression of the kind described in the text is not a strategy that is readily available to a Democratic administration, which needs red states to accept federal funds to implement its policies. See, for example, Bulman-Pozen and Metzger, "The President and the States," 330 (noting the Obama administration's flexibility vis-à-vis Republican states in implementing the ACA). Instead, a Democratic administration will tend to resort to regulatory repression of the opposing state bloc.

66. David Weigel and Amy Goldstein, "GOP Tries One More Time to Undo ACA with Bill Offering Huge Block Grants to States," the *Washington Post* online, September 13, 2017, last accessed February 28, 2018, https://www.washingtonpost.com /powerpost/gop-bill-to-block-grant-major-parts-of-the-aca-unveiled/2017/09/13 /bdcd1872-988b-11e7-87fc-c3f7ee4035c9_story.html.

67. "It may be that the [Trump] White House will achieve unilaterally what several Republican senators . . . hoped to accomplish with legislation: turn [Medicaid] funds and policy discretion over to the States. It is highly unlikely, however, that this devolution will succeed without national standards that impose conservative policies on state and local governments." Milkis and Jacobs, "I Alone," 603.

68. See generally, Michael S. Greve, Jonathan Klick, Michael A. Petrino, and J. P. Sevilla, "Preemption in the Rehnquist and Roberts Courts: An Empirical Analysis," *Supreme Court Economic Review* 23, no. 1 (2015): 353.

69. James Madison, *Federalist* 39, in Alexander Hamilton, James Madison, and John Jay, *The Federalist Papers*, ed. Clinton Rossiter (New York: Signet Classics, 2003).

70. Douglas Kendall and Simon Lazarus, "Broken Circuit: Obstructionism in the Environment's Most Important Court," *The Environmental Forum* 30, no. 3 (May/June 2013): 36.

71. Michael S. Greve and Ashley C. Parrish, "Administrative Law without Congress," 22 *George Mason Law Review* 22, no. 3 (Spring 2015): 501, 522–534.

72. "The hydraulic pressure inherent within each of the separate Branches to exceed the outer limits of its power, even to accomplish desirable objectives, must be resisted." See INS v. Chadha, 462 U.S. 919, 951 (1983).

73. Levinson and Pildes, "Separation of Parties," 2314.

74. Neomi Rao, "Administrative Collusion: How Delegation Diminishes the Collective Congress," *New York University Law Review* 90, no. 5 (November 2015): 1463.

75. See Daniel Farber and Anne Joseph O'Connell, "The Lost World of Administrative Law," *Texas Law Review* 92 (2014): 1137; and Greve and Parrish, "Administrative Law without Congress."

76. Whitman v. American Trucking Associations, 531 U.S. 457, 472 (2001); and Mistretta v. United States, 488 U.S. 361, 372 (1989).

77. See generally, Greve and Parrish, "Administrative Law without Congress"; and Sohoni, "On Dollars," 1681.

78. See, for example, Zachary Price, "Enforcement Discretion and Executive Duty," *Vanderbilt Law Review* 67, no. 3 (April 2014): 671; and Barron and Rakoff, "In Defense of Big Waiver," 272 (noting the paucity of doctrines to govern "big waivers").

79. See Gregory v. Ashcroft, 501 U.S. 452 (1991).

80. National Federation of Independent Business v. Sebelius, 567 U.S. 519, 642 (2012).

81. "Well before the creation of the modern administrative state, we recognized that States are not normal litigants for the purposes of invoking federal jurisdiction." Massachusetts v. EPA, 549 U.S. 407, 518; and "[The States] are not relegated to the role of mere provinces or political corporations, but retain the dignity, though not the full authority, of sovereignty." See also Alden v. Maine, 527 U.S. 706, 715 (1999).

82. See Daniel Francis, "The Decline of the Dormant Commerce Clause," *Denver Law Review* 94 (2017): 255; Michael S. Greve, "The Dormant Coordination Clause," *Vanderbilt Law Review En Banc* 67 (2014): 269, 287–307; and Heather K. Gerken and Ari Holtzblatt, "The Political Safeguards of Horizontal Federalism," *Michigan Law Review* 113, no. 1 (October 2014): 57, 59, which argues that political safeguards may adequately protect states against horizontal externalities and exploitation.

83. See Connor N. Raso and William N. Eskridge Jr., "Chevron as a Canon, Not a Precedent: An Empirical Study of What Motivates Justices in Agency Deference Cases," *Columbia Law Review* 110, no. 7 (November 2010): 1727.

84. See Gillian E. Metzger, "Administrative Law as the New Federalism," *Duke Law Journal* 57, no. 7 (May 2008): 2023.

85. National Federation of Independent Business v. Sebelius; and King v. Burwell, 135 S.Ct. 2480, 2485 (2015).

86. See generally, Bensel, *Sectionalism and American Political Development*.

87. Jonathan A. Rodden, *Hamilton's Paradox: The Promise and Peril of Fiscal Federalism* (Cambridge: Cambridge University Press, 2006).

88. Rodden, *Hamilton's Paradox*, 55–67.

89. For examples and discussion, see Michael S. Greve, *Federalism and the Constitution: Competition Versus Cartel* (Arlington, VA: Mercatus Center at George Mason University, 2015).

90. Conlan and Posner, "American Federalism," 284–285.

91. 11 U.S.C. §§ 901 et sec. (2012). See Melissa B. Jacoby, "Federalism Form and Function in the Detroit Bankruptcy," *Yale Journal on Regulation* 33, no. 1 (2016): 55.

92. Puerto Rico Oversight, Management, and Economic Stability Act, Pub. L. No. 114-187, 130 Stat. 549 (2016).

93. Steven Malanga, *The Public Pension Problem: It's Much Worse Than It Appears*, Manhattan Institute (July 22, 2016), https://www.manhattan-institute.org/html/public -pension-problem-its-much-worse-it-appears-9095.html.

94. Malanga, *The Public Pension Problem*.

95. See several contributions in *When States Go Bankrupt: The Origins, Context, and Solutions for the American States in Fiscal Crisis*, ed. Peter Conti-Brown and David Skeel (New York: Cambridge University Press, 2014).

96. 12 U.S.C. §§ 5211 et sec. (2012) (Troubled Asset Relief Program, "TARP").

97. I frankly doubt that any such program could be enacted. State debt relief and the harrowing question of allocating losses among all pensioners and bond holders would trigger harsh sectional, ideological, partisan, and class divisions—all of them running along the same line. The discussion in the text serves simply to illustrate federalism's predicament.

98. Bulman-Pozen, "Executive Federalism," 993–1015. For a similar, equally judicious assessment, see Bulman-Pozen and Metzger, "The President and the States," 325–332.

99. See Jonathan Rauch, *Political Realism: How Hacks, Machines, Big Money, and Back-Room Deals Can Strengthen American Democracy* (Washington, DC: Brookings Institution Press, 2015).

100. Lowande and Milkis, "We Can't Wait," 21–24.

101. Peter H. Schuck, *Why Government Fails So Often and How It Can Do Better* (Princeton, NJ: Princeton University Press, 2014), 12–13.

102. Steven M. Teles, "Kludgeocracy in America," *National Affairs* 17 (2013): 97.

103. Juan J. Linz, "The Perils of Presidentialism," *Journal of Democracy* 1 (1990): 51; and Matthew Yglesias, "American Democracy Is Doomed," *Vox*, October 8, 2015, last accessed February 28, 2018, http://www.vox.com/2015/3/2/8120063/american -democracy-doomed.

104. See Ganesh Sitaraman, *The Crisis of the Middle-Class Constitution* (New York: Knopf, 2017); Steven Levitsky and Daniel Ziblatt, *How Democracies Die* (New York: Crown, 2018); and "The joining of presidential prerogative and partisanship creates the false illusion that the executive of a vast bureaucratic state . . . can truly function as a representative democratic institution with meaningful links to the president's party

and the public. Instead, we have learned the hard lesson that executive partisanship leads to a plebiscitary politics, which exposes the American people to leaders who scorn the institutional restraints that are a vital ingredient of constitutional government as well as the collaboration that is the sine qua non of organized party politics." Milkis and Jacobs, "I Alone," 612.

105. In the aftermath of President Trump's election, liberal scholars and pundits have emphasized that potential, and urged like-minded constituencies and state officials to act accordingly. See Cristian Farias, "A New Romance: Trump Has Made Progressives Fall in Love with Federalism," *New York Magazine*, August 24, 2017; and Heather K. Gerken and Joshua Revesz, "Progressive Federalism: A User's Guide," *Democracy: A Journal of Ideas* (Spring 2017), last accessed February 28, 2018, http://democracyjournal.org/magazine/44/progressive-federalism-a-users-guide.

CHAPTER 8

Parties against the Constitution

Zachary Courser

Understanding the polarized politics of America requires close study of the conflict between contemporary American political parties and the Constitution.[1] Until the twentieth century, the two-party system operated within the Constitution's republican limits on majority rule and protections for individual rights. The principle of majority rule was understood to be circumscribed by principles of republican government, such as separation of powers, checks and balances, bicameralism, enumerated rights, and other constitutional limitations on popular power. Consequently, a mere partisan majority could not achieve unilateral control over policy without coordination between the branches of government or a supermajority in the legislative. This arrangement was accepted by both parties as a salubrious republican principle of governance that required a degree of consensus and took account of various minority views and objections. Today, instead of reaching for political consensus and expressing a republican concern for the rights of the minority, contemporary parties seek unfettered majority rule under an exacting principle of democracy.[2] As this chapter will demonstrate, today's party system embraces democracy as its one legitimizing political principle, casting a long shadow over the Constitution's formal, republican limitations on popular rule. As parties insist on unlimited majority rule, party politics increasingly conflicts with the roadblocks the Constitution places on the majority rule. Whereas nineteenth-century parties accepted and respected these limitations as bulwarks against majority tyranny, today's parties seek to overcome them as undemocratic and illegitimate. Yet these limits endure, frustrating the will of partisan majorities to effect policy change. Thus, a conflict between today's

157

democratic parties and the republican Constitution has resulted in much of
the gridlock we observe in American politics today.

A consequence of the grinding conflict over majority rule has been the
gradual disappearance of moderate voters from politics.[3] Extreme ideological
voices are now over-represented in elections and policymaking, while a growing plurality of voters struggles to find representation and expression within
the party system.[4] According the Pew Research Center, the "overall share of
Americans who express consistently conservative or consistently liberal opinions has doubled over the past two decades from 10% to 21%. And ideological
thinking is now much more closely aligned with partisanship than in the past."[5]
However, the majority of Americans "do not have uniformly conservative or
liberal views," and "most do not see either party as a threat to the nation."
In fact, most Americans want their representatives to "meet halfway to resolve contentious disputes, rather than hold out for more of what they want."[6]
While partisans today are more ideologically consistent and feel a stronger
antipathy toward one another, a plurality of voters prefers to be thought of as
independent or unaffiliated with any political party.[7] Polarization might not be
the result of a strong party system but rather the consequence of weak parties
unable to resist the influence of ideologically entrenched activists and interest
groups, and therefore unable to meet the interests of median voters.[8] Weak
parties allow activist partisans and interest groups to colonize the machinery
of parties, amplify ideological appeals, polarize issues, and drive moderates
out of politics. Even beyond polarization and gridlock, this dissonance has
serious side effects for the health of American political institutions. Of particular concern is the damage that has been done to popular perceptions of the
legitimacy of political parties, Congress, the presidency, and the courts. Protest movements like the Tea Party on the right and Indivisible on the left have
seized on popular misgivings about American political institutions, helping to
create a volatile populist political climate that amplifies voters' loss of confidence in parties, politicians, and American politics in general. [9]

A MADISONIAN THEORY OF MAJORITIES

To fully appreciate the conflict between today's parties and the Constitution,
one must understand the republican theory upon which the Constitution is
based. The Constitution delineates the powers and institutional arrangements
of the federal government, with a focus on limiting the political reach of majorities, in the interest of protecting minority rights. What makes American
constitutionalism distinct from parliamentary systems is an overriding concern
for the potential abuses majorities pose to liberty. Through indirect represen-

tation and the separation of powers, the Constitution requires a broad consensus to create policy not only within the electorate but also within coordinate branches of government. Simple popular majorities can accomplish little to influence any one election or session of Congress.

The character of the federal government as organized by the Constitution is essentially and explicitly republican, shielded from the direct influence of simple majorities. Examples of the indirect representation of popular will in the selection of federal offices are numerous. As originally ratified, the Constitution requires that members of the US Senate be selected by state legislatures. Senators serve six-year terms and only one-third of the body is up for election every two years. Successive layers of mediating institutions insulate the election of the executive from popular opinion: state legislatures, the Electoral College, and in the absence of a majority, the House of Representatives. The Supreme Court is selected by two indirectly elected institutions—the Senate and the executive. The only truly popular federal institution, directly elected by the people, is the House of Representatives.

The separation of governmental power into distinct branches further bolsters the Constitution's republican character against the influence of simple majorities. No branch of government can accomplish much politically without the cooperation and consent of the others. Congress relies on the executive to pass legislation, and both must submit to the Supreme Court's judgment as to its constitutionality. The only exception to this principle is a supermajority in Congress. Two-thirds of Congress can override the executive's veto, and the same supermajority joined with three-fourths of the states can change the Constitution itself.

The Framers of the Constitution based these limitations on majority rule on their understanding of the limits of human nature as applied to politics. James Madison's account of human nature in *Federalist* 10, and the necessity of a republican government to safeguard liberty and individual rights from the baneful effects of faction, remains a cornerstone of American constitutional theory. Madison acknowledged that policy in the states was often made on the basis of a "superior force of an interested and overbearing majority," not the "rules of justice and the rights of the minor party."[10] He carefully observed that this tendency toward overbearing majorities was not the result of a defect of government, but a defect in the judgments of the people in the democratic conduct of their affairs. As Madison demonstrated in his account of democratic governments throughout history, the fallibility of reason, human self-love and self-interest, and the vulnerability of majorities to intemperate passions have always caused democracies to distort considerations of justice and disregard minority rights. Madison made an axiom of the reality that, due to these defects in human nature, citizens in a self-governing society will develop into factions that are "actuated by common impulse or passion, adverse to the rights of other citizens"—or the entire society.[11]

To Madison, this potential for majority factions to form is of particular concern. He sees securing "the public good and private rights against the danger of such a faction" while also preserving "the spirit and the form of popular government" as a fundamental problem the Constitution must address.[12] Madison's well-known "republican remedy" to this problem involves both a properly constituted representative legislature and an extended republic. As such, no factious passion or impulse that would endanger so vast and diverse a nation as the United States could concert its efforts and find a majority to support it.[13] Madison's arguments regarding the frailties of human nature with regard to democratic governance extend beyond *Federalist* 10 to inform the many limitations the Constitution places on majorities to govern unopposed. These limitations create, as political theorist Harvey Mansfield describes, a "constitutional space" between the people and their government, making political conditions more likely for generating consensus and allowing for deliberation. The US Constitution is "government by the people but it keeps the government at a distance from the people, so that the government, while remaining popular, will be as wise and moderate as possible."[14]

While explicit about the dangers of majority faction and the necessity of securing minority rights, the Constitution is nearly silent on the role of citizens in creating or sustaining popular consent for its institutions and process to function. For the Framers, effective government under the Constitution would not rely primarily on an active, politically engaged citizenry but on "the reliable inclination of men to follow their own interests, fairly narrowly understood."[15] The Constitution was meant to create a self-perpetuating "system of channeled self-interest."[16] To this end, the Framers fashioned a Constitution that relied on an assumption that the mass of American citizens can and will provide this necessary popular input through their participation in elections, with no regard as to how. This deficiency was a key objection of anti-Federalists to the Constitution. They insisted that attention to republican virtue could not be ignored, and that the nation would always depend upon the republican virtue of its people. To anti-Federalists, this "community of mere interest"—devoid of a concern for republican virtue—was insufficient to command the people's confidence or their security.[17]

The advocates for the ratification of the Constitution—the Federalists—offered "no account of the critical role for intermediate political actors in mobilizing and organizing voters in elections."[18] In fact, Federalists "took for granted a certain kind of public-spirited leadership" and "the republican genius of the people."[19] Instead of relying on the republican virtue of citizens, as ancient republics had, Federalists put their faith in the effective operation of the Constitution in securing stable and effective governance. This, in turn, would act as the primary means of securing the necessary attachment of the people to the Constitution. Alexander Hamilton observes in his defense of a strong executive in *Federalist* 68 that "the true test of a good government is its aptitude and tendency to produce a good administration."[20] He argues that the enemy fought against in the revolution was not government but tyranny, and that excessive hostility to governmental power imperiled the *"strength* and *stability* in the organization of our government, and *vigor* in its operations."[21]

In summary, the critical contribution of the Federalists to American political thought is their dedication to republican forms *and* their distrust of majorities to safeguard rights and maintain liberty. This belief informs the institutional arrangements of the Constitution, its emphasis on dividing power and protecting the rights of the minority, and the space it creates between the people and their government. It makes majorities in American politics uniquely limited, and requires a greater degree of consensus in policymaking than in other democratic nations. It could also be said that the Federalists created the Constitution in a "political vacuum" that had little regard for the problems of mobilization or the organization of public opinion in a republic.[22]

NINETEENTH-CENTURY PARTIES: POLARIZATION WITHOUT GRIDLOCK

The corrective for the Constitution's silences on voter mobilization and organization of public opinion was eventually found in the establishment of political parties. The advent of the two-party system in the lead up to Andrew Jackson's 1828 presidential campaign initiated a process of democratizing the Constitution and connecting a growing electorate to the operation of elections.[23] Parties helped to correct some of the democratic deficiencies of the Constitution by organizing citizens to supply its political system with voters, candidates, policies, and most critically, consent.[24] Parties proved extremely effective in turning out the electorate to vote and in doing so made American politics more popular. Despite their democratic nature, parties as originally established accepted the republican limitations on majority rule that the Constitution imposed, aligning citizens around broad but distinctive constellations of ideas that commanded the loyalty of an equally broad coalition of voters.[25] At their peak power in the late nineteenth century, however, parties did polarize voters and candidates into two sharply opposed political camps but did not polarize each camp ideologically, leaving constitutional and ideological space for compromise in the development of government policy.

Party organization developed reluctantly at first but quickly became a legitimate and commonplace means of organizing elections and government policy. Despite George Washington's warnings against the "spirit of party," and the founding era's general equating of parties with factions, Thomas Jefferson's Democratic-Republican Party legitimized party opposition to the Federalists' vision of the Constitution in the election of 1800.[26] However, Jefferson's intention was not to establish party competition, but to rescue the Constitution from what he and his followers deemed the antidemocratic politics of the Federalists. He declared in his first inaugural address, "We are all republicans, we are all federalists," and he sought to move the country toward a universal acceptance of his democratic vision of the Constitution.[27]

In Jackson's defeat in the presidential election of 1824, Martin Van Buren identified many deficiencies in the presidential selection process and how a political party could remedy them. In fact, it was in part a concern for the direct popular appeal of General Jackson to the people, and the potential for this informal popular power overwhelming the limits of the Constitution, that motivated Van Buren to "substitute party principle for personal preference" by having Jackson nominated by the Democratic Party.[28] Van Buren sought to place party principle above the popular appeal of particular candidates, and built a disciplined party organization to hold government accountable to the people's choice. He helped to anchor party power in the president's ability to dispense government jobs as a reward for party loyalty and service during elections.

Despite some resistance from the early Whig Party, partisanship gradually came to be deeply engrained in the political life of Americans and shaped nearly every aspect of politics. Ninety-five percent of newspapers in America by 1850 had some loyalty to a party.[29] Campaigns during the nineteenth century were not fought along policy lines, but waged as spectacular displays of support for parties and candidates. The chief goal during elections was not to convince undecided or independent voters, who largely did not exist, but to mobilize party supporters.[30] Politics at the electorate level was a very simplified affair, with elections working to "reduce the complex, daunting process of thinking through many issues and choosing among hundreds of candidates to a matter of black-and-white opposites."[31] Around 80 percent of the eligible electorate turned out to vote for president between 1868 and 1896. Michael McGerr concludes in his study of the partisanship of this period that "the nineteenth century marked the highpoint of voter turnout in the North."[32]

Between 1878 and 1910, roll call votes between Republicans and Democrats in Congress were highly polarized.[33] Despite the sharp differences in opinion between parties, and the virtual absence of independent voters, both the Democratic and Republican parties respected the limitations on majority rule imposed by the Constitution. While dedicated to the idea of democracy in principle, the Democratic Party saw in these limitations a bulwark against the encroachments of national power on local rights.[34] They were more comfortable with limited democratic majorities in state and local governments, due to their smaller size and proximity to their constituencies. According to John Gerring, "The constitutional restrictions that Democrats lauded were intended to hem in the powers of government, not the powers of the people."[35] This preference for democratic localism and a weak national government also helped to insulate southern states from federal enforcement of civil rights. The Republican Party respected the Constitution's limitations on majority power, but from a different vantage. Their support for restrictions on majority rule derived from their fear of "popular misrule," in line with the Federalists' concerns about the dangers that the majority faction posed to liberty.[36]

Despite a deeply polarized Congress and a divided electorate, a political culture existed on both sides and accepted the idea that majorities did not have the right to rule in an unlimited fashion. For example, in their study of tariff legislation between the 1860s and 1880s—an issue that strongly divided both parties during the nineteenth century—Gregory Wawro and Eric Schickler found that "narrow majorities were generally sufficient to pass major policy changes" in the Senate despite the omnipresent threat of a minority filibuster.[37] This infrequent resort of the minority to filibuster divisive legislation mirrors the record of the antebellum period. It wasn't until 1917 that the Senate had to institute a two-thirds majority vote for cloture to end the unlimited right of the minority to filibuster legislation. Despite major policy differences and a polarized partisan environment, majorities found ways to accommodate minority interests in the Senate through regular legislative order during a very polarized period.

DEMOCRATIZING PARTISANSHIP AND THE RISE OF RESPONSIBLE PARTIES

Though deeply engrained partisanship was a fait accompli by the mid-nineteenth century, there were still detractors of various stripes. In fact, anti-partisanship has long been part of the American political character, dating from the founding era.[38] Washington, Madison, and others knew of parties such as they existed in the British Parliament, and they initially saw them as

incompatible with the Constitution and its protections against faction and majority tyranny. Liberal reformers after the Civil War saw parties and patronage
as inefficient, corrupt, and based in excessive reliance on mass participation in
elections.[39] Civil service reform became a key issue for antiparty activists, striking as it did at the heart of parties' organizational strength and administrative
weakness.[40] And, for the first time since before Jackson, the idea of being a
conscientious independent voter, and judging politics without a partisan lens,
gained legitimacy.[41]

Alongside complaints about excesses, a new species of argument was directed against partisan government in the late nineteenth century. Woodrow
Wilson was one of the first political theorists to build an argument against
parties being capable of managing the complex affairs required of modern
governments.[42] He complained about the dilute nature of political participation that parties required from citizens and the lack of national purpose in the
operations of the federal government. Beginning with his earliest writings as
a Princeton undergraduate in 1879, Wilson was the first to expound a theory
of party government that required direct popular control of government.[43]
He complained of how the voice of the majority was lost in the diffusion of
power the Constitution required, and that it was "a thing of despair to get any
assurance that any vote he may cast will even in an infinitesimal degree affect
the essential course of administration."[44] Wilson's first book, *Congressional Government* (1885), was a critique of the weakness of the Constitution in achieving
programmatic policy changes to match the demands of a shifting and growing
nation in the late nineteenth century. He demonstrated an admiration of the
capacities of the British Parliament and its cabinet system to accomplish these
goals, but he saw that the US Constitution would not be amended under any
normal circumstances to eliminate the separation between the president and
Congress that a parliamentary system requires.[45]

As constitutional reform was not an option, Wilson eventually sought to
connect voters directly with the "course of administration" through a reform
of political parties. Wilson came to see the Constitution's limitations on popular rule as outmoded and based on the assumptions of an earlier social and
economic order. As he styled it in a 1912 campaign speech, "The Constitution
of the United States Had Been Made under the Dominion of the Newtonian
Theory," which was due to evolve according to the Darwinian theory of adaptation and change.[46] However, amending the Constitution to overcome its
limits on democracy presented a real, though not insurmountable, challenge
for reformers. For example, the Seventeenth Amendment, ratified in 1913, allowed for a degree of democratization and undermined federal limits on popular majorities, shifting power from state legislatures directly to state residents

in selecting their Senators.[47] But a direct assault on the constitutional limits on majority rule was not possible. Wilson saw in political parties a means of holding the "disconnected and dispersed" powers of the Constitution together, directing their energies toward building "national judgments upon national questions."[48] Endowed with the mandate from a majority in the electorate, parties could coordinate national policy and overcome the limitations of the Constitution to achieve policy with a national purpose.

Wilson's ideas took hold in the Democratic Party and among Progressive reformers in the early twentieth century. Progressives sought to establish a standard of responsible party government in service of national programmatic policy and the expansion of democracy generally. Reformers like Herbert Croly were particularly enamored of the idea that national politics should have national purpose and that each citizen would be somehow ennobled by his or her participation in achieving it.[49] He believed establishing a more direct and unmediated role for citizens in politics would allow the people to collectively achieve a national political purpose.[50] Theodore Roosevelt, despite his origins as a Republican Party stalwart, came to embrace Croly and other Progressives' theory of the collective purpose of American democracy. By the time of the 1912 election, Roosevelt—as the Progressive Party candidate—expounded upon the virtues of a more directly democratic politics in America.[51] The traditional two-party system persisted in thwarting these innovations, despite their popular appeal. During the 1912 campaign, the Republican Party was the home of the defense of this view. According to Sidney Milkis, Progressives like Wilson and Roosevelt had "faith in unmediated, national mass opinion" that appeared to threatened "valued traditions in the United States, such as federalism and the separation of powers."[52] William Howard Taft, battling for reelection with Roosevelt and Wilson, blasted Progressive innovations on majority rule as threatening constitutional norms and republican government itself. He accused his opponents of proposing to "utterly tear down all the checks and balances of a well-adjusted, democratic, constitutional, representative government" and "the limitations on executive and legislative power as between the majority and minority."[53]

The Republican Party dominated federal elections during the 1920s, as voters grew tired of Wilson and other Progressives' attempts at innovating American democracy. During this "return to normalcy," Republicans maintained their traditional views on political parties and the Constitution's limits of majority rule. The crisis of the Great Depression swept the Democrats back into power in 1933 and opened new opportunities to continue the work of establishing Progressive ideas in American government. As president, Franklin Delano Roosevelt (FDR) attempted to complete the work of Wilson and other

Progressive reformers in using political parties to overcome the Constitution's limits on majority rule.[54] Like Wilson, FDR saw transformation of the political parties as a key to achieving the policy program of the New Deal. His reforms required extravagant use of executive power that was resisted by the constitutionally minded, locally oriented party organization he found in the Democratic Party in the 1930s. At the peak of his popularity, FDR pressed his party organization, which held ample majorities in Congress, as hard as possible to overcome the constitutional roadblocks that had been placed before the New Deal. From 1937 to 1938, his court-packing plan, his purge campaign, and his executive reorganization act, were all aimed at centralizing administrative and policymaking control in his hands as president. He was, however, beaten back by his own party out of respect for the Constitution's separation of powers doctrine. While this frontal assault on the Constitution did not succeed, FDR was able to transform American political parties into being ideological and programmatic. FDR disliked the broad platforms and loose ideological commitments of parties before the New Deal. He wanted parties to present slates of decisive policy differences and policy proposals before the American people, and to have the people reward or punish parties based on their ability to enact their policies. He wanted parties to present sharp definition and dueling conceptions of national purpose, and elections to be contests that engaged the public on these ideas. FDR wrote that he would see to it "that the Democratic party and the Republican party should not be merely Tweedledum and Tweedledee to each other."[55] He didn't want the hodgepodge, loosely constructed regime of constitutional parties that cleaved to founding ideas of limited majority control. He wanted ideological parties. From then on, the Democratic Party was to be the party of liberals, and the Republican Party that of conservatives.

POST-1950 POLITICAL PARTIES

It is in the context of FDR's battle against constitutional limits on majority control of government that the American Political Science Association composed a report on "responsible" parties.[56] E. E. Schattscheider, chairman of the Committee on Political Parties that authored the report, was a well-respected expert on parties. He popularized the idea of responsible parties in his well-known textbook *Party Government* (1942), and was a force in building the arguments against an American party system that operated "as two loose associations of state and local organizations, with very little national machinery and very little national cohesion."[57] The limited and localized party system that existed then was not capable of organizing national opinion in support of a partisan policy program. Therefore, holding a particular party responsible for their policies "at the polls thus tends to vanish." The report's purpose was to outline various party reforms to help make parties responsible to voters during elections, and "to bring about fuller public appreciation of a basic weakness in the American two-party system."[58]

The report's proposed reforms reflect Progressive theories of democracy and of the role of the citizen in government affairs. The authors observe the limitations that are placed on democratic rule by the Constitution, but contemplate that "it is easy to overestimate . . . the rigidity of the existing constitutional arrangements in the United States."[59] A thorough reform of party organization was required to democratize every aspect of their operations, placing the will of the majority of the party membership at the center of power. The committee proposed a thorough "intraparty" democratization of "internal processes" to make party leadership accountable to party members.[60] They wanted party membership, which had never required dues or internal registry, to be more formal. It was insufficient to consider just anyone who cast a ballot for a party's candidate to be a member. In order for party conventions, caucuses, and primaries to be answerable to the party, membership had to be formally defined. According to the report, conventions were "unwieldy, unrepresentative and less than responsible in mandate and action."[61] The authors approvingly reference Wilson's proposal to have a national primary for the selection of the president, suggesting that the parties adopt "a convention of not more than 500–600 members, composed mostly of delegates elected directly by the party voters on a more representative basis," in addition to a handful of party leaders.[62] It is notable that the report dismisses the idea that direct participation of members in every aspect of party conduct would cause a polarizing effect in American politics. The authors insist that the sharply defined ideological landscape shaped by these reforms would "not cause parties to differ more fundamentally or more sharply than they have in the past."[63] In fact, this "clarification of party policy" would initiate a "more reasonable discussion of public affairs" and not "cause the parties to erect between themselves an ideological wall."[64]

Austin Ranney, an accomplished party scholar in his own right, was a dogged critic of the report on responsible parties and the Progressive view of parties. According to Ranney, the proposal for more intraparty democracy meant "participation as well as control." He therefore presented the report's suggestion of getting "twenty-seven million Democrats to 'participate' in the close supervision of the affairs of the Democratic party" as highly unworkable.[65] His most severe critique of the report is that it "clearly rejects the notion that the nature of American parties is basically determined by our constitutional system," and that the doctrine of responsible parties "is indispensable to a system of 'unlimited' majority rule."[66] Ranney recounts the Madisonian theory of the Constitution in limiting the power of majorities, and argues contrary to the report's conclusions that the Framers "did not contemplate the growing need for party responsibility when [the Constitution] was set up," that they sought to make sure that "no unified and disciplined majority 'faction' would ever be able to trample upon the rights of minorities."[67] He points out that the "decentralized and irresponsible parties" that are complained of in the report made "it difficult for strong-willed and self-conscious popular majorities even to form."[68] Ranney finds the theory behind responsible parties to be contrary to both the Constitution and the sentiments of most Americans, suggesting that "the prevailing attitude in the United States is that we want *both* majority rule *and* inviolable minority rights, and that neither deserved any priority over the other."[69] Ranney concludes that the whole concept of responsible parties will always be unworkable unless "the American people have fully accepted the doctrine of majority-rule democracy" and, one assumes, rejected the limitations the Constitution places on it.[70]

Although the APSA report, Ranney, or indeed any individual political scientist failed to have much of a direct effect on the course of party reform post-1950, the parties clearly did in fact continue to develop along lines established under FDR and the Progressive theory of democracy. Reforms of the presidential nomination process in the 1970s created significantly more intraparty democracy in the Democratic Party. Democratically controlled state governments created a system of state primaries that bound delegates directly to the choice of the mass of voters. These primary laws applied to both parties equally—due to the domination of state legislatures by the Democratic Party from the 1970s through the 1990s. Therefore, both parties have experienced takeovers by ideological factions during presidential nomination contests. According to John Kenneth White and Jerome Mileur, "The institution of a primary system greatly facilitated the conservative takeover of the GOP, already begun by Barry Goldwater in 1964 and given renewed impetus by Ronald Reagan a decade later."[71] The intraparty reforms of the Democratic Party, particularly those of the McGovern-Fraser Commission, were so successful in making their candidates ideologically extreme that they had to institute a system of party leader control by introducing "superdelegates" in 1984. Despite the protests of the authors of the responsible parties report, and the expectations of Progressives generally, intraparty democratization has built an ideological wall between the parties.

CONTEMPORARY POLARIZATION
AND AMERICAN DEMOCRACY

In 2011, William Galston observed how the responsible parties doctrine had largely come to be established in American politics: "Two major parties had become less diverse internally and more unlike one another. The public now had a clear choice between competing programs and principles, and more voters were aware of the difference between the parties. The electorate could more reliably predict what the policy consequences of its choices would be. Not surprisingly, the links among partisanship, ideology, and voting patterns had tightened."[72] As parties have become more ideologically homogeneous and programmatic, American politics has become extremely polarized. And it is beyond question that American politics today is extremely polarized.[73] Since the late 1990s, polarization in roll call votes in the House of Representatives has exceeded that of the late nineteenth century.[74] The Senate has reached similar extremes of polarization during the same period. This polarizing effect is not limited to parties in government, as the electorate has recently come to reflect the same sharp divide.[75] The Pew Research Center reported that as of 2014, "partisan animosity has increased substantially" in the electorate, with voters increasingly dividing themselves into distinctive ideological camps.[76] And, according to a study by political scientist Matthew Levendusky, there is also less and less ideological overlap between the Republican and Democratic parties today, with partisans actively sorting into clear and defined ideological groups.[77]

Polarization in the electorate today is not simply a sharp divide between party principles but a thorough ideological sorting between liberals and conservatives. Levendusky demonstrates that today's polarized electorate is not the product of ideologically extreme parties but more of ideologically homogenous parties. More ideologically coherent parties leave little space for parties to engineer compromise and increase the incentive for one party to dominate the federal government. The behavior of parties in government increasingly becomes either minority obstructionism or majority absolutism, with little or no space for moderation or compromise. According to political scientist Alan Abramowitz, the center between the parties, where compromise was once achieved, has all but disappeared.[78] He observes how "the conditions for responsible party government have largely been met" by today's political parties, and "ideologically defined parties [offer] voters a clear choice between alternative sets of policies."[79] He also notes, "The institutions of American government remain a major obstacle to effective party governance." Under the new incentives set up by ideologically homogenous parties, unlimited majority rule is preferred to compromise. Abramowitz concludes that unless there is some kind of constitutional reform, "the antimajoritarian features of the American political system will remain important obstacles to effective party governance."[80] The outcome of this conflict is that American politics will be defined by either partisan dominance of government, with a supermajority ignoring interests of the minority, or near total gridlock.

An equally unmistakable feature of contemporary American politics is the unwillingness of Americans to publicly own up to their partisan affiliation. As Samara Klar and Yanna Krupnikov observe in their book on political independents, as of July 2015, "more than 40 percent of people reported that they were independents, a nationwide increase in the number of independents even from as recently as 2010. In the four years between 2010 and 2014, in states that require party registration, the total number of people registered as either Democrats or Republicans has declined by 2,847,353."[81] The authors conclude that this phenomenon of being "both anti-partisan and politically polarized" has to do with the negative perception of partisanship in the electorate and an unwillingness of committed ideological partisans to reveal their preferences.[82] In examining the attitudes of independent voters, Klar and Krupnikov found that independent partisans are "going undercover," seeking to hide their beliefs due to their negative perception of being a partisan due to their fears of being thought of negatively. The authors note that these perceptions make party mobilization problematic because as "partisans go undercover, parties will no longer be able to count on grassroots campaigns, word-of-mouth efforts, and simple mobilization through social networks."[83] However, "the people who are most willing to be vocal about their partisanship . . . are more often the people who are least concerned with what others think. These people may continue to vocalize their preferences openly, publicly, and without concern for the perceptions of others, creating the image that partisanship is everywhere."[84] Thus, as negative perceptions of partisanship grow, increasing numbers of voters will not actively associate with a political party, breaking a vital precondition for responsible parties. Instead of an engaged electorate, the authors conclude, ideological parties in America will likely produce "widespread political inaction" while overrepresenting extreme ideological activists in elections and government.

CONCLUSION

In 1969, Richard Hofstadter described the Constitution as being "against parties," with its various limits on majority rule.[85] Today it is perhaps more appropriate to say we have "parties against the Constitution." Our increasingly uncompromising parties have come into continual and sometimes extreme conflict with the Constitution. And while the constitutional space between the people and government has eroded significantly, the formal limits on majority rule endure. Harvey Mansfield observed in 1993 that this space is "unrenewable capital," as there is no sure way to reduce or limit democratic power in a democratic society. He writes, "The very difficult task for a party today is to arrest the tendency of democracy to become more extreme and to recapture the constitutional sense of the American people."[86] Today, this task seems almost impossible given the shift in favor of unlimited majority rule that has become embedded in American partisanship. As Austin Ranney observed in the 1950s, the American people wanted "*both* majority rule *and* inviolable minority rights, and that neither deserved any priority over the other."[87] Based on the evidence, Americans today have come to prioritize a "doctrine of majority-rule democracy" over the protections for minority rights the Madisonian constitutional system provides.

In considering reforms to reduce the negative effects of polarization, many scholars recommend *more* democracy.[88] Thomas Mann and Norman Ornstein, in their study of how parties clash with the Constitution today, conclude American parties need to "expand the vote," "modernize registration," "make attendance at the polls mandatory," and effect other similar prodemocracy reforms. However, given the nature of the conflict between the republican Constitution and the desire for unlimited majority rule, these reforms would likely only amplify gridlock and disengagement. Bruce Cain observes that creating more opportunities for participation rarely succeeds in engaging voters because voters lack the capacity to engage at the level these reforms demand. He writes, "Questions that are not asked frequently enough, despite decades of empirical research on this topic, are whether individual citizens have the resources, motivation, and capacity to undertake these new civic opportunities, and, if not, what this means for the design of effective reforms."[89]

Voters require parties to help them engage in politics and to mediate their interests in the actual conduct of government.[90] The Progressive theory of citizenship, as applied through the responsible parties doctrine, misconstrues this fact. Responsible parties have been capable of transforming the party system into two uniform ideological camps, and in polarizing government, but they have been much less successful at engaging citizens with their government. Moreover, the gridlock and partisan rancor that has resulted from polarization has tested the resilience of the Constitution in promoting a system of effective administration. If the Federalists were correct that a primary means of securing the affection and loyalty of Americans to their Constitution is effective administration, then the ongoing conflict between the desire for majority rule—as embodied in responsible parties theory—and the republican theory of the Constitution may ultimately endanger the popular legitimacy of the Constitution itself.

NOTES

1. Daryl J. Levinson and Richard H. Pildes, "Separation of Parties, Not Powers," *Harvard Law Review* 119, no. 8 (June 2006): 2311–2386; Thomas E. Mann and Norman J. Ornstein, *It's Even Worse Than It Was: How the American Constitutional System Collided with the New Politics of Extremism* (New York: Basic Books, 2016); and Peter W. Schramm and Bradford Wilson, eds., *American Political Parties and Constitutional Politics* (Lanham, MD: Rowman & Littlefield, 1993).

2. Richard Pildes, "Romanticizing Democracy, Political Fragmentation, and the Decline of American Government," *Yale Law Journal* 124, no. 3 (December 2014): 804–852.

3. Alan I. Abramowitz, *The Disappearing Center: Engaged Citizens, Polarization, and American Democracy* (New Haven, CT: Yale University Press, 2011).

4. Pew Research Center, "Political Polarization in the American Public," June 2014, last accessed May 11, 2018, http://www.people-press.org/2014/06/12/polit ical-polarization-in-the-american-public.

5. Pew Research Center, "Political Polarization," 6.

6. Pew Research Center, "Political Polarization," 8.

7. Shanto Iyenger and Sean Westwood, "Fear and Loathing across Party Lines: New Evidence on Group Polarization," *American Journal of Political Science* 59, no. 3 (July 2015): 690–707; Matthew Levendusky, *The Partisan Sort: How Liberals Became Democrats and Conservatives Became Republicans* (Chicago: University of Chicago Press, 2009); and Pew Research Center, "Political Polarization."

8. See Nathaniel Persily, "Introduction," in *Solutions to Political Polarization in America*, ed. Nathaniel Persily, 3–14 (New York: Cambridge University Press, 2015); and Pildes, "Romanticizing Democracy."

9. Scott Rasmussen and Doug Schoen, *Mad as Hell: How the Tea Party Movement Is Fundamentally Remaking Our Two-Party System* (New York: Harper, 2010); and Melissa Deckman, "How the Resist Trump Movement Could Transform into the Tea Party of the Left," *American Politics and Policy Blog*, London School of Economics (March 3, 2017), http://blogs.lse.ac.uk/usappblog/2017/03/03/how-the-resist-trump-move ment-could-transform-into-the-tea-party-of-the-left/.

10. James Madison, *Federalist* 10, in Alexander Hamilton, James Madison, and John Jay, *The Federalist Papers*, ed. Clinton Rossiter (New York: Mentor, 1999), 45.

11. Madison, *Federalist* 10, 46.

12. Madison, *Federalist* 10, 48.

13. Madison, *Federalist* 10, 52.

14. Harvey C. Mansfield, "Political Parties and American Constitutionalism," in *American Political Parties and Constitutional Politics*, ed. Peter W. Schramm and Bradford Wilson (Lanham, MD: Rowman & Littlefield, 1993), 14.

15. Herbert Storing, *What the Anti-Federalists Were For* (Chicago: University of Chicago Press, 1981), 72.

16. Storing, *What the Anti-Federalists Were For*.

17. Storing, *What the Anti-Federalists Were For*, 76.

18. Pildes, "Romanticizing Democracy," 815.

19. Storing, *What the Anti-Federalists Were For*, 73.

20. Hamilton, *Federalist* 68, 382.

21. Storing, *What the Anti-Federalists Were For*, 71.

22. Storing, *What the Anti-Federalists Were For*, 71; and Nancy Rosenblum, *On the Side of the Angels: An Appreciation of Parties and Partisanship* (Princeton, NJ: Princeton University Press, 2008), 89–92.

23. James Ceaser, *Presidential Selection* (Princeton, NJ: Princeton University Press, 1979); and Robert V. Remini, *Martin Van Buren and the Making of the Democratic Party* (New York: Columbia University Press, 1959).

24. Michael E. McGerr, *The Decline of Popular Politics: The American North, 1865–1928* (New York: Oxford University Press, 1986); and Rosenblum, *On the Side of the Angels*.

25. John Gerring, *Party Ideologies in America, 1828–1996* (New York: Cambridge University Press, 1998).

26. Dumas Malone, *Jefferson and the Ordeal of Liberty* (Boston: Little, Brown, 1962).

27. Thomas Jefferson, First Inaugural Address, March 4, 1801, last accessed May 10, 2018, http://avalon.law.yale.edu/19th_century/jefinau1.asp.

28. Quoted in Sidney Milkis, *Political Parties and Constitutional Government: Remaking American Democracy* (Baltimore, MD: Johns Hopkins University Press, 1999), 25.

29. McGerr, *The Decline of Popular Politics*, 14.

30. McGerr, *The Decline of Popular Politics*, 38.

31. McGerr, *The Decline of Popular Politics*, 41.

32. McGerr, *The Decline of Popular Politics*.

33. Michael J. Barber and Nolan McCarty, "Causes and Consequences of Polarization," in *Solutions to Political Polarization in America*, ed. Nathaniel Persily (New York: Cambridge University Press, 2015), 17.

34. Gerring, *Party Ideologies*, 179–180.

35. Gerring, *Party Ideologies*, 180.

36. Gerring, *Party Ideologies*, 92.

37. Gregory J. Wawro and Eric Schickler, *Filibuster: Obstruction and Lawmaking in the US Senate* (Princeton, NJ: Princeton University Press, 2007), 144.

38. Rosenblum, *On the Side of the Angels*, 25–107.

39. John G. Sproat, *The Best Men: Liberal Reformers in the Gilded Age* (New York: Oxford University Press, 1968).

40. Ari Hoogenboom, *Outlawing the Spoils: A History of the Civil Service Reform Movement, 1865–1883* (Urbana: University of Illinois Press, 1968).

41. McGerr, *Decline of Popular Politics*, 42–68.

42. Austin Ranney, *The Doctrine of Responsible Party Government—Its Origins and Present State* (Urbana: University of Illinois Press, 1954), 25–47.

43. Ranney, *The Doctrine of Responsible Party Government*, 25.

44. Quoted in Ranney, *The Doctrine of Responsible Party Government*.

45. Woodrow Wilson, *Congressional Government: A Study in American Politics* (New York: Houghton Mifflin, 1885).

46. Woodrow Wilson, *The New Freedom, A Call for the Emancipation of the Generous Energies of a People* (New York: Doubleday, 1913).

47. Ironically, this amendment was also in part the result of persistent partisan deadlock on nominations in state legislatures that left Senate seats unfilled. Ralph Rossum, *Federalism, the Supreme Court, and the Seventeenth Amendment: The Irony of Constitutional Democracy* (Lanham, MD: Lexington Books, 2001); and Wendy J. Schiller and Charles Stewart III, *Electing the Senate: Indirect Democracy before the Seventeenth Amendment* (Princeton, NJ: Princeton University Press, 2014).

48. Quoted in John Kenneth White and Jerome M. Mileur, "In the Spirit of Their Times: 'Toward a More Responsible Two-Party System' and Party Politics," in *Responsible Partisanship: The Evolution of American Political Parties since 1950*, ed. John C. Green and Paul S. Herrnson (Lawrence: University of Kansas Press, 2002), 17.

49. Herbert Croly, *The Promise of American Life* (New York: Macmillan, 1909).

50. Herbert Croly, *Progressive Democracy* (New York: Macmillan, 1915).

51. Sidney M. Milkis, *Theodore Roosevelt, the Progressive Party, and the Transformation of American Democracy* (Lawrence: University Press of Kansas, 2009), 27–74.

52. Sidney M. Milkis, *Political Parties*, 56.

53. Quoted in White and Mileur, "In the Spirit of Their Times," 18.

54. Sidney Milkis, *The President and the Parties: The Transformation of the American Party System since the New Deal* (New York: Oxford University Press, 1993).

55. Milkis, *Political Parties*, 92.

56. White and Mileur, "In the Spirit of Their Times."

57. American Political Science Association (APSA), *Toward a More Responsible Two-Party System, a Report* (Menasha, WI: American Political Science Association, 1950).

58. APSA, *Toward a More Responsible*.

59. Quoted in Austin Ranney, "Toward a More Responsible Two-Party System: A Commentary," *The American Political Science Review* 45, no. 2 (June 1951): 493.

60. Ranney, "Toward a More Responsible,"489.

61. APSA, *Toward a More Responsible*, 37.

62. APSA, *Toward a More Responsible*, 38.

63. APSA, *Toward a More Responsible*, 20.

64. APSA, *Toward a More Responsible*, 20.

65. Ranney, "Toward a More Responsible," 491.

66. Ranney, "Toward a More Responsible," 493, 495.

67. Ranney, "Toward a More Responsible," 496.

68. Ranney, "Toward a More Responsible," 496.

69. Ranney, "Toward a More Responsible," 498.

70. Ranney, "Toward a More Responsible," 499.

71. White and Mileur, "In the Spirit of Their Times," 28.

72. William Galston, "Can a Polarized American Party System Be 'Healthy'?," *Issues in Governance Studies* 34 (April 2011): 3.

73. Christopher Hare and Keith T. Poole, "The Polarization of Contemporary American Politics," *Polity* 46, no. 3 (July 2014): 411–429; Pew Research Center, "Political Polarization"; Iyenger and Westwood, *Fear and Loathing*; and Barber and McCarty, *Causes and Consequences*.

74. Barber and McCarty, *Causes and Consequences*, 17.

75. Pew Research Center, "Political Polarization."

76. Pew Research Center, "Political Polarization."

77. Levendusky, *Partisan Sort*.

78. Abramowitz, *Disappearing Center*.

79. Abramowitz, *Disappearing Center*, 60.

80. Abramowitz, *Disappearing Center*, 165.

81. Samara Klar and Yanna Krupnikov, *Independent Politics* (New York: Cambridge University Press, 2016), 152.

82. Klar and Krupnikov, *Independent Politics*, 128.

83. Klar and Krupnikov, *Independent Politics*, 36.

84. Klar and Krupnikov, *Independent Politics*, 156.

85. Richard Hofstadter, "A Constitution against Parties: Madisonian Pluralism and the Anti-Party Tradition," *Government & Opposition* 4, no. 3 (July 1969): 345–366.

86. Mansfield, "Political Parties."

87. Ranney, "Toward a More Responsible," 489.

88. Thomas E. Mann and Norman J. Ornstein, *It's Even Worse Than It Was* (New York: Basic Books, 2016).

89. Bruce Cain, *Democracy More or Less: America's Political Reform Quandary* (New York: Cambridge University Press, 2014).

90. Steven J. Rosenstone and John Mark Hansen, *Mobilization, Participation, and Democracy in America* (New York: Longman, 2003).

CHAPTER 9

In Defense of Polarization

Joseph M. Bessette

The English term *polarization,* which originated in the science of optics, was apparently first used to describe divisions in political thought in 1862 when a social critic in Britain complained of "that wretched polarization of our whole national thought, since 1688, into the two antagonistic currents of common Whiggism and common Toryism."[1] The *Oxford English Dictionary* defines the social and political meaning of the term as "the accentuation of a difference between two things or groups; division into two sharply contrasting groups or sets of beliefs." A century after this first political use of the term polarization, commentators and scholars began to describe and largely decry the polarization of American politics. Indeed, in Google's vast digitized database of works in American English dating back to 1800, none of the terms *political polarization, party polarization,* or *ideological polarization* makes an appearance until 1940. Use of these terms then grew rapidly, peaking between 1989 and 2004.[2]

The American Founders did not speak of "polarization" as such, either as a characteristic of political life or as a problem that had to be addressed. They did, however, speak of party and often of "the spirit of party." The major American political parties always have, of course, been polarized. No one would deny that the Jeffersonian-Republicans and the Federalists of the nation's first party system embraced "sharply contrasting . . . sets of beliefs," as did their successors, the Democrats and the Whigs, and later the Democrats and the Republicans. Indeed, the commonly accepted theory of critical, or realigning, elections (particularly the elections of 1800, 1828, 1860, 1896, and 1932) turns on the existence of real ideological differences between the major parties, with the voters choosing one set of beliefs, principles, or policies over another. The absence of an indisputably critical election since 1932 is not evidence that the parties are no longer polarized. On the contrary; although Republicans since former president Eisenhower have made their peace with the essential features of the welfare state ushered in by Franklin Delano Roosevelt's New Deal, Republicans and Democrats today seem both more ideologically homogeneous internally and more ideologically distant from each other than at any time in recent decades. So, the point is not that polarization is a new feature of our two major political parties; indeed, they have always been polarized but may be more so now than in the recent past.

POLARIZATION, THE PARTY SPIRIT, AND DELIBERATIVE DEMOCRACY

As the preceding chapters document in some detail, contemporary critics blame polarization for a variety of pathologies. Polarization, some charge, divides the citizenry and their representatives into warring camps, with each side viewing the other less as fellow citizens with different ideas about how to achieve common goals than as enemies who must be defeated if the good is to be achieved. Polarization fosters self-righteousness as it destroys civility. It empowers extremists of the left and right. It renders compromise across the party divide virtually impossible, fostering deadlock in our governing institutions. Perhaps most seriously, it corrodes the very foundations of deliberative democracy by undermining the openness to information and arguments necessary for fully informed reasoning on the merits of public policy.

Strikingly, many of these criticisms of polarization closely echo the Founders' early critique of political parties. Search through the eighty-five essays of *The Federalist Papers* defending the proposed Constitution of 1787, and you will find repeated criticisms of parties and the party spirit—and not a word in praise. In *Federalist* 1, Alexander Hamilton includes "*party opposition*" (emphasis added here and below) with "ambition, avarice, [and] personal animosity" as among the "not . . . laudable" motives that would likely influence the debate over the proposed Constitution.[3] In *Federalist* 9, he decries the "*party rage*" that had beset the republics of Greece and Italy.[4] In *Federalist* 10, James Madison warns against the effects of "the *spirit of party* and faction in the necessary and ordinary operations of government"—a warning Hamilton reiterates in *Federalist* 26: "The *spirit of party*, in different degrees, must be expected to infect all political bodies."[5] Fortunately, as Madison explains in *Federalist* 37, the deliberations of the body that wrote the Constitution were largely uncontaminated by the party spirit: "The convention must have enjoyed, in a very singular degree, an exemption from the *pestilential influence of party animosities*—the disease most incident to deliberative bodies and most apt to contaminate their proceedings."[6] In his discussion of the treaty power in *Federalist* 64, John Jay defends the selection of senators by state legislators as "vastly" superior to direct popular election because in popular elections, "the activity of *party zeal*, taking the advantage of the supineness, the ignorance, and the hopes and fears of the unwary and interested, often places men in office by the votes of a small proportion of the electors."[7] In introducing the subject of the new executive branch in *Federalist* 67, Hamilton charges that opponents of the Constitution engage in misrepresentation and distortion that "far exceed the usual though *unjustifiable licenses of party artifice*."[8] In *Federalist* 79, in defending the Constitution's failure to explicitly include "inability" as a cause for removing federal judges, Hamilton warns that "personal and *party attachments and enmities*" would more likely decide the matter than would "the interests of justice or the public good."[9] Two essays later, Hamilton again cites the ills of party when he explains why the judicial power should be vested in a body distinct from the legislature:

> The members of the legislature will rarely be chosen with a view to those qualifications which fit men for the stations of judges; and as, on this account, there will be great reason to apprehend all the ill consequences of defective information, so, on account of the natural propensity of such bodies to *party divisions,* there will be no less reason to fear that the pestilential breath of faction may poison the fountains of justice. The habit of being continually marshaled on opposite sides will be too apt to stifle the voice both of law and of equity.[10]

And, in the final essay, Hamilton cautions his reader to allow "no partial motive, no particular interest, no pride of opinion, [and] no temporary passion or prejudice" to affect his judgment about the merits of the proposed Constitution. He must at all times "beware of an *obstinate adherence to party*," for "the object upon which he is to decide is not a particular interest of the community, but the very existence of the nation."[11]

To adhere to a party, then, is to side with a part against the whole, to identify with a particular interest rather than with the interest of the broader community. This attachment to a part engages the citizen's interests and emotions and can result in animosities, enmities, zeal, and even rage. This spirit of party corrodes the electoral process by inflaming passions and preying on the hopes and fears of the ignorant. It corrupts the deliberative process by turning lawmakers away from the interests of the whole and by habituating them to embrace party loyalty over their duty to justice and the common good. It is not surprising then that the deliberative democracy the Framers designed was intended to work without political parties and, one might even say, against parties.[12]

Although Madison's famous *Federalist* 10 essay focuses on the dangers of majority factions, his argument can reasonably be read as applying to majority parties more generally. The great danger that republics face is control by a majority of citizens united by an "impulse of passion, or of interest, adverse to the rights of other citizens, or to the permanent and aggregate interests of the community."[13] Small republics have no solution to this problem, which explains why stable, just, and effective long-lived republics are absent from the historical record. By contrast the large republic "extend[s] the sphere," so that "you take in a greater variety of parties and interests," making it less likely that no one group would come to dominate the government.[14] The "multiplicity of interests" of a large commercial republic counteracts the deep divisions that often arise from "[a] zeal for different opinions concerning religion . . . [and] government . . . an attachment to different leaders ambitiously contending for pre-eminence and power . . . the various and unequal distribution of property."[15] In the past, these sources of disagreement and strife "divided mankind into parties, inflamed them with mutual animosity, and rendered them much more disposed to vex and oppress each other than to co-operate for their common good."[16] Now, it is precisely "different opinions . . . concerning government," often linked to "attachment to different leaders," that constitute the very basis of the American party system. Thus, the James Madison of 1787–1789, whose prodigious efforts rightly earned him the informal title "Father of the Constitution," was no friend of political parties. Remarkably, by early 1792 he was trying to convince his countrymen that party spirit was necessary to save the republic.

MADISON AS POLARIZER

As Ralph Ketcham recounts in his biography of Madison, during the first session of the First Congress (March–September 1789), the Virginia congressman functioned as "the floor leader [in the House of Representatives] of essentially nonpartisan programs necessary to . . . establish the new government."[17] In the second and third sessions (January–August 1790 and December 1790–March 1791), however, divisive controversies arose over plans urged by Secretary of the Treasury Alexander Hamilton to pay off the outstanding national debt at full face value, to assume the debts incurred by the states during the Revolutionary War, and to establish a national bank.[18] Madison opposed all three measures, largely because they would enrich speculators and others in the financial class and would dangerously concentrate power in the national government. By the end of the First Congress, Madison was the de facto leader of the de facto opposition party in Congress. He and his friend (and mentor) Thomas Jefferson (then secretary of state) concluded that the battle over republican principles could not be confined to the governing institutions but must engage the larger public. They convinced Madison's college friend Philip Freneau to establish a national newspaper in Philadelphia, called the *National Gazette*, to serve as a voice for republican principles "to counteract the influence of John Fenno's *Gazette of the United States*, which Madison and Jefferson regarded as 'a paper of pure Toryism, disseminating the doctrines of monarchy, aristocracy, and the exclusion of the influence of the people.'"[19] On October 31, 1791, the *National Gazette* published its first issue.

Between November of 1791 and December of 1792, Madison wrote eighteen unsigned essays for the *National Gazette* on a wide range of topics.[20] One of his first was a 220-word piece, "Public Opinion," which began, "Public opinion sets bounds to every government, and is the real sovereign in every free one."[21] He adds, "In proportion as government is influenced by opinion, it must be so, by whatever influences opinion."[22] A month later he wrote, "All power has been traced to opinion. The stability of all governments and security of all rights may be traced to the same source. . . . How devoutly it is to be wished, then, that the public opinion of the United States should be enlightened."[23] Thus the political battlefield could not be confined to the institutions of government. "Internal checks on powers," which Madison himself had done much to design, did not guarantee that republican principles would guide national policy. Such checks "are neither the sole nor the chief palladium of constitutional liberty. The people who are the authors of this blessing, must also be its guardians."[24] Public opinion, then, must be enlightened and marshaled against the oligarchic, aristocratic, and even monarchical tendencies of the policies of Hamilton and his allies in Congress.

Throughout his essays, Madison outlines the essential elements of republican dogma. The American states should not be consolidated into one government because this would result in "so great an accumulation of powers in the hands of [the national executive], . . . as might by degrees transform him into a monarch."[25] Each generation should "bear the burden of its own wars, instead of carrying them on, at the expense of other generations."[26] National policy should favor independent farmers because "they are the best basis of public liberty, and the strongest bulwarks of public safety."[27] Just government secures not only man's possessions but also his right to "his opinions and the free communication of them." Indeed, "conscience is the most sacred of all property . . . being a natural and unalienable right."[28] The enemies of the

Union are those who would "by arbitrary interpretations and insidious precedents . . . pervert the limited government of the Union, into a government of unlimited discretion, contrary to the will and subversive of the authority of the people."[29]

In his penultimate essay, Madison canvasses the state of political parties in the United States and their relationship to republican principles.[30] He identifies three periods in the history of parties in the new nation: (1) the division over whether to seek independence from Britain, (2) the division over whether to ratify the Constitution of 1787, and (3) the division that arose over the administration of the new government. This third division, which emerged in just two short years under the Constitution, was "natural to most political societies, [and was] likely to be of some duration in ours."[31] But this was not the case of two different, but equally legitimate, sets of beliefs and principles competing for control of policy—in the way, for example, that many today think of the competition between the Democratic and Republican parties. Rather, one side was an "antirepublican party" and the other a "Republican party," which later became the name of the party founded by Madison and Jefferson, usually referred to as the Democratic-Republican Party or the Jeffersonian-Republican Party to distinguish it from the Republican Party founded in the 1850s.

The antirepublicans were "partial to the opulent," had "debauched themselves into a persuasion that mankind are incapable of governing themselves," and believed that government must function through "the pageantry of rank, the influence of money and emoluments, and the terror of military force."[32] The Republicans, by contrast, believed "that mankind are capable of governing themselves," "hat[ed] hereditary power," and opposed "every public measure that does not appeal to the understanding and to the general interest of the community."[33] In his final essay, presented as a debate over "Who Are the Best Keepers of the People's Liberties," Madison has the "Anti-republican" saying that "the people are stupid, suspicious, [and] licentious" and "should think of nothing but obedience [to government], leaving the care of their liberties to their wiser rulers."[34] The Republican acknowledged that because the people are often "ignorant," "asleep," and "divided," they sometimes "betray themselves." The lesson, however, was not that the people should "give themselves, blindfold, to those who have an interest in betraying them." Instead, "the people ought to be enlightened, to be awakened, to be united, that after establishing a government they should watch over it, as well as obey it."[35]

Madison's project, then, was to "enlighten[]," "awaken[]," and "unite[]" Americans around true republican principles, to engage them in "a common cause, where there is a common sentiment and common interest, in spite of

circumstantial and artificial distinctions."[36] The antirepublicans, knowing
that they were outnumbered by the other side, sought "to weaken their opponents by reviving exploded parties, and taking advantage of all prejudices,
local, political, and occupational, that may prevent or disturb a general coalition of sentiments."[37] Here the Madison of 1792 appears to contradict the
Madison of 1787–1788. Where before the "multiplicity of interests" of the
large commercial republic was the essential prerequisite to the success of self-
government, now it appears to be a dangerous impediment to the formation
of majority republican opinion. Where the Madison of *Federalist* 10 and 51
hoped that the large number and variety of interests in the new nation would
depolarize the deep divisions engendered by "a zeal for different opinions concerning religion, . . . government, . . . [and] an attachment to different leaders," as well as by the "unequal distribution of property," the Madison who
authored the partisan essays of 1791–1792 was preeminently a polarizer—
someone exhibiting zeal for a particular opinion about government and doing
his best to "accentuat[e] . . . [the] difference between two things or groups; [to
divide the citizenry] into sharply contrasting groups or sets of beliefs." By the
end of the 1790s the nation's first party system—Republicans versus Federalists—was firmly established, and in the election of 1800 the Republicans won
a resounding victory in what Jefferson called, in his First Inaugural Address, a
"contest of opinion," and then some years later, a "revolution."[38]

Though some scholars deny any fundamental discontinuity between the
Madison of the *Federalist Papers* and that of the *National Gazette* essays (see, especially, the works by Lance Banning and Colleen Sheehan, cited above), the
former Madison feared and discouraged political parties while the latter en-
thusiastically promoted them.[39] The Madison who praised the multiplicity of
interests in the new nation in *Federalist* 10 and *Federalist* 51 feared the kinds of
deep societal cleavages over religion, government, leaders, and property that
cause party divisions and can lead to majority tyranny. Yet just a few years later,
Madison sought to mobilize opinion around the true principles of republicanism and thus to divide opinion in the nation between the poles of republican
and antirepublican. A new national republican party was needed to resist the
antirepublican forces that threatened to undo the revolution. What was at stake
for Madison was nothing less than the fundamental character of the regime.

LINCOLN AS POLARIZER

The Missouri Compromise of 1820, which, except for the new state of Missouri, "forever prohibited" slavery in the vast national territory north of the
latitude 36° 30' (which was most of the Louisiana Purchase of 1803), settled

for a time the national controversy over the extension of slavery to the territories. In the 1830s, however, the ideological divide over slavery deepened with the emergence of both a reinvigorated abolitionist movement—William Lloyd Garrison and others founded the *Liberator* in 1831 and then the American Anti-Slavery Society in 1833—and the "positive good" school of slavery, which was launched by John C. Calhoun on the floor of the US Senate in 1837. A decade later, the addition of a large new territory resulting from the Mexican-American War (1846–1848), encompassing the present-day states of Arizona, California, Nevada, and Utah, as well as parts of New Mexico, Colorado, and Wyoming, rekindled the debate over the extension of slavery. A new compromise engineered in 1850 seemed once again to settle the matter by admitting California as a free state and allowing the residents of New Mexico and Utah to decide for themselves whether to permit slavery. Yet, another provision of the same compromise—a new Fugitive Slave Law to replace the largely ineffective one of 1793—led to a firestorm in the North because of provisions that tilted toward claims by slave owners and thus endangered free blacks in the North. Many in the North simply refused to cooperate with the federal officials who enforced the law, and some states passed "personal liberty laws" that weakened the federal law by, for example, requiring jury trials for those accused of being escaped slaves and by prohibiting state officials from assisting in their capture and return. During these years, Southerners continued to push to open up the territories that the Missouri Compromise had marked "forever" off-limits to slavery.

By the early 1850s Senator Stephen Douglas of Illinois, leader of the Democratic Party in Congress, had come to believe that a crisis was fast approaching that could rend the Union. Southerners increasingly saw slavery as a positive good that ought to expand across the continent, whereas Northern abolitionists opposed all compromises with slavery, and some such as Garrison, denounced the Constitution itself as "a pact with the devil," "a covenant with death," and "an agreement with Hell" for its concessions to slavery. As Harry Jaffa characterizes Douglas's thinking in his seminal work on the Lincoln-Douglas debates, the growing polarization over slavery in the 1850s "was threatening to wrench American politics from its normal channels, within which national majorities and minorities could peacefully divide, and substitute a sectional issue upon which compromise would not be possible. When that was accomplished, the Union he loved would perish."[40] To combat this polarization Douglas led the fight in Congress to pass the Kansas-Nebraska Act of 1854, which repealed the Missouri Compromise and allowed slavery to spread into the national territories (whether above or below the old 36° 30' line) if the residents there approved. Popular sovereignty, expressed through local majorities, would settle the matter, freeing the national government from having to address such a deeply divisive issue. For this strategy to work, Northern opinion would have to be reconciled to the idea of opening up free territories to slavery as the price required for propitiating the South.

There is reason to believe that Douglas and his supporters were confident that slavery would not, in fact, take root in the newly opened lands—largely for economic reasons—and that the residents there would write free constitutions for their new states. Thus in Douglas's eyes the Kansas-Nebraska Act was something of a masterstroke: it placated Southerners by granting them an equal opportunity initially to settle the territories with their property while it established a legal regime that would likely result in the spread of free institutions westward. Passions would cool throughout the nation as the large moral questions that slavery raised would be channeled into numerous local debates in the sparsely populated territories. In effect the nation as a whole would be relieved of the need to confront the rightness or wrongness of slavery: "Douglas came increasingly to the conviction that practical measures directed toward the containment of slavery could succeed only if they did not involve the abstract question of the intrinsic good or evil of slavery."[41] Douglas saw himself as promoting an "essentially moderate and middle ground" between the extremes of abolitionism and the "positive good" school, a polarization that endangered the Union.[42] We might then, call Douglas the "Great Depolarizer: the enemy of extremists North and South" who fashioned a grand compromise that would defuse the destructive division over the morality and extension of slavery.[43]

As the successful lawyer, one-time congressman from 1847 to 1848, and Illinois Whig Party activist, Abraham Lincoln later recounted (referring to himself in the third person): "The repeal of the Missouri Compromise aroused him as he had never been before."[44] Within months, Lincoln, who had spoken little about slavery in the past, launched a rhetorical campaign against Douglas and his principles that would culminate in the Lincoln-Douglas debates of 1858 and lead to victory in the presidential election of 1860. As Lincoln articulated in his very first confrontation with Douglas in the fall of 1854, the Kansas-Nebraska Act represented no less than an overturning of the essential moral foundations of the nation:

> This *declared* indifference, but as I must think, covert *real* zeal for the spread of slavery, I can not but hate. I hate it because of the monstrous injustice of slavery itself. I hate it because it deprives our republican example of its just influence in the world—enables the enemies of free institutions, with plausibility, to taunt us as hypocrites—causes the real friends of freedom

to doubt our sincerity, and especially because it forces so many really good men amongst ourselves into an open war with the very fundamental principles of civil liberty—criticising the Declaration of Independence, and insisting that there is no right principle of action but *self-interest.*[45]

Slavery directly violated the very principle of human freedom upon which the nation was founded. It had been tolerated at the beginning out of practical necessity but was never accepted as morally right. Now, with the passage of the Kansas-Nebraska Act, the national government took a position of indifference to its spread, which necessarily implied indifference to its injustice: "I particularly object to the NEW position which the avowed principle of this Nebraska law gives to slavery in the body politic. I object to it because it assumes that there CAN be MORAL RIGHT in the enslaving of one man by another." This was a position that "the fathers of the republic eschewed, and rejected." "Let us re-adopt the Declaration of Independence," Lincoln urged, "and with it, the practices, and policy, which harmonize with it. . . . If we do this, we shall not only have saved the Union; but we shall have so saved it, as to make, and to keep it, forever worthy of the saving."

Four years later, when Lincoln accepted the new Illinois Republican Party's nomination for US Senate, he feared that the people of the North were growing increasingly indifferent to the spread of slavery to the territories. In his speech in Springfield on June 16 to the Republican delegates, he got right to the point:

Mr. President and Gentlemen of the Convention.

If we could first know *where* we are, and *whither* we are tending, we could better judge *what* to do, and *how* to do it.

We are now far into the fifth year, since a policy was initiated, with the *avowed* object, and *confident* promise, of putting an end to slavery agitation.

Under the operation of that policy, that agitation has not only, *not ceased*, but has *constantly augmented*.

In *my* opinion, it *will* not cease, until a *crisis* shall have been reached, and passed—"A house divided against itself cannot stand."

I believe this government cannot endure, permanently half *slave* and half *free*.

I do not expect the Union to be *dissolved*—I do not expect the house to *fall*—but I do expect it will cease to be divided.

It will become *all* one thing, or *all* the other.

Either the *opponents* of slavery, will arrest the further spread of it, and place it where the public mind shall rest in the belief that it is in course of ultimate extinction; or its *advocates* will push it forward till it shall become alike lawful in *all* the States, old as well as new—*North* as well as *South*.[46]

There was no middle position, no middle ground between slavery and freedom. Either the nation would eventually become entirely free, or slavery would become legal everywhere within it. By its very nature, slavery was a polarizing issue. It allowed for only two, diametrically opposed, positions: either it is wrong or it is right. Indifference to its spread meant indifference to its injustice; a nation indifferent to the injustice of slavery would eventually become a nation that tolerated it everywhere. And what would become of the sacred principle that all men are created equal once it was accepted that some men were not equal and therefore were not "endowed by their Creator" with "inalienable rights"? The year before, in a speech decrying the Supreme Court's decision in *Dred Scott v. Sandford*, Lincoln described the Declaration's principle of human equality as "a stumbling block to those who in after times might seek to turn a free people back into the hateful paths of despotism." For future tyrants, it would be "one hard nut to crack."[47] Thus what was at stake in the controversy over the extension of slavery to the territories was not just the freedom of blacks but the freedom of all—the very principle on which the nation had been founded.

Lincoln devoted much of the House Divided Speech to detailing the evidence of the "*tendency* to the latter condition [the legalization of slavery]" through the "*machinery* so to speak" of national policy involving Congress, the president, and the Supreme Court.[48] Lincoln saw "evidence of design and concert of action, among its chief architects, from the beginning [the first days of 1854]." Yet the architects of the new policy knew full well that their eventual success depended on public endorsement of this radical change. Hence, an essential purpose of "the Nebraska doctrine," insisted Lincoln, was "to *educate* and *mould* public opinion, at least *Northern* public opinion, to not *care* whether slavery is voted *down* or voted *up*." Indeed, according to Lincoln, Douglas's "avowed *mission is impressing* the 'public heart' to *care* nothing about [slavery]." Once Douglas and his allies were successful, once indifference to slavery became the norm in the North, then a single new Supreme Court decision, a kind of second *Dred Scott* decision, would complete the work. Where the first decision had denied Congress's constitutional authority to exclude slavery from the territories,

another Supreme Court decision [could] declar[e] that the Constitution of the United States does not permit a *state* to exclude slavery from its limits. And this may especially be expected if the doctrine of "care not whether slavery be voted *down* or voted *up,*" shall gain upon the public mind sufficiently to give promise that such a decision can be maintained when made. Such a decision is all that slavery now lacks of being alike lawful in all the States.

All depended, then, on public opinion in the North. If it remained steadfast in its opposition to slavery as a great moral wrong that violated the nation's central founding principle, then the prospect of massive popular resistance to such a second *Dred Scott* decision would stay the Court's hand, and the battle for freedom would eventually be won. But if the compromisers and appeasers succeeded in persuading white Americans not to care about slavery, then the battle was surely lost. As Lincoln went on to say in the first of his debates with Douglas, "In this and like communities, public sentiment is everything. With public sentiment, nothing can fail; without it nothing can succeed. Consequently he who moulds public sentiment, goes deeper than he who enacts statutes or pronounces decisions. He makes statutes and decisions possible or impossible to be executed."[49]

In Lincoln's view, at its beginning the nation was not polarized over the rightness or wrongness of slavery. Slavery's fundamental injustice was widely acknowledged and arguably universally recognized among those of the founding generation. Thus in a moral sense the nation had not existed from its founding as "half slave" and "half free," as Douglas claimed. It did not begin half antislavery and half proslavery, though it had largely become so by the 1850s. Douglas sought to defuse this polarization through compromise but that compromise could only take hold if Northerners became indifferent to the spread of slavery. Northerners had to be moved off the pole of adamant opposition to slavery to some middle position of indifference. Lincoln saw that if that effort were successful, the proslavery position would carry the day. So Lincoln was, indeed, a polarizer, doing everything in his power to sharpen the moral distinctions and to preserve principled opposition to slavery. But Lincoln understood that the nation could not survive permanently polarized over the morality of slavery. Like a knife balanced on its edge, it would eventually topple to one side or the other. Lincoln's short-term polarizing was to keep the nation from titling proslavery, but his ultimate goal was to restore the original, very much nonpolarized, national consensus for freedom.

LESSONS FOR THE PRESENT AGE?

Although comparisons between James Madison and Abraham Lincoln are not particularly common, viewed through the lens of polarization, the similarities are striking. Both men viewed developments in national policy as deeply threatening to the republican character of the regime. Both recognized that the battle to preserve American republicanism had to be fought not only within the governing institutions but also in the larger arena of American public opinion. Both recognized that in the end the character of public opinion would prove decisive and that, therefore, a rhetorical campaign had to be waged that sharpened the ideological issues at stake and in so doing clarified and even accentuated the divide with the polity.

Thus both Madison and Lincoln were polarizers and, indeed, were denounced for just that. In early 1792 Federalist Congressman Fisher Ames called Madison "a desperate party leader," and a few months later Hamilton wrote that Madison had become "the head of a faction decidedly hostile to me and my administration, and actuated by views in my judgment subversive of the principles of good government."[50] In 1858 even Lincoln's friends, who were shown an advance copy of the House Divided Speech, "regarded the speech as too radical for the occasion."[51] As if to prove the point, Douglas later denounced the speech as propounding a doctrine that "is revolutionary and destructive of the existence of this Government."[52] Moreover, as Harry Jaffa, writes, "Lincoln's rhetoric with its frequent appeals to the universalism of the Declaration of Independence . . . involved the deliberate risk of civil war."[53]

To decide rightly whether to risk civil war (Lincoln) or to potentially foment deep and lasting divisions and antagonisms within the political community (Madison) when compromising measures seem to be at hand requires all the practical wisdom that the democratic statesman can command. Surely, at such critical junctures in the life of a nation, compromise will seem the easier and safer path. That Lincoln chose the right path—promoting more, not less, polarization on the slavery issue in the 1850s—seems to be largely the judgment of history. That Madison was correct in 1791–1792 in castigating his political opponents as enemies of popular rule is in retrospect more debatable. Yet by the late 1790s the Madisonian/Jeffersonian critique of Federalist principles and policies had broadened considerably and with the election of 1800 ushered in a period of such dominance by the new Republican Party that the opposition party simply faded away. Madison's and Jefferson's short-term polarizing efforts had in their view saved the Republic and restored a national (nonpolarized) consensus true to the nation's founding principles.

Today some believe that the nation faces dangers comparable to those addressed by Madison in the 1790s and Lincoln in the 1850s. Alarms come from both the left and the right. Growing numbers on the left charge that democracy has given way to plutocracy as corporate money corrupts our politics, and the economic system fosters massive and unjust income inequality, freezing millions at the bottom of the economic ladder. Voices on the right decry the evils of the vast modern administrative/welfare state, which, they maintain, spreads dependency, undermines personal character, threatens to bankrupt the nation, and, by empowering bureaucrats and judges, destroys the genuine self-government embodied in the American Constitution.

To compromise or to polarize? If these and like critiques of modern American government are mistaken or at least grossly overdrawn, then we should very much regret a polarization that replaces collective deliberation about common goals with the kind of divisiveness and rancor that makes reasonable compromises impossible. If, however, the situation is as dire as some maintain, then a polarization that clarifies the threats to modern American constitutional democracy and points the way to securing and preserving the "Blessings of Liberty" promised by the Constitution might be the very thing that is most needed. As Lincoln so aptly put it in 1858, "If we could first know *where* we are, and *whither* we are tending, we could then better judge *what* to do, and *how* to do it."[54]

NOTES

1. *Oxford English Dictionary*, s.v. "polarization," last accessed December 30, 2016, http://www.oed.com/view/Entry/146757.

2. Search on the terms "ideological polarization," "party polarization," and "political polarization" since 1800, Google Ngram Viewer, last accessed March 1, 2018, https://books.google.com/ngrams/.

3. Alexander Hamilton, *Federalist* 1, in Alexander Hamilton, James Madison, and John Jay, *The Federalist Papers*, ed. Clinton Rossiter (New York: New American Library, Mentor Book, 2003), 28.

4. Hamilton, *Federalist* 9, 66.

5. Madison, *Federalist* 10, 74; and Hamilton, *Federalist* 26, 167.

6. Madison, *Federalist* 37, 227.

7. Jay, *Federalist* 64, 389.

8. Hamilton, *Federalist* 67, 406.

9. Hamilton, *Federalist* 79, 473.

10. Hamilton, *Federalist* 81, 483.

11. Hamilton, *Federalist* 85, 522.

12. See, for example, Richard Hofstadter, "A Constitution against Parties," in *The Idea of a Party System: The Rise of Legitimate Opposition in the United States* (Berkeley: University of California Press, 1969).

13. Madison, *Federalist* 10, 72.

14. Madison, *Federalist* 10, 78.

15. Madison, *Federalist* 51, 321; and Madison, *Federalist* 10, 73, 74.

16. Madison, *Federalist* 10, 73.

17. Ralph Ketcham, *James Madison: A Biography* (Charlottesville: University Press of Virginia, 1990), 304.

18. See Ketcham, *James Madison*; and Jack N. Rakove, *James Madison and the Creation of the American Republic*, 2nd ed. (New York: Longman, 2002), 107–121.

19. Ketcham, *James Madison*, 326.

20. For an overview, see "Madison's National Gazette Essays 19 November 1791–20 December 1792," last accessed March 1, 2018, http://founders.archives.gov/documents/Madison/01–14–02–0103. Some scholars report nineteen, rather than eighteen, essays. This is simply a matter of whether one counts the two-part essay "Money" as one or two. In the widely used one-volume Library of America edition of Madison's writings, editor Jack Rakove includes sixteen essays (excluding "Money" and "British Government"). All eighteen essays are reprinted in Colleen Sheehan's *The Mind of James Madison* (New York: Cambridge University Press, 2015), 228–270. For major scholarly interpretations of these essays, see especially Lance Banning, *The Sacred Fire of Liberty: James Madison & the Founding of the Federal Republic* (Ithaca, NY: Cornell University Press, 1995), 347–365; Colleen A. Sheehan, *James Madison and the Spirit of Republican Government* (New York: Cambridge University Press, 2009), esp. 57–175; Sheehan, *The Mind of James Madison*; Richard K. Matthews, *If Men Were Angels: James Madison and the Heartless Empire of Reason* (Lawrence: University Press of Kansas, 1995), 212–220 and passim (see his index entry for *National Gazette*); and Jeremy D. Bailey, *James Madison and Constitutional Imperfection* (New York: Cambridge University Press, 2015), 104–113.

21. "Public Opinion," December 19, 1791, in *James Madison: Writings*, ed. Jack Rakove (New York: Library of America, 1999), 500–501.

22. Rakove, "Public Opinion," December 19, 1971, 501.

23. Rakove, "Charters," January 19, 1792, 503.

24. Rakove, "Government of the United States," February 6, 1792, 509.

25. Rakove, "Consolidation," December 5, 1791, 498.

26. Rakove, "Universal Peace," February 2, 1792, 506.

27. Rakove, "Republican Distribution of Citizens," March 5, 1792, 512.

28. Rakove, "Property," March 29, 1792, 515, 516.

29. Rakove, "The Union: Who Are Its Real Friends?," April 2, 1792, 518.

30. Rakove, "A Candid State of Parties," September 26, 1792, 530–32.

31. Rakove, "A Candid State of Parties," September 26, 1792, 531.

32. Rakove, "A Candid State of Parties," September 26, 1792, 531.

33. Rakove, "A Candid State of Parties," September 26, 1792, 531.

34. Rakove, "A Candid State of Parties," September 26, 1792, 531; and Rakove, "Who Are the Best Keepers of the People's Liberties," December 22, 1792, 532–533.

35. Rakove, "Who Are the Best Keepers of the People's Liberties," December 22, 1792, 533.

In Defense of Polarization 191

36. Rakove, "Who Are the Best Keepers of the People's Liberties," December 22, 1792, 533; and Rakove, "A Candid State of Parties," 532.

37. Rakove, "A Candid State of Parties," 531–532.

38. Thomas Jefferson, First Inaugural Address, March 4, 1801, at http://www.presidency.ucsb.edu/ws/?pid=25803; and Thomas Jefferson to Spencer Roane, September 6, 1819, The Founders' Constitution, at http://press-pubs.uchicago.edu/founders/documents/a1_8_18s16.html.

39. Banning, *Sacred Fire of Liberty*; Sheehan, *James Madison and the Spirit of Republican Government*; and Sheehan, *The Mind of James Madison*.

40. Harry V. Jaffa, *Crisis of the House Divided: An Interpretation of the Issues in the Lincoln-Douglas Debates* (Garden City, NY: Doubleday, 1959), 43–44.

41. Jaffa, *Crisis of the House*, 54.

42. Jaffa, *Crisis of the House*, 50.

43. Jaffa, *Crisis of the House*, 102.

44. Quoted in William Lee Miller, *Lincoln's Virtues: An Ethical Biography* (New York: Vintage Books, 2002), 232.

45. Abraham Lincoln, "Peoria Speech," October 16, 1854, last accessed March 1, 2018, https://www.nps.gov/liho/learn/historyculture/peoriaspeech.htm.

46. Abraham Lincoln, "House-Divided Speech," June 16, 1858, last accessed March 1, 2018, https://www.nps.gov/liho/learn/historyculture/housedivided.htm.

47. Abraham Lincoln, "Speech on the Dred Scott Decision," June 26, 1857, last accessed March 1, 2018, http://teachingamericanhistory.org/library/document/speech-on-the-dred-scott-decision.

48. Lincoln, "House Divided Speech," emphasis in the original throughout unless otherwise noted.

49. "First Debate: Ottawa, Illinois," August 21, 1858, last accessed March 1, 2018, https://www.nps.gov/liho/learn/historyculture/debate1.htm.

50. Ames and Hamilton quoted in Ketcham, *James Madison*, 333, 336.

51. Roy P. Basler, ed., "House Divided Speech," in *Collected Works of Abraham Lincoln*, last accessed March 1, 2018, http://www.abrahamlincolnonline.org/lincoln/speeches/house.htm.

52. First Lincoln-Douglas Debate, https://www.nps.gov/liho/learn/historyculture/debate1.htm.

53. Jaffa, *Crisis of the House*, 61–62.

54. Lincoln, "House-Divided Speech."

About the Contributors

Joseph M. Bessette, PhD, is a professor of government and ethics at Claremont McKenna College. He is the author of many essays and books on the subject of American constitutionalism, democracy, and politics. Co-editor and contributor to *The Constitutional Presidency* and *The Mild Voice of Reason: Deliberative Democracy and American National Government*, Bessette's work focuses on how the Constitution creates the framework for democratic deliberation in US politics. He is currently working on a book about the death penalty in the United States.

Amanda Hollis-Brusky, PhD, is an associate professor of politics at Pomona College. Author of *Ideas with Consequences: The Federalist Society and the Conservative Counterrevolution*, Hollis-Brusky's work focuses on the dynamics of constitutional change and the role "support structures"—networks of lawyers and academics, nongovernmental institutions, and ideas—play in that process. Her second book project, on the rise and efficacy of the support structure for conservative Christian legal mobilization, is currently titled *Higher Counsel: Training the Conservative Christian Legal Movement*, coauthored with Joshua C. Wilson of University of Denver and under advanced contract with Oxford University Press.

Zachary Courser, PhD, is a visiting professor of government and research director of the Dreier Roundtable at Claremont McKenna College (CMC). He has published articles on populist political movements, American political parties, and American democracy, including "Protest without a Party: The Tea Party as a Conservative Social Movement," in *Society* and "The Tea Party at the Election," in *The Forum*. Courser has experience working in policy and government, both on Capitol Hill and as the director of CMC's Washington

193

Program, and he co-directs CMC's Policy Lab. He has taught and researched at the Institut d'Études Politiques de Lyon (Sciences Po Lyon) and worked as a senior program director and fellow for the Legatum Institute in London. He is currently working on an edited volume on the spread of populism in the United States and Europe.

Michael S. Greve, PhD, is a professor of law at George Mason University Law School. He is the author of nine books and a multitude of articles appearing in scholarly publications, as well as numerous editorials and book reviews. Author of *The Upside-Down Constitution* and *Real Federalism: Why It Matters, How It Could Happen*, Greve is an expert on the development of American federalism and its effect on public policy.

Eric Helland, PhD, is a professor of economics at Claremont McKenna College and an economist at the RAND Corporation, whose research focuses on law, economics, and regulation. He has served as a senior economist on the Council of Economic Advisers, currently serves as an editor of the *International Review of Law and Economics*, and co-directs the Dreier Roundtable. His recent articles include "Stock Ownership and Patterns of Recusal in Federal Courts," in the *Georgetown University Law Review*; "The Impact of Fetal Alcohol Exposure: Evidence from the End of Prohibition," in *Economic Inquiry*; and "Estimating Effects of English Rule on Litigation Outcomes," in *Review of Economics and Statistics*.

Benjamin Kleinerman, PhD, is an associate professor of constitutional democracy at Michigan State University. His research focuses on the relationship between executive power and the constitutional order. He is the author of *The Discretionary President: The Promise and Peril of Executive Power*. He is currently working on a second book, tentatively titled *Becoming Commander-in-Chief: A Constitutional Success Story*, that continues the investigation of executive power.

Kenneth P. Miller, JD, PhD, is an associate professor of government, co-director of the Dreier Roundtable, and associate director of the Rose Institute for Local Government at Claremont McKenna College. Miller's primary research focuses on state government institutions, with emphasis on direct democracy (initiative, referendum, and recall) and the interaction between law and politics. His publications include *Direct Democracy and the Courts*, and he is currently working on a book comparing Texas and California as models of red- and blue-state politics and policy.

Kathryn Pearson, PhD, is an associate professor of political science at the University of Minnesota. The author of *Party Discipline in the U.S. House of Representatives* and articles in the *Journal of Politics*, *Perspectives on Politics*, and *Legislative Studies Quarterly*, her research focuses on the US Congress, congressional elections, political parties, and women and politics. She is working on a new book project, currently titled *Gendered Partisanship in the House of Representatives*, that analyzes congresswomen's pursuit of power in a partisan era.

George Thomas, PhD, is a professor of government at Claremont McKenna College. Author of *The Founders and the Idea of a National University: Constituting the American Mind* and *The Madisonian Constitution*, Thomas's research focuses on the American constitutional order, constitutional law, and American political thought.

Index

Union, *continued*
  and James Madison, 17, 28, 181
  and Stephen Douglas, 12–13, 183

Van Buren, Martin, 66, 78n16, 162
veto
  legislative, 28, 104–105
  points, 6, 16, 22, 87
  presidential, 2, 59, 64, 84, 109
  vetocracy, 15
voting
  in Congress, 36, 38, 39, 73
  and polarization, 6, 169
  racial discrimination in, 90
  rights, 80, 83, 85, 90
  roll-call, 1, 36, 39, 163, 169
  in Supreme Court, 83, 89
  Voting Rights Act (1965), 89, 92, 95

Wallace, George, 5
war
  in Afghanistan, 21
  Civil War, 3, 69, 126, 188
  in Iraq, 4, 21
  in Vietnam, 4
  World War II, 71

Warren, Chief Justice Earl
  Warren Court, 83, 90
Washington, George, 35, 63, 65–66, 75,
    162, 163
Watergate, 40
welfare
  general, 7
  public, 16
  reform, 122–123
  state, 177, 189
Whig Party, 33n49, 67–68, 162, 176,
    184
  view of presidential power, 64, 66, 70
White House, 82, 144
  Democrats in, 36
  Obama in, 109, 132
  Republicans in, 46, 73, 113
Wilson, Woodrow, 15, 64, 70, 113
  and checks and balances, 60
  and parties, 164–166, 167
  as polarizing, 27
  as reformer, 101, 166
women, 4
worker safety, 103
World War II, 71